Roman Beck

The Network(ed) Economy

WIRTSCHAFTSINFORMATIK

Roman Beck

The Network(ed) Economy

Economy

The Nature, Adoption and Diffusion
of Communication Standards

With forewords by Prof. Dr. Wolfgang König
and Prof. Dr. Rolf T. Wigand

Deutscher Universitäts-Verlag

Bibliografische Information Der Deutschen Bibliothek
Die Deutsche Bibliothek verzeichnet diese Publikation in der Deutschen Nationalbibliografie;
detaillierte bibliografische Daten sind im Internet über <http://dnb.ddb.de> abrufbar.

Dissertation Universität Frankfurt/Main, 2006

1. Auflage Juli 2006

Alle Rechte vorbehalten
© Deutscher Universitäts-Verlag | GWV Fachverlage GmbH, Wiesbaden 2006

Lektorat: Ute Wrasmann / Anita Wilke

Der Deutsche Universitäts-Verlag ist ein Unternehmen von Springer Science+Business Media.
www.duv.de

Umschlaggestaltung: Regine Zimmer, Dipl.-Designerin, Frankfurt/Main
Druck und Buchbinder: Rosch-Buch, Scheßlitz
Gedruckt auf säurefreiem und chlorfrei gebleichtem Papier
Printed in Germany

ISBN-10 3-8350-0364-X
ISBN-13 978-3-8350-0364-4

Foreword

Modern communication channels together with new electronic media standards are constantly changing traditional interaction patterns of humans and even machines in an increasingly globalized and networked world. Such a communication-based interaction is of pivotal economic importance in order to manage efficiently inter-organizational cooperation and business information flows. Consequently, the availability of generally accepted electronic communication standards is essential in order to decrease communication-related transaction costs.

Roman Beck elaborates in his dissertation *The Network(ed) Economy* the importance of the so far independently from each other discussed diffusion theory on the one hand and network effect theory on the other hand. However, Roman Beck not only connects the two theories epistemologically, but also develops and extends those theories by providing a network diffusion model. The core of his model is the so-called network effect helix, where a dynamic and self-enforcing interplay between direct and indirect network effects is deployed to simulate diffusion patterns and paths of communication standards. In his analysis, Roman Beck especially focused on the critical diffusion period between the market launch of a new communication standard and (in case of a successful diffusion) the achievement of a critical mass of adopters. His research results and consequently the chosen title of the thesis are capable to illustrate the overall topic of his work in the interesting area between an incompletely interconnected "networked economy" on the one hand and a completely interconnected "network economy". The difference between those two scenarios is defined by the way electronic communication standards are adopted and implemented. The traditional view on network economies is strongly influenced by Coase and his model of hybrids or alliances as alternative coordination forms for markets and hierarchies. Sourcing through the market is communication costs efficient when the asset specificity is extremely low making additional communication or coordination with suppliers unnecessary. On the other hand, in the case of products with a high asset specificity the necessary amount and consequently costs of communication and coordination with business partners can be extremely high. Then, a hierarchical sourcing or self-production can be cost-advantageous compared to sourcing through the market. However, the properties of most sourced goods are somewhere in-between with average asset specificity and moderate necessity of communication. In this mid-range goods spectrum, improvements in communication and system integration can help to further decrease transaction costs for cooperatively sourced and produced goods in a networked economy whereas the sourcing of goods with extremely low or high asset specificity will furthermore be cost efficient by employing market or hierarchy as sourcing mechanism.

The different sourcing models already illustrate the importance of interorganizational communication and cooperation for efficient business transactions. Therefore, developing a network diffusion model in order to be able to explain agents' independently and locally made adoption decisions for communication standards and furthermore, conceptualizing new business processes and prototypical applications in order to increase the degree of interorganizational integration is a highly complex and challenging task Roman Beck is mastering brilliantly. Apart from the thorough description and extension of current knowledge and theories, Roman Beck's outstanding thesis captivates by its true abundance of original, methodologically precisely compiled results. In particular, Roman Beck was able to combine and extend network effect theory by adapting and integrating models and constructs from diffusion of innovation theory. He classified for the first time sponsored and unsponsored network effect goods into Musgrave's classification scheme of private and public goods and demonstrates convincingly why digital goods (and here especially communication standards) are so particular. Roman Beck is intensely reflecting and discussing the nature of network effect goods what finally allows him to derive his network diffusion model with direct and indirect network effects as primary utility sources and drivers of communication standards diffusion.

Altogether, Roman Beck has substantially increased the knowledge within the area of network effect theory, standardization, and diffusion theory. His groundbreaking results disclose not only important methodical progress but are also of significant importance for practitioners.

Prof. Dr. Wolfgang König,
Dean of the Faculty of Business Administration
and Economics, Johann Wolfgang Goethe University Frankfurt

Foreword

The Network(ed) Economy is a timely and important book. The play of words in "network(ed)" is most appropriate and descriptive for today's global economy, as networks are at the core of all economic and organizational life. Roman Beck's perspective of a networked, dynamic and multi-layered economy shows convincingly how we rely today on the intricate web of relationships among processes, structures, integration and innovation and how information and information technology enable many of these reciprocal interactions. The networked economy is shaped by the linkages among individuals, firms and institutions resulting in patterns of economic behavior that drive and inhibit actions. Moreover, we have realized how the fundamental structure of firms has been altered and that networked structures enable new organizational forms.

Roman Beck sheds new light on essential characteristics of the networked economy such as network effects, a new goods classification model, externalities and entire network industries as well as the underlying communication standards making this economy possible in the first place. A good number of economic phenomena may be explained via such concepts. Based on a multitude of definitions in the literature, broad network effects could explain many non-intended observations. Roman Beck, however, elegantly delineates his own definition so that this problem does not arise.

This work is broadly influenced by the writings of Ronald Coase's transaction cost theory, the late Ev Rogers' diffusion theory as well as the numerous writers on network effects. The subject of the book is the economic analysis of the characteristics of communication standards in the information economy, as well as their adoption and diffusion within a network effect context. Roman Beck succeeds in demonstrating the adoption and diffusion behavior of potential users of network effect goods. Moreover, we learn about the resulting diffusion paths and dynamics within the emerging networks. Lastly, the author offers a diffusion model, the network effect helix, that contributes to identify network-specific diffusion influence factors. This network effect helix analyzes how the diffusion of pure network effect goods gets started, how their utility changes over their life cycle and which factors are significant in order to establish a standard per se in the market.

This writer saw many chapters and concepts in this book evolve over the last few years as Roman Beck and he met frequently in Frankfurt, but also at ICIS,

ECIS, AIS, HICSS, the Bled International Electronic Commerce Conference and other conferences. Additional insights were gained and idea exchanges occurred at an MIS Quarterly (MISQ) workshop on standards in Seattle, WA, resulting in a special issue on standards by MISQ edited by John King and Kalle Lyytinen, as well as a special issue on vertical information systems standards of Electronic Markets: An International Journal, edited by this writer, M. Lynne Markus and Charles W. Steinfield. Many concepts and ideas found their impetus in the large-scale National Science Foundation-funded multi-year Global Electronic Commerce (GEC) project conducted within ten nations, as well as through ideas gained at the semi-annual meetings at the Center for Research on Information Technology and Organizations (CRITO), University of California at Irvine. Roman Beck, Wolfgang Koenig and this writer were responsible for the report on Germany as one of the ten nations participating in the Global Electronic Commerce project. This project demonstrated how the Internet and electronic commerce are bringing countries together to create a global networked economy. The GEC project addressed: (1) scientific understanding of the relationship between national environments and the use and impacts of e-commerce, (2) benchmarks for future studies of national and global trends, (3) business metrics for global e-commerce markets; and (4) insights for policy makers who seek to maximize the benefits of e-commerce.

This book is a must-read for and belongs into the personal library of all those, i.e. academicians as well as practitioners and policy makers, who strive to shape our new digital world by harnessing information and information technology.

Prof. Dr. Rolf T. Wigand,
Maulden-Entergy Chair and Distinguished Professor of Information Science
and Management, Department of Information Science
CyberCollege, University of Arkansas at Little Rock

Preface

An advice a young PhD student gets very soon in his academic career is: Make it short! Well, some of us at least tried to write an as short as possible dissertation but naturally each of us failed. Nevertheless, in order to stay on track and to remain focused good advisors, colleagues, and friends are indispensable for all of us to complete our personal PhD adventure successfully.

Therefore, I am deeply indebted to my advisor, Prof. Dr. Wolfgang König, for his guidance and support and for giving me the freedom to conduct my own research. He was encouraging me to improve my work and to submit my results to conferences and journals, which definitely was a good exercise for the final preparation of my dissertation.

I am also thankful to Dr. Tim Weitzel, Daniel Beimborn, and Jochen Franke for their support, fruitful discussions and several research papers we have written together. Thank you friends!

I am also grateful to the members of my committee, Prof. Dr. Gerriet Müller, Prof. Dr. Dr. h.c. Dieter Biehl, and Prof. Dr. Roland Holten. In particular, Dieter Biehl has helped me to furnish the public goods and infrastructure theory part for what I am very thankful. Furthermore, I would like to thank Prof. Dr. Rolf T. Wigand and Prof. Dr. John L. King for their support throughout all the years and for their thorough cross reading of my thesis. Both have been invaluable sources of inspiration for my work.

The author is indebted to the German as well as the U.S. National Science Foundation for their funding and financial support of the two research projects "IT Standards and Network Effects" (funded by the German National Science Foundation) and "Globalization and E-commerce" (funded by the U.S. National Science Foundation). Both projects have been invaluable and essential for me and my research.

Everybody who survived his or her personal PhD project knows that the darkest hour is just before dawn. The last months before completing a thesis are the most difficult of all: often you cannot see the light at the end of the tunnel. In such moments, you definitely need somebody who believes in you and encourages you. Therefore, my special thanks go to you, Claudia.

Dr. Roman Beck

Table of Contents

Figures

Tables

Equations

Variables and Symbols

β	Constant Parameter
B_0^R	Installed Base of Already EDI-capable Retailers in Period 0
B_0^S	Installed Base of Already EDI-capable Suppliers in Period 0
B_t^R	Installed Base of EDI-capable Retailers in Period t
B_t^S	Installed Base of EDI-capable Suppliers in Period t
B_{qt}	Installed Base of Standard Adopter of the Same Technology q in Period t
b_i	Financial Contribution
c_C^C	Customer Complaint Costs
c_S^C	Supplier Complaint Costs
c_{ij}^D	Direct Costs for i with Neighbor j
c_i	Costs
$C_{i-\text{mode},i,t}^N$	Costs for all i-mode Adopter
$C_{WAP,i,t}^N$	Costs for all WAP Adopters
c_{ijt}^R	Communication Saving of Retailer i in Period t, if i and j use EDI
c_{jit}^S	Communication Saving of Supplier j in Period t, if i and j use EDI
d	Defective Shipment
$E\left[INE_{it}\right]$	Estimated Utility of Indirect Network Effects for Agent i in Period t
$E\left[B_{i-\text{mode},t}\right]$	Estimated Adoption of i-mode in Period t
$E\left[U_{it}\right]$	Estimated Utility for i in Period t
$E\left[U_{jt}\right]$	Estimated Utility for j in Period t
$E\left[U_{it}^{INE}\right]$	Estimated Utility of Indirect Network Effects in Period t
$E\left[U_{jt}^{INE}\right]$	Estimated Indirect Network Effect Net Benefit of the Neighbors j in Period t
$E\left[U_{i-\text{mode},i,t}\right]$	Estimated Utility of i-mode Adoption for Agent i in Period t

G	Quality
i	Network Participant Index i
INE_{it}	Indirect Network Effects for i in Period t
j	Network Participant Index j
K	Cost of Technology Adoption
k_{it}^{R1}	Decision-relevant Costs of Retailer i in State 1 and Period t
k_{it}^{R2}	Decision-relevant Costs of Retailer i in State 2 and Period t
k_{jt}^{S1}	Decision-relevant Costs of Supplier i in State 1 in Period t
k_{jt}^{S2}	Decision-relevant Costs of Supplier i in State 2 in Period t
$\mu\left(nu_{ij}^{d}\right)$	Average Direct Network Utility
$\mu\left(nu_{i-\mathrm{mode},i}^{N}\right)$	Average Indirect Network Utility of i-mode
$\mu\left(nu_{WAP,j}^{N}\right)$	Average Indirect Network Utility of WAP
N	Total Population
N^{R}	Total Number of Retailers
N^{S}	Total Number of Suppliers
n	Number of Agents
n_{i}	Network Agents or Participant
nb_{j}	Number of Communication Partners of Agent j
nu_{ij}^{D}	Net Utility Coefficient for i with Neighbor j
$nu_{i-\mathrm{mode},i}^{N}$	Indirect Net Utility Coefficient i-mode
$nu_{WAP,i}^{N}$	Indirect Net Utility Coefficient WAP
p_{ij}	Probability of Technology Adoption of i on the Part of Agent j
p_{r}	Price of Product r
q_{r}^{i}	Aggregated Quantity of Product r Ordered by Customer i
q_{r}^{j}	Aggregated Quantity of Product r Ordered by Customer j
q_{r}^{d}	Quantity of Reclaimed Defective Product r

r	Product
s_i	Asset Specificity
sub_i	Substitution Rate
t	Time
T	Total Time Horizon
θ	Efficiency Indicator
u_i	Utility for Agent i
u_j	Output Variable
u_{it}^I	Indirect Network Utility Coefficient for Agent i in Period t
u_{ij}^D	Direct Network Utility for Agent i with Neighbor j
$U_{i,t}^{INE}$	Overall Individual Net Utility from Indirect Network Effects in Period t
$U_{i-mode,i,t}^N$	Indirect Network Utility for all i-mode Adopters
$U_{WAP,i,t}^N$	Indirect Network Utility for all WAP Adopters
v	Value of Defective Shipment
v_i	Input Variable
VB	Virtual Installed Base
w_i	Total Capital
x	Public Good
x_i	Decision Variable
x_j	Indicator for the i-mode Adoption by Agent j
y	Private Good

Abbreviations

ACE	Agent-based Computational Economics
ASCII	American Standard Code for Information Interchange
ASP	Application Service Provider
ATM	Automated Teller Machine
B2B	Business-to-Business
B2C	Business-to-Consumer
CCR	Charnes Cooper Rhodes
cHTML	compact HTML
COMDIS	Commercial Dispute
DEA	Data Envelopment Analysis
DESADV	Dispatch Advice
DK	Denmark
DMU	Decision Making Unit
DNA	Deoxyribonucleic Acid
EDI	Electronic Data Interchange
EANCOM	European Article Numbering Communication Association
EDIFACT	Electronic Data Interchange for Administration, Commerce and Transport
EFT	Electronic Funds Transfer
EMS	Enhanced Messaging Service
ERP	Enterprise Resource Planning
F	France
G	Germany
GPRS	General Packet Radio Service
GSM	Global System of Mobile Communication
HTML	Hypertext Markup Language
HTTP	Hypertext Transfer Protocol
ICT	Information and Communication Technology

ILN	International Location Number
INVOIC	Invoice
IS	Information Systems
IT	Information Technology
IP	Internet Protocol
LAN	Local Area Network
MMS	Material Management System
MSP	Mobile Service Providers
NTSC	National Television Systems Committee
OEM	Original Equipment Manufacturer
PAL	Phase Alternating Line
R&D	Research and Development
PC	Personal Computer
PRICAT	Price and Catalog Data
SGML	Standard Generalized Markup Language
SME	Small- and Medium-sized Enterprise
SMS	Short Message Service
SWIFT	Society for Worldwide Interbank Financial Telecommunications
TAM	Technology Acceptance Model
TCP/IP	Transmission Control Protocol / Internet Protocol
TOE	Technology Organization Environment
UMTS	Universal Mobile Telecommunication System
UN	United Nations
US	United States
VAN	Value Added Network
VCR	Video Cassette Recorder
VDA	Verband der Automobilindustrie
VHS	Video Home System

W3C	World Wide Web Consortium
WAP	Wireless Application Protocol
WiFi	Wireless Fidelity
WiMAX	Worldwide Interoperability for Microwave Access
WLAN	Wireless Local Area Network
WP	Word Processor
WWW	World Wide Web
XML	Extensible Markup Language

1 Introduction

Although we are living in a globalized and networked world, people seldom care about the necessary underlying communication infrastructure and standards. From an economic point of view, the diffusion of network-constitutive standards and their economic impacts are analyzed in countless publications, e.g., for allocation impacts and emerging market structures. Accordingly, the diffusion results of communication standards or standards with network effects in general (none or too many standards, monopolistic dominated markets, etc.) have considerable consequences for the individual but also overall welfare of network participants. However, the question of how such standards can overcome the start-up problem and critical diffusion phase between the market rollout and the critical mass remains unanswered. A fundamental problem of the diffusion of standards and at the same time the reason for the start-up problem is the existence of network externalities: the individually achievable benefit of a communication standard depends on the adoption decision of further potential network participants. Consequently, the individual benefit is hard to predict, in contrast to the individual costs of adopting a standard.

An implicit assumption in a large part of the literature is the identical strength in principle of direct and indirect network effects in all phases of diffusion. Not only direct, but also indirect, network effects influence the size of networks positively, since both network effects are part of positive adopter network externalities in growing networks. Emerging networks under development change their size steadily so one can also assume a constantly changing magnitude of both types of network effects. Although this argumentation seems to be intuitively obvious, it is not considered methodologically in current network effect diffusion models. This is even more astonishing when considering that the early path of diffusion of a new communication standard determines the overall market success or failure, which is known as the start-up-dilemma. The model developed in this contribution incorporates both types of varying network effects and analyzes the start-up and diffusion phase until the critical mass of adopters is reached. This allows us not only to analyze the observable past diffusion paths of communication standards based on direct and indirect network effects but also to forecast possible diffusion scenarios under certain premises.

Therefore a network effect helix model and simulation has been developed in this contribution incorporating elements of the network effect and diffusion theory firstly to describe methodically the adoption or decision situation of prospective network participants, and secondly to solve or at least relax the inter-temporal and inter-network problem of benefit estimation. While network effect theory primarily examines the characteristics of network effect markets and their influence on the existence and efficiency of equilibria and typical coordination problems resulting from compatibility requirements respectively, diffusion models are more focused on the prognosis of the adoption of innovations. Diffusion theory usually tries to examine the change in the number of users between two sequential periods. If social interactions or more specifically communication among (prospective) users is important for the diffusion of innovations, then the diffusion problem is subject to the diffusion and the network effect theory.

The two research strands also symbolize representatively the difference between a networked economy and a network economy, as indicated in the title of this dissertation. While diffusion theory is concerned with the diffusion of goods (in our case: communication standards) constituting a network of users, network effect theory is more focused on the economic dynamics inside such networks. Since the diffusion of all kinds of communication and e-business standards has reached a high saturation level in almost all industries and developed countries, the goal of being networked with each other seems to have been reached or to be at least reachable in the near future. The next step towards a fully integrated, intermeshed, and friction-free network economy might remain an idealistic vision or goal, but can also help to identify the potentials of a network economy that have not been utilized or discovered so far.

In order to explain the diffusion of communication standards, the nature of communication standards as part of the group of public goods has to be clarified, followed by the examination of why individuals adopt an innovation. In this way the reasons for the adoption indirectly determine thereby the overall diffusion. In particular, the diffusion of communication standards in pure network markets depends on the way the expected utility value is estimated and which parameters are used to calculate it, e.g., how the adoption decision of further potential network participants is made. Furthermore, the value of a communication standard and therefore the mix and strength of network effects are changing over the life cycle of a standard or growing network, which must also be considered by a new adopter. Such interactions between potential adopters and network participants can be simulated by agent-based computational economics (ACE) approaches, which are used here to formulate the network effect helix model. By applying ACE, it is possible to analyze economically complex, double-sided dependencies between individual adoption decisions on the microeconomic and resulting diffusion structures on the macroeconomic level. Such simulation models are at the same time suitable to contribute to network effect theory by helping to explain the dynamics of decentralized coordination or standardization problems among agents.

The normative model in this contribution is supplemented by the empirical results of the diffusion of communication technologies and standards in three different industry sectors (retail & wholesale, manufacturing, and banking & insurance) in Denmark, France, Germany, and the US. Furthermore, two applications are developed by this author to solve the identified compatibility problems among business partners in order to increase the degree of interorganizational process automation.

1.1 Motivation and Research Questions

Apart from the formation of hierarchically organized and well defined firms to produce goods and services, further possible market-oriented solutions are conceivable, e.g., by establishing and sourcing through decentralized virtual firms on the market. As already as 1937, Coase argued that firms and markets are alternative organizational forms which can be used for organizing transactions (Coase 1937). The central question is why firms emerge at all in a specialized exchange economy where the sourcing can be provided by markets. The answer can be found in his famous transaction costs approach: firms only exist because there are costs of using the market and its price mechanisms, such as costs for searching, negotiating, monitoring, and enforcing. These costs occur when goods or services are transferred across separate interfaces between organizations. It is a matter of common knowledge that organizations emerge when the coordination of transactions through hierarchies is more advantageous than coordination through markets (Coase 1937; Williamson 1985). As a result, economic benefits from vertical integration (collaboration) arise when internalization (or partial internalization) dominates transaction difficulties associated with market exchanges (Lee et al. 2002). Such an organizational disintegration (Picot et al. 1996) is cost efficient if the sourcing by market or hierarchical mechanisms is more cost intensive and no monopolies exist (Economides 1999).

The more specific an asset or good is the better is the sourcing not by the market but by hybrid or hierarchically organized solutions. Referring to Williamson (Williamson 1991), Figure 1 illustrates the three possible forms of coordination mechanisms. Instead of using the term "hybrid" for variants such as collaborative or alliance-based sourcing (Malone et al. 1987; Picot et al. 1996; Williamson 1991), here the more general term "networked" is used, emphasizing the potentials offered by communication standards to reduce transaction costs when coordinating various intercompany processes. Since the asset specificity is the main determinant for transaction costs, an increasing specificity is always related to an increase in transaction costs. Sourcing through the market is cost efficient when the specificity is low since competition on the market will lead to low prices (specificity between $0 < s_1$). A hierarchical sourcing or self-provided organization of an asset with low specificity is less attractive because comparatively cost-advantageous, necessary skills and machines are not easily replicable on demand.

With increasing specificity and heterogeneity of assets to be sourced, the necessary amount of coordination is also rising. The hierarchy performs best ($> s_2$) in the case of sourcing highly specific or heterogeneous assets or goods because strict control instruments and internal contracts can be applied.

However, these two coordinating mechanisms are not the only ones observable within industry sectors. Variants or networked solutions of the two pure sourcing concepts can be identified, e.g., to coordinate value or supply chains. This indicates that there is an area ($s_1 < s_2$) where on the one hand the specificity is high and therefore the market coordination is too expensive, but on the other hand the hierarchical souring is also not applicable, e.g., due to low frequency of sourcing or due to small numbers. Because of the advent of modern communication standards that have reduced the coordination complexity and therefore transaction costs significantly, the ability to collaborate with other market participants is becoming more and more attractive. In such a networked economy, apart from the cost reduction due to standardized communication frameworks, additional network effect benefits can be achieved when all market participants adopt and support the same standards while gaining the full potential of a network economy in the long run.

Figure 1: Coordination Mechanism related Transaction Costs

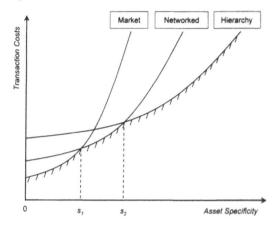

As mentioned above, transaction costs are mainly the costs of coordinating comprising costs of information and communication. Such costs can be interpreted as the "economic equivalent of friction in physical systems" (Williamson 1985, p. 19). With technical progress and the ongoing diffusion of information technology and communication standards, this "friction" will be reduced continuously. For a detailed discussion of how information technology and communication standards also effect markets and hierarchies see (Picot et al. 1996).

If the process of ongoing reduction of coordination frictions continues and accelerates with each new automation and communication application in the future, network-based sourcing might become an increasingly attractive and cost efficient alternative to pure market or hierarchical sourcing, enjoying some properties of markets and some of hierarchies (Jarillo 1988). From a macroeconomic point of view, such an interaction-based sourcing is socially cost efficient but not necessarily profit maximizing for all network participants because competitive advantage also results from cost heterogeneity among competitors (Farrell et al. 1998). Figure 2 depicts the "natural" borders of such an economically efficient development. The situation, now described as network economy will never be better than the market for assets with a very low specificity and contrariwise will never exceed the efficient sourcing of highly complex, heterogeneous, and specific assets, which will always be provided by centrally coordinated hierarchies. Although coordination by market and hierarchy will also benefit from new communication standards and IT solutions lowering the transaction costs, the overall net effect will be in favor of networked coordination for the whole continuum between these two poles. At least theoretically, it is imaginable that sophisticated communication solutions together with trustable contract mechanisms will be able to coordinate all kinds of demand and supply in developed and mature networked environments. Although some steps towards this goal have already been made, e.g., in the form of EDI, e-business, electronic supply chain management, electronic marketplaces, etc., the targeted vision seems to be still in the far distant future. In the meantime, we should concentrate on the development and diffusion of technologies and standards that are necessary in order to reach this goal.

Figure 2: Coordination Mechanisms: from a Networked to a Network Economy

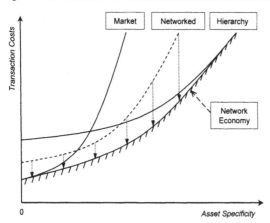

The primary target of this contribution is the economic analysis of the nature, adoption, and diffusion of network effect goods and standards such as EDI or communication standards in modern e-business applications in the light of network effects, since those standards are the foundation of a networked and especially a network economy. The aim is to explain socio-economic interactions in the adoption process, as well as the implications of process automation approaches and the impact of communication or e-business standards on the overall business performance in and among companies. Based on an

analysis of the nature of communication standards, their potential paths of diffusion, as well as the properties of network effect goods supplemented by empirical results from a global survey on the use and impacts of e-business standards comprising ten countries, two new EDI-based automation approaches
are developed, and two inductive simulation models are presented. The so-
called network effect helix model allows an in-depth focus on direct and indirect network effects related to the adoption, growth, and potential impact of a
network. At the same time, the model reveals new insights into the dynamics
of the very early phase of diffusion of network effect goods.

The challenge here lies in the advancement of the network effect theory
through diffusion-cycle-dependent communication standards benefits in order
to be able to explain and design the adoption decision of potential participants
(individuals and enterprises) in networks. Ultimately, the task is to develop a
consistent model of the interplay of microeconomic effects (individual adoption
decisions) with macroeconomic effects (network effects) to explain real world
phenomena like interorganizational communication integration (e.g., by EDI) or
diffusion of data communication standards in mobile phone markets (e.g., the
battle between i-mode vs. WAP). The network effect helix explanation model
developed is capable of defining and integrating individual and social goals
that can be used to improve adoption decision models for network effect
goods.

Consequently, the simulation-based network effect helix model considers the
dynamically changing strength of direct and indirect network effects with each
new adopter inside the developing network over time. This allows potential
adopters to determine the expected benefit value by considering the direct and
indirect network effects of communication standards for different environmental conditions. Therefore, various networks are analyzed, such as EDI networks (EDIFACT or XML-EDI standards), as well as mobile phone networks
with data communication standards. Those networks are characterized by decentral adoption and increasing returns with each new network participant.
Furthermore, such markets can be regarded as potential candidates for market
failure due to the public good property of such networks.

Through the application of the developed network effect helix model, prospective adopters can anticipate the interplay and dynamic changes of direct and

indirect network effects of a certain communication standard according to the assumed increasing attractiveness of a growing network on the market over time. This phenomenon of a mutually increasing attractiveness is described as the network effect helix, because of the two kinds of network effects, which complement each other in a self-supporting up-forcing spiral. Based on the network effect helix model, market strategies focused on the changing importance of the two network effects can be formulated to overcome the start-up problem of unsponsored communication standards and to ensure successful diffusion.

Unlike existing static procedures for the determination of the diffusion process, which are based on regressions of previous diffusion paths, thus underestimating the importance of technical progress and innovation, or on net present value based approaches assuming unrealistic rational behavior, the network effect helix model uses the expected network benefits derived from the combination of both network effects and the available information about the quality and features of a communication standard. The model assumes that this information is evenly distributed among the potential network participants that can be described as the result of a decision building process in a group. Although all group members have the same information available, they still do not know the adoption threshold or preferences of all network participants with the exception of the decision of their direct communication partners or neighbors.

Based on these parameters, a potential adopter can derive his/her optimal adoption moment for a communication standard to join the bandwagon. On the other hand, service providers for such standards can formulate more customized and diffusion phase-related market strategies to attract heterogeneous adopters during the diffusion process. In doing so, they can attract early innovators to overcome the start-up problem, as well as late adopters to keep the bandwagon rolling until critical mass is reached in terms of their preferences structure and different bundles of services (depending on the different bundles of direct and indirect network effects available at that point in time of the diffusion process).

In order to identify and model the economic effects accompanying the diffusion of communication standards and to be able to illustrate the real world importance of communication standards in the broadest sense, an empirical study provides an overview of differently deployed e-business standards and their relevance for the improvement of internal and external business processes. The underlying survey contained questions dealing with the business process changes necessary due to the implementation of the e-business standard, as well as questions targeted on the perceived or realized benefits based on the deployment of those e-business standards. While the empirical survey allows a snapshot of networked industries and economies, the communication solutions introduced in chapter 1 contribute to the next level of interoperability towards a network economy.

The two communication solutions are developed to enable SMEs to participate in communication networks and to increase the degree of EDI-based process automation. Both solutions illustrate that the benefits of automated communication channels have not yet been exploited completely and that more processes could be conducted in a standardized way.

1.2 Structure of the Dissertation

This dissertation analyzes the diffusion patterns of network effect goods and standards with positive network externalities. Network analyses are often based upon the theory of positive network effects, which describes a positive correlation between the number of users of a network good and its utility (Katz et al. 1985). A common finding is the existence of network effects, i.e. the increasing value of a network as the number of its participants increases (demand side economies of scale) leading in many cases to unfavorable welfare outcomes (Pareto-inferior results of diffusion processes) (Clements 2004; Katz et al. 1986b; Weitzel 2004). Katz and Shapiro (Katz et al. 1985) differentiate between direct network effects in terms of the direct "physical effects" (Katz et al. 1985) of being able to exchange information and *indirect network effects* arising from interdependencies in the consumption of complementary goods.

Such complementary or network effect goods constitute network effect markets where the demand of customers is attached to an existing or expected installed base of users and where the linkage between those independent customers is initiated by network effects (Köster 1998). If a network effect good generates a benefit exclusively to the adopter in connection with further adopters and therefore has no stand-alone utility, then one speaks of pure network markets. Communication standards and communication networks belong to a special group of goods, which have a lot in common with public goods. As quasi-public goods, they also constitute (virtual) infrastructures, which are compatible, non-rivalry, and non-excludable in consumption (Musgrave 1959 p. 43; Samuelson 1954). Since network effects are found especially where compatibility is important, the term network often describes the "network of users" of certain technologies or standards such as the network of MS Word or SAP R/3 users (Besen et al. 1994). Therefore, the adoption of compatible technologies (or standards) is considered to constitute networks.

Since compatibility is important in many markets, the individual adoption decisions directly affect the decisions of others. In the economic literature such interdependencies are discussed in detail as bandwagon, snowball, or avalanche effects (Ceci et al. 1982; Leibenstein 1950; Rohlfs 2003). This implies a positive relation between the readiness to adopt network effect goods and the number of other users of the same good or standard. Prominent examples are markets for information and communication technologies, such as for instance the telephone. The benefit of a telephone depends on the number of persons who can be reached. In this simple example the telephones resembles the "nodes", while the telephone circuits represent the "edges" of a network.

Strong network effect phenomena can be found on many markets with compatibility issues. For a successful diffusion of network effect goods or standards in particular the achievement of a critical mass of users is important (Economides et al. 1995a; Economides et al. 1995b; Mauboussin et al. 2000). While traditionally the phenomenon of the critical mass was subject to economic or sociological analyses (Rogers 2003), today there are several information systems approaches which analyze the diffusion of network effect goods by applying neural networks (Plouraboue et al. 1998) or ACE-based models (Wendt et al. 2000). According to the results of the last-mentioned literature, opinion leaders might be able to start a learning process or an exchange of experience about an innovation but, however, they cannot accelerate the diffusion or even solve the start-up problem itself. They can only initiate the learning process which is a product of their own experience (Arrow 1962). Consequently, prospective adopters develop their decision for themselves primarily considering the product information they are acquainted with and their own experience with an innovation, and are not simply focussed on the decision of opinion leaders.

From an economic point of view, open communication standards belong to the group of public goods (Musgrave 1959; Samuelson 1954) due to their simultaneous usability (non-rivalry) and their free accessibility (non-excludable) to. Lack of rivalry in consumption is a central element of standards. Beyond that, for network effect goods it is not only important that no one can be excluded: it is essential for the success of a communication standard that as many adopters as possible use it. The condition of non-excludability is not fulfilled in the case of proprietary or sponsored communication standards and therefore cannot be regarded as "pure" public goods, but rather correspond to the category of club goods (Nicholson 1992, p. 757).

Church, Gandal and Krause (Church et al. 2002) also emphasize that network effects arise if the utility of consumption is related positively to the absolute number of further adopters, which likewise acquire compatible standards or goods. At the same time they deny the connection between the strength of indirect network effects and the size of a network. However, especially for communication networks it is true that the number and variants of compatible products and services increases with the network size, e.g., in hard- and software markets (the so-called hardware and software paradigm). In such networks not only the achievable direct network effects affect the adoption decision, but likewise the realizable indirect network effects (Church et al. 2002; Gupta et al. 1999; Katz et al. 1985). Since both network effects are part of positive network externalities and their magnitude undisputedly increases with the size of a network (Cabral et al. 1999; Csorba 2002), then indirect network effects must also be affected by the size of a network.

The pattern of argument in network effect theory is always the same· the discrepancy between private and collective gains in networks under increasing returns may possibly lead to Pareto-inferior results. With incomplete information about other agents' preferences, excess inertia ("start-up problem") can occur, as no agent is willing to bear the disproportionate risk of being the first adopter of a technology and then becoming stranded in a small network if all others eventually decide in favor of another technology. This *start-up problem* prevents any adoption at all of the particular technology under risk aversion and declining costs, even if everyone prefers it.

While the traditional models contributed greatly to the understanding of a wide variety of problems associated with the diffusion of standards (and consequentially, the evolution of networks), more research is still needed especially when trying to develop solutions to the aforementioned problems (Liebowitz et al. 1994b). Additionally, there are only a few contributions aimed at supporting standardization decisions on an individual level. Furthermore, the specific interaction of potential technology adopters within their personal socio-economical environment and the potential decentralized coordination of network efficiency are neglected. As a result, important phenomena of modern network effect markets such as the coexistence of different products despite strong network effects or the fact that strong players in communication networks force other participants to use a certain solution cannot be sufficiently explained by the existing approaches (Liebowitz et al. 1994b; Weitzel et al. 2000a).

Other areas of research are also concerned with networks. In contrast to network effect theory focusing on compatible technologies constituting networks, diffusion theory analyses relational and structural interaction patterns to explain the diffusion of innovations. Besides these essentially economic research approaches, many (mostly empirical) studies of network phenomena in the form of diffusion processes can be found in various research areas such as anthropology, early sociology, rural sociology, education, medical sociology, communication, etc. Other related areas include actor network theory emphasizing the social construction of networks (Callon 1991), contributions concerning the dispersion of the Internet (David et al. 1996c), policy issues in networks (David 1995; Liebowitz et al. 1996) and inter-temporal coordination problems when building infrastructures (Thum 1995).

When discussing network efficiency, quite often the objective is an overall measure, such as the duration of production processes throughout an entire value chain or aggregate (i.e. supply-chain wide) cost efficiency (centralized solution). Still, in corporate reality such an overall solution, derived from an implicitly assumed collective utility function, does not describe the strategic investment decisions of each participant in a supply chain. Instead, they seek an individually rather than collectively optimal decision (decentralized solution). This discrepancy is partly responsible for many network infrastructures staying far behind their potential and is known as the start-up problem in network effect theory. This start-up problem can also be described as the so far insufficiently described components and properties of a network effect good. Unfortunately, network effects as a constitutive particularity in networks can be a part of externalities with particular influences on the automatic transmission from local to global efficiency which are hard to predict (Weitzel et al. 2000a).

In economics, an externality is considered to be present whenever the utility function of some economic agent includes variables whose values are chosen by another economic agent without particular attention to the welfare effect on the other agent. Generally speaking, in accordance with traditional literature on economics, a network externality exists if market participants fail to internalize somehow the impact of a new network adopter on others in some way. Thus, the question of how to internalize these effects, or in other words, how to find coordination designs to build better networks arises. The answer to this question may be found in a more differentiated analysis of the Penguin effect (Farrell et al. 1986, p. 943). Hungry penguins sit on a floe and wait until the first one jumps into the water because they fear the presence of predators. Each prefers to wait and see what happens with the first one. This wait-and-see behavior occurs with each new standard adoption decision, but it is still unclear why the first one jumped into the water. In the case of unsponsored communication standards, there is no real stand-alone utility of, e.g., being the only one with a telephone device, which would possibly justify jumping first. Analogous to the first moving penguin, which has seen the first fish, or a special dish only it prefers while the rest are waiting for the dish of the day, there are also heterogeneous preferences, as well as different risk aversions and network market determinations which are responsible for the first-mover's adopting a new standard and which are different from the determinants of subsequent adopters. As the network grows, the ratio of achievable direct and indirect network benefits grows and varies in an upwards spiral with positive feedback to each other. This network effect helix phenomenon will be described in more detail in the following sections.

Figure 3 depicts the further structure of this book. After the introduction in chapter 1, the necessary theoretical foundations is provided in chapter 2 and

3, followed by results of an empirical survey in chapter 4 supporting the assumed importance of communication and e-business standards in networked
economies. Subsequently, the two approaches developed to increase the degree of networking are discussed in chapter 5, followed by the diffusion simulation and the network effect helix approach in chapter 6. Finally, chapter 7
concludes and provides some interesting and promising future paths of information systems research in that area.

Figure 3: Structure of the Thesis

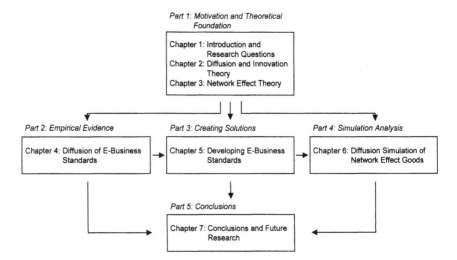

2 Diffusion and Innovation Theory

The diffusion of new goods or standards is an object of interest in innovation as well as diffusion theory. Both fields of research differ from each other by examining the genesis or formation of innovations until the first implementation and usage in the market entrance phase (Bierfelder 1994) in the first case while the research on diffusion analyzes the interplay between the adoption and penetration of innovations in a market regardless of the origin of an innovation (Witt 1987). A further difference exists based on a different understanding of the term innovation. While innovation theory regards an innovation as a process, in diffusion theory an innovation is an object or the result of technological progress.

Both theories are connected by the profit and growth-oriented approach of the Schumpeterian trilogy of invention, innovation, and diffusion (Schumpeter 1947). The Schumpeterian trilogy divides technological progress, for example, into three stages of taxonomy. In the first stage, the invention, creative response or entrepreneur phase, new ideas are generated. In the innovation process stage, new ideas are used to develop or transform new products or processes while the third or diffusion stage is concentrated on the adoption and penetration of these new products or processes (Cantwell 2001).

The analysis of invention and innovation, as well as the diffusion of innovations in the context of information goods has a certain tradition in information systems research, especially in the context of standards setting and diffusion such as EDI or more general E-Business (Beck et al. 2005b; Beck et al. 2005c; Brynjolfsson 1993; Brynjolfsson 1994; Brynjolfsson et al. 1993). Communication standards such as those used for data transmission among mobile phone users can also be regarded as such an innovation.

2.1 Business Environment

Every discussion about the diffusion of innovations such as new communications standards or information goods with a network effect character would be incomplete if the environmental parameters influencing the speed and path of diffusion were not taken into account. Generally, the environmental framework defines the conditions and boundaries of free individual or business activities. The framework comprises certain conditions and excludes other impacts or conditions at the same time, e.g., different legal systems in different countries.

Different frameworks define different drivers or inhibitors for the diffusion of new technologies or standards on the macroeconomic, as well as the company level.

In organizational research literature, business environment or environmental framework are normally synonymous with environmental conditions (Kreikebaum 1998), environmental factors (Meffert 1997), general conditions, or global surroundings (Kubicek et al. 1976).

Kreikebaum (Kreikebaum 1998) characterizes business environment as a set of rules and facts (e.g. the number of competing enterprises in a market) which cannot easily be changed by one's own business activities and therefore are an externally given constant. In the context of multinational companies, business environments can be seen as global changes and developments in competition or—from a more technical point of view—as business improvements based on new standards or technologies adopted on a global level. Meffert argues from an environmental factor point of view differentiating between politically, socio-culturally and economically related general frameworks (Meffert 1997). The lack of distinction between the chosen definitions is the result of the underlying habitual language use.

Kubicek and Thom follow a more corporate policy type of discussion and describe the business environment as general conditions necessary to produce goods and services which are the same for all enterprises or at least for most in a certain geographic region (Kubicek et al. 1976). This general definition can be subsumed under the term "global surrounding" including all conditions in a geographic area. The geographic area is therefore relevant for enterprises with different corporate goals and has an impact on the development and execution of different economic strategies. Economically inspired differences in the definition of business environments comprises:

1. Economic factors: general economic situation in a certain region or market influencing the competitiveness of an enterprise
2. Technological factors: technological progress and development in terms of new products or processes relevant for enterprises in the same market to remain competitive

3. Legal-political factors: legal regulations and executive authority, as well as judiciary can be subsumed under this factor, which are relevant for the business activities of an enterprise

4. Socio-cultural factors: societal and culturally fundamental structures and differences in mentality which have an effect on the behavior and education of persons within an enterprise

5. Physical factors: physical factors are all geographical, infrastructural or topological circumstances which have an impact on the effectiveness of an enterprise

The corporate policy-related factors offer only the perception that a business environment is similar for all enterprises in the same region. However, the differentiation helps to identify further important theoretical foundations beside the theory of the diffusion of innovations, namely the infrastructure theory that also analyzes the diffusion of communications infrastructure. Subsequently, starting with environmental theory, the relevant aspects of innovation and diffusion theory are introduced, followed by aspects of public goods and network effect theory to develop the nature of communication standards responsible for the special paths of their adoption and diffusion.

National business environments can be regarded as specific circumstances or data set at the national level affecting the activities and strategic decisions of individuals as well as enterprises who may potentially adopt communication standards. Due to the universal validity of the previous definitions the question of which factors are of special importance for the diffusion of network effect goods arises. Answering the question will be delayed until the following sections which analyze how deeply the diffusion and innovation theory is affected by environmental circumstances.

2.2 Innovation Theory

Innovations in terms of innovation theory can be both, i.e. completely new innovations (inventions) having the power to revolutionize processes or even markets or innovations in the form of process or product improvements. While inventions have the potential to open completely new markets, process innovations advance existing products or processes and increase the competitiveness of innovators. In fact, most innovations are based on earlier innovations by enhancing former innovations and so on (just as e-business is based on the Internet and before that EDI, which is based again based on protocols, etc.).

Considering the overall innovation creation process, the innovation itself is only one stage. It begins with the R&D phase, where new ideas or solutions are generated, followed by creating prototypes and finally with the production of marketable product or process improvement. A product innovation might be an extreme enhancement of existing products or services, while a process innovation might be an improved production method for goods or services.

The information systems literature identifies two controversial approaches juxtaposed to each other: either innovative information technology (IT) and IT standards have an overall impact on growth and productivity or not at all. Although the IT landscape has changed dramatically, starting with the diffusion of mainframes, then PCs and later on the integration of PCs in networks such as the Internet, the ongoing research on IT and its impact on business processes is still in progress. The statistical problem of identifying empirically a positive impact or rather correlation between the information technologies implemented and productivity is the central point of critique of the so-called productivity paradox (Brynjolfsson 1993; Brynjolfsson et al. 1996a; Hitt et al. 1996; Strassmann 1999; Triplett 1999). The possible benefits of deploying IT are the reduction of processing and communication costs due to automation, or the increasing performance and quality of business processes (Goodhue et al. 1995; Liebowitz 2002). The degree of IT impact can also be classified by the degree of innovativeness. Swanson differentiates between three types of innovation: innovations confined to tasks of information systems, those supporting business administration, and innovations embedded in core business technologies (Swanson 1994). Depending on the category of the innovation, the impact increases when the innovation is part of the core business and decreases when the innovation affects a single business task only.

2.2.1   Determinants of Innovations

The innovative power of an enterprise depends on certain pivotal determinants for the genesis of innovations. Characteristics such as leadership, corporate structure (openness for innovations, creativity, etc), active conflict management, valuation of employees and their skills, customer care and information technology infrastructure are identified as important drivers for innovative enterprises. Based on these facets of an innovatively acting enterprise it is obvious that innovation cannot easily be reduced to the sole responsibility of an R&D department. It is even more a corporate culture and policy challenge which has to be incorporated into enterprise strategies.

Innovations are ideas, behaviors or objects, which are recognized as new by potential adopters and distinguished by their (1) relative advantage, (2) compatibility, (3) complexity, (4) trialability, and (5) observability (Rogers 2003, p. 221).

1. *Relative advantage* describes the degree to which an innovation is better in comparison to the replaced idea or solution (Rogers 2003, p. 229). It can be measured in economic scales, social prestige, convenience or satisfaction and depends less on the objective advantage—which the innovation of the decision unit offers—than subjectively noticed advantage (Rogers et al. 1997). The more the subjectively noticed relative advantage is, the faster an innovation becomes adopted (Mahler et al. 1995).

2. *Compatibility defines the degree to which an innovation is noticed as* compatible with the existing values, experiences and needs of potential adopters (Rogers 2003, p. 240) or (Weiber 1992). Since the adoption of non-compatible innovations usually requires a change of values—which usually takes place very slowly—an innovation which does not conform to the existing values and standards of a social system will diffuse more slowly than a compatible one (Rogers et al. 1997).

3. *Complexity* is defined as the degree to which an innovation is perceived as difficult to understand and to use (Rogers 2003, p. 257) and (Weiber 1992). The more simple an innovation is to understand, the faster it will diffuse (Mahler et al. 1995).

4. *Trialability* describes the degree to which an innovation can be tested on a limited basis. This is important to reduce the adoption decision uncertainties (Rogers 2003, p. 258) and (Rogers et al. 1997). Again, innovations that can be tested are adopted faster than innovations that cannot be tested before they are adopted.

5. *Observability* is defined as the degree to which the consequences of an innovation are visible for others. Visibility promotes the discussion about

an innovation among further potential adopters, since business partners and competitors evaluate the new experiences of the adopter (Rogers 2003, p. 258). Thus the adoption is affected positively by earlier adopters (Rogers et al. 1997).

The following section provides an overview of the Schumpeterian perspective on innovation from a profit and productivity point of view. Since the adoption and deployment of new communication standards can be regarded as a form of innovation, it is important to estimate the value or accompanied profit of such innovations in advance.

2.2.2   Profit resulting from Innovations

Schumpeter's contribution to the transmission mechanism of innovation on entrepreneurial profit and growth is based on the assumption of enterprises' dynamic ambition towards profit maximization (Schumpeter 1983, p. 129). The central element of innovation is a competitive market where innovations enable market participants to reach a more competitive position to realize higher output and profit margins. The competition of dynamic enterprises and the permanent threat of monopolistic price settings of a competitor on the one hand and the striving for reputation and higher profits on the other hand motivate enterprises to be innovative.

This so-called Schumpeterian hypothesis includes two categories to generate profit. The first category is based on market power as the source of profits because otherwise in the case of perfect competition the margins would be reduced to zero. It is argued that perfect polypolystic markets have never existed and will never exist and therefore such assumptions are not very useful. Accordingly, Schumpeter ascribes increasing profits to market power based, e.g., on a first mover advantage.

The second category is based on the idea that external shocks such as new information generate economic activities and value added behavior resulting in a new profit allocation. In this approach, growth is regarded as a destructive process (creative destruction) (Schumpeter 1942, p. 62) or creative response (Schumpeter 1947) accompanied by the transformation of an existing market or the creation of new ones (Cantwell 2001). The intensity of the degree of innovation behavior defines the market structure and ousts enterprises that cannot keep pace. An extraordinary profit increase is therefore not necessarily based on increasing market power but the result of a value adding activity. The additional market power of innovative enterprises is not the source of additional value but is a coincidental byproduct. Due to the imponderable and experimental nature of innovation processes which are more like a trial and error cycle, the second category of profits is best described by the search for higher profits rather the direct orientation towards maximizing profits (Cantwell 2001).

Both latter categories can be combined with Penrose's thesis of the different functions of an enterprise. On the one hand, an enterprise sets a price and output decision, which is a function of its profit, especially if an enterprise can increase its market power at the same time. On the other hand, an enterprise develops innovations to find new solutions and to increase its knowledge. Therefore, the underlying motivation of enterprises to strive for more profits generates new knowledge and productivity opportunities (Penrose 1956).

Although the Schumpeterian differentiation of profit into two categories is disputable, the separation is useful to underline the importance of interorganizational cooperation, as well as competition. Winners and losers characterize competitive markets. Some enterprises perform better in following innovative trends and attract further imitators or business partners that perpetuate further success. This concentration process generates a new market structure with again increasing competitive pressure until a new innovation occurs (Nelson 1997). The business environments necessary in terms of Schumpeter's hypothesis to gain profits from innovations are freedom of competition and an existing business law framework to protect knowledge property such as property rights (see also 2.1).

A critical point for being innovative and successful at the same time is the size of an enterprise. Schumpeter argues that established large enterprises have larger reservoirs of knowledge, business networks, authority, as well as financial resources to survive during recessions (Schumpeter 1983). Therefore, according to Schumpeter, large enterprises can be regarded as dominating locomotives starting the innovation train based on technical progress. Innovative profits are determined by the size of an enterprise and its domination in different markets, as well as market entrance barriers into a certain market. In order to stay innovative, large enterprises internalize the R&D process in an organized way where technical progress is developed by highly specialized experts with market-oriented focus, unlike small firms (Malerba et al. 1996). In more detail, large enterprises can benefit from economies of scale and better funding of R&D, but might possibly also have to bear more risk. Accompanied by the accumulation of innovative knowledge and the last mentioned financial situation (which is not least necessary to patent an innovative idea) large enterprises create entrance barriers for smaller ones by creating a stable but competitive core of persistent innovators (Malerba et al. 1996, p. 470).

2.2.3   Allocation of Innovation-based Profits

In an increasingly networked and globalized economy where process and product innovations are more and more produced in cooperation and where the benefits of innovative standards or network effect goods are used by all adopters, it is necessary to focus on the incentives to innovate, namely the diffusion of innovation-based profits. Innovators and imitators often depend on each other because in the case of network innovations the increase in productivity yielded is often only achievable if further adopters of the innovation or the underlying infrastructure are in place and evenly distributed among the market participants. Such complementary relations therefore complicate every profit forecast relating to an innovation (Rosenberg 1982). According to Schumpeter, innovators gain the largest benefit out of their innovations. This assumption is at least questionable if the innovation is a product or service with public goods property as most information goods are in a network economy. The underlying assumption is that a first-mover-advantage exists but this is not always the case, especially when competitors are following a fast-second-mover-strategy (Liebowitz et al. 1995c). Furthermore, in certain cases it might be necessary that imitators follow soon in order to gain profits at all, e.g., when imitators find the most productive means of producing an innovation or improving an innovation until it is ready for the market. Not bearing the costs of developing an innovation, imitators may have the resource to improve a newly adopted innovation.

Based on the character of innovations, R&D-based knowledge spillovers have an impact on both the private and the social return or profit. This view presumes that an innovation has public goods properties (non-excludable, non-rivalry in consumption, etc.) with positive external network effects or spillovers to other market participants or even other industries (Bernstein et al. 1988).

Technological progress or innovations are often context-related and highly specific. Therefore, additional improvements are often necessary to build a general innovation in order to make it useable for other processes, products, or adopters. If an innovator or even adopter is able to identify and transfer further implementation options onto similar or complementary processes or products, the probability of making such a generalized or standardized innovation successful increases (Cantwell 2001). The abolishment of the difference between innovators and imitators of an innovation emphasizes Schumpeter's view of innovation profits as described above. Innovation-based profits should not be regarded as the consequence of monopolistic first-mover advantage but as profits which increase the productivity of the overall market with imitators using the innovation in new combinations (Cantwell 2001). Innovations created in cooperation networks have the potential to increase the total profit by combining R&D capacity on the one hand and the transformation and integration capacity on the other hand. The highest profits will therefore not necessarily occur on the first-to-discover or first-to-commercialize innovator's side, but on the side of the innovator capable of integrating and advancing an innovation in a real-world scenario. This result directly supports the assumed importance of cooperation in a grid network—or more generally—in a network economy.

2.3 Diffusion Theory

Unlike innovation theory, diffusion theory deals with the adoption, the speed and degree of penetration, and the distribution of an innovation. This diffusion of an innovative standard or product is based on the number of adopting "imitators" (individuals or enterprises) and characterized by uncertainty about the success, the compatibility with existing solutions, and the ability to be more innovative on their part (Rosenberg 1982). Diffusion is regarded as an adjustment process towards a future equilibrium depending on the learning curve of potential imitators. To a certain degree, the innovation process is overlaps with the diffusion process and vice versa. Therefore, in diffusion theory the innovation phase is the first step towards the distribution of a new standard on the market.

2.3.1   Development of Diffusion Theory

Diffusion theory has its roots in different scientific disciplines (Rogers 2003, p. 40). In general, each discipline analyzes domain-specific innovation diffusion behaviors based in its own tradition. Rogers identified the main roots of diffusion theory by analyzing publications from anthropology, sociology, agriculture, education, medicine, communication, economics, and psychology, to mention only the most important ones. Not least due to Rogers' first diffusion book in 1962, diffusion theory became a unified and independent field as an integrated concept in many different research disciplines.

The research on diffusion patterns is mainly focused on the path of dispersion of an innovation, on the dispersion speed, on dispersion related factors and the impact of dispersion-manipulating activities (Hecker 1997) to explain the path of innovation diffusion. For that purpose, diffusion is observed from different perspectives such as from an economic history, adoption behavior, market and infrastructure or development point of view (Brown 1981).

The economic history perspective analyzes the process of adapting innovations to existing requirements and situations which are the essential prerequisites for potential adopters and therefore diffusion. Innovation in this context is regarded as a continuously changing process during the diffusion process which influences the form and function of an innovation, as well as the adopting environment. Such an assimilation to market requirements increases the probability that an innovation will be adopted by further users and therefore be successful (Brown 1981).

2.3.2   Pivotal for Diffusion: The Adoption Decision

A dominating aspect in the research on diffusion is the adoption and decision process, or more precisely, the demand aspect of diffusion. This aspect is based on the idea that the adoption of an innovation is primarily the result of learning or communication processes. Therefore what is examined are predominantly factors which are connected to an effective information flow, as well as characteristics of information flows, the information access, and resistance during the process of deciding whether or not to adopt. Substantial aspects of innovation adoption resistances are innovation-readiness and the congruence between the innovation and the social, economic and psychological characteristics of the potential adopter (Brown 1981).

While the adoption perspective is based on the assumption that all potential adopters have the same opportunity to accept an innovation, the market and infrastructure perspective assumes that the possibilities of adoption may differ substantially. Therefore, the latter focuses on the process by which innovations and the conditions for their adoption are brought to the potential adopters, representing the supply aspect of diffusion. This perspective is based on the assumption that individual behavior is the result of the alternatives offered, limited by the market and controlled by the government and private institutions rather than representing free will. Thus, diffusion is determined substantially by the behavior of institutions. The development perspective deals with both the impact of diffusion on phenomena such as economic development, social change and individual welfare, as well as the resulting effects on diffusion based on this impact (Brown 1981).

Only two of the four perspectives address the diffusion process directly, namely the adoption perspective and the market and infrastructure perspective. Both perspectives are based on the assumption that an innovation does not change during the entire diffusion process. Furthermore, it is assumed that the diffusion process is characterized by the fact that the potential adopters of an innovation do not adopt at the same time or even never will adopt. In addition, the diffusion process exhibits a certain regularity at a given level of population, so that by a comparison of the adopters with the non-adopters of a given innovation systematic differences may be revealed concerning the economic, social, regional, and demographic characteristics of each group (Brown 1981).

2.3.3   Impact of Institutions on the Diffusion Process

In what follows, diffusion and its determining factors are discussed in more detail. It is widely agreed that diffusion is the aggregated result of the adoption decision of all members of a social system (Felten 2001; Gierl 1987; Kortmann 1995; Röck 2000; Weiber 1992). The adoption designates the decision to take over and/or completely use an innovation (Felten 2001; Rogers 2003). The adoption decision usually does not take place immediately, but after a certain information-gathering phase to diminish uncertainty about the pros and cons of the innovation. This process is also called the innovation decision-making process. It differs from other decision-making processes by the fact that the novelty of the innovation has been noticed and the associated increase in uncertainty (Rogers 2003, p. 20).

The process cycle depends on whether the adoption decision is made by an individual or an organization. The individual decision is typically subdivided in an ideal case into the phases: knowledge, persuasion, decision, implementation and confirmation (Rogers 2003, pp. 168-218). In the knowledge phase, the decision-making unit acquires information about the existence of an innovation, followed by gathering experiences to become acquainted with the properties and functions of an innovation. In the following decision-making phase, the decision unit collects and evaluates further relevant information in order to judge the innovation and to form an attitude in relation to the innovation. In the decision phase, e.g., tests are conducted which lead to the adoption or refusal of the innovation. In the implementation phase, the innovation is adopted and integrated into existing systems or infrastructures. In the confirmation phase the decision unit tries to eliminate cognitive dissonances that arise or tries to reduce them at least by looking, e.g., for further information about the innovation in order to confirm or revise the decision. Between these phases, forward and backward jumps and/or feedbacks can occur (Weiber 1992).

Thus, institutions and the business environment affect the decision whether or not to adopt an innovation in various ways, and the adoption depends, e.g., on the existing infrastructure already in place (Gierl 1987). The innovation's relationship to an existing infrastructure can be neutral, complementary or competitive (Kortmann 1995). While from an open infrastructure no influence on the innovation adoption decision results, complementary infrastructure increases the applicability or attractiveness of an innovation and thus promotes the willingness to adopt.

Furthermore, it depends on the business environment whether an existing condition is felt to be an unsatisfactory problem the solving of which may be the reason for intervention or innovative behavior. The perceived need for changes increases if the problem or inefficiency identified is not eliminated. Such needs can occur as a result of the perception or awareness of an innovation or can occur after an active search for problem solving solutions on the market. In each case, the availability of innovation-referred information will increase (Rogers 2003, p. 15).

The social environment affects the behavior and with it the decision of the potential innovation adopter by means of norms, standards, and role-expectation. Standards form the opinions and attitudes of the decision unit. They restrain the adoption of innovations which are not compatible with them. Role-expectation is defined by the profile or behavior of a person while the expectations of the social system and controlled is defined by positive and negative sanctions. Positive sanctions are, e.g., social acknowledgment, increase in prestige and praise while imprisonment and mockery are possible examples of negative sanctions. Consequently, positive sanctions stimulate the adoption of innovations while negative sanctions impede their adoption. Examples of environmental factors which affect the adoption of new technologies by enterprises are tax law, patent law, license rights, market size, market structure, financial supply, and availability of work (Mohr 1977).

During the entire innovation decision-making process, an information exchange takes place between the potential adopter and their surrounding environment, using different kinds of communication. Diffusion research differentiates between interpersonal communication and mass communication. Interpersonal communication takes place via personal contact among two or more persons. With mass communication such as radio, television, and newspapers information is communicated through mass media. While interpersonal communication is important and is more suitable when influencing opinions and attitudes, potential adopters can also be informed about the existence of an innovation quickly and more efficiently by mass media.

Therefore, mass communication in the perception phase of the innovation adoption decision-making process plays an important role, while a more important role can be assigned to interpersonal communication in the forming of the adoption decision in the decision making phase (Rogers 2003, p. 36).

2.4 Diffusion of Public Goods and Infrastructure

The importance of communication standards and network effects in corporate systems can also be analyzed from a more general perspective. Standards and their implementation in the form of adopted licenses, software, or even complete ERP-systems constitute both a physical as well as a virtual infrastructure which provides benefits for all network participants using the same network infrastructure.

2.4.1 Public Goods: Emergence and Definitions

The origin of the theory of public goods goes back to an essay of Samuelson from 1954, in which he identifies substantial properties of public goods, or in his own words "collective consumption goods" (Samuelson 1954, p. 387). First of all the fundamental characteristic of public goods is based on the ability to be used simultaneously by several consumers or individuals. Secondly, Samuelson recognizes the characteristic of the interpersonal indivisibility of public goods. Based on Samuelson's definition, two elementary principles are finally developed in the literature. The principles of non-rivalry and non-exclusion in consumption to classify goods go back to (Samuelson 1954) and are illustrated in Table 1.

Table 1: Classification of Public and Private Goods

	Excludable	Non-excludable
Rivalry	**Private Goods**	Common Goods
Non-rivalry	Club Goods	**Public Goods**

Source:(Musgrave 1959, p. 43) and (Nicholson 1992, p. 757).

If a good is characterized by non-rivalry, then the consumption of the product or standard is not interfered with by the simultaneous use of the same product or standard by another consumer. Several individuals can use the same good to the same extent under same conditions. Use by additional individuals causes opportunity costs of zero. A typical example of a non-rivalry good is a public television program or the beam of a lighthouse, but in principle all digital goods belong to this category to a certain degree. If a good possesses the property of non-exclusion, then no individual can be excluded from the consumption of the good. The ability to exclude someone from consumption is a necessary condition for the supply of private goods. But the ability to exclude someone is not given per se, but by assignment of property rights (Musgrave 1959, p. 9).

Pure public goods are given if a good fulfills both criteria, e.g., in the case of the lighthouse. The opposite of it is the pure private good, characterized by rivalry in consumption and the ability to exclude others from consumption: if a unit of the private good is consumed, then it is no longer available to other consumers. Furthermore, private goods are divisible, unlike public goods, since different persons can consume different quantities of a good.

Public goods are freely available for all individuals in the same quantity, while the total quantity of the private goods corresponds to the sum of the subsets controlled by the economic agents. Table 1 depicts a classification of pure public and private goods together with possible combinations.

Club goods are characterized by the fact that consumers are excludable and—to a certain degree—that they are non-rivalry in consumption. Typical examples of this category are motorways with toll or cable television channels. Common goods are rivalry in consumption, but exclusion is not possible (e.g., freely accessible meadow).

2.4.2 Noncontributors, Free-riders and Market Failure

Products and services with public goods properties or "publicness" can lead to substantial problems and inefficiencies both from an allocation and distribution point of view. Often consumers cannot be excluded from the use of public goods such as information or digital goods. Therefore, they have no interest in revealing their true preferences or willingness to pay because in doing so they must fear that they have to contribute financially to the creation of the public good (Musgrave 1959, p. 8). In fact, consumers hope that others or society itself will acquire the public good, in order to take a free ride at their expenses. If all consumers behaved opportunistically, society (or the supplier of public goods) would underestimate the demand and under-allocate resources to their production (Musgrave 1959, pp. 8-9).

The free-rider problem can be clarified by introducing the game theoretical prisoner's dilemma with two households considering independently from each other whether they want to provide a public good or not. Let us assume that the price of the public good concerned amounts to 3 monetary units per unit. The two households have each a maximum willingness to pay of 2 monetary units per unit. If both households make a unit available, each receives a net utility of 4 - 3 = 1. The households i can decide between the two strategies: to contribute (b_i) and not-to-contribute (n_i). If household 2 decides for the strategy (b_2), then household 1 will select strategy (n_1) since it promises a higher net advantage. If household 2 behaves as a free rider (n_2), then household 1 will decide for the same strategy (n_1). This strategy is always the best alternative for household 1, independently of the behavior of household 2. Due to the symmetrical game arrangement, the same applies to household 2, so that a stable equilibrium (n_1, n_2) can be identified. In this equilibrium, both participants have the incentive to act as free riders while hoping that the other one takes over the costs of the supply of the public good. In contrast, the solution (b_1, b_2) is an unstable equilibrium.

The strategy not-to-contribute (n_i) is dominant for both households and leads in this case to an inefficient equilibrium, since both households could benefit from a joint strategy of (b_1, b_2). (n_1, n_2) is a Nash equilibrium where no participant can improve its benefit by deviating in behavior or changing strategy if the other participant retains his/her strategy (Nicholson 1992, p. 625). Due to the characteristics of public goods, consumers have a free-rider incentive: they can use the public good to the same extent as those who have paid for it, which results in too low a supply of public goods. A market undersupply or failure of goods with public goods property occurs. In extreme cases not a single unit of the public good might be supplied, with the consequence that the market fails, since no private supply of public goods is provided (Musgrave 1959, pp. 6-17) (Andel 1992, p. 383). In this way one can see the substantial difference to the price mechanisms of private goods. Unauthorized customers can be excluded from the use and consumption of private goods. The utility of a good is therefore only available for customers who are willing to pay as an expression of their preferences on the market for a certain product. In the ideal case, a supplier decides now if she or he wants to produce the demanded quantity. The market for private goods reaches a Pareto-optimal allocation if the marginal utility corresponds to the marginal costs of each person. In a Pareto-optimal equilibrium no agent is able to position her- or himself better without at the same time positioning another individual worse (Musgrave 1959).

The analysis of a Pareto-optimal allocation of public goods has its roots in an essay by Lindahl, published in 1919 (Musgrave 1959; van de Nouweland et al. 2002). Based on a graphically-oriented model introduced in Lindahl's contribution, Samuelson developed his own model to explain the circumstances influencing the Pareto-optimal diffusion of public goods (Samuelson 1954). The model assumes two individuals or agents considering whether or not to acquire a public good which they can use together. Both must decide individually how much they are willing to pay to finance the public good. The total capital is described by w_1 and w_2 respectively, while x_1 and x_2 are the remaining amount for consumption and g_1 and g_2 are the money used to acquire the public good. The utility function of the agents depends on the private consumption and the quality G of the public good. Therefore, the individual utility is a function of $u_1(x_1,G)$ and $u_2(x_2,G)$ respectively. The cost function of a certain quality of the public good is given by $c(G)$. Both agents must pay at least $c(G)$ if they want to acquire the public good with the quality G. Consequently, the budget restrictions of the two agents are:

$$x_1+x_2+c(G)=w_1+w_2$$

A Pareto-optimal allocation of public goods is realized, when no agent or person can be made better off without someone else being made worse off (Nicholson 1992, p. 224), i.e. if the sum of the marginal payment willingness corresponds accurately to the marginal costs. This is the so-called Samuelson condition or Lindahl equilibrium (Musgrave 1959, p. 74).

2.4.3   Standards and Network Goods: Private or Public Goods Category?

In the following, an analysis of some special properties of communication standards or network goods that violate several assumptions necessary to explain an efficient functioning market, such as, e.g., for private goods are provided. This is equivalent to the conclusion that in the absence of subsidies coordination mechanisms in purely private markets are not adequate to coordinate the diffusion or allocation of communication standards and are not capable of overcoming the start-up problem. Due to consumption externalities, marginal prices determined by the private market may lead to a socially undesirable outcome.

Communication standards as part of digital or information goods can be represented as binary-coded data or bits and therefore can be transferred or processed electronically worldwide. Examples of such digital goods are digital television programs, electronic books, music, films, web pages, telecommunication services, and software (Shapiro et al. 1998). Hardware is not part of digital goods, but a necessary complementary infrastructural prerequisite to make digital goods available.

The potential application and usability of digital goods are considerably wider when compared with non-digital, tangible, or physical goods (Choi et al. 1997). Consequently, information goods are, like public goods, of different importance or value for different consumers.

In general, digital goods are, like public infrastructure goods, expensive in the creation phase while in the power output phase the usage costs are marginal or even zero. The diversification and multi-usability together with the non-rivalry in consumption are further indicators of similarities between public goods and digital goods. In contrast to public goods, customers of privately supplied digital goods such as certain information, data exchange standards, software, etc. can be excluded from consumption. Even more, the supplier can control the diffusion of digital goods if the good belongs to the category of sponsored network goods.

The production of digital goods such as software can be characterized by high fixed costs, due, for example, to research and development costs or the expensive equipment necessary to establish a grid (Shy 2000, p. 53). On the other hand, the pure production process is in most instances reproduction, providing electronic copies of the original. The resulting variable costs and marginal costs, e.g., for copies, are thereby constant and negligibly low.

The average production costs of physical goods are characterized by a U-shaped gradient. Initially, the costs of an additionally produced unit are small but rise steeply after the capacity border is reached, since further costs of maintenance work, substantial investments in network infrastructure, or overtime emerge. Digital goods are not subject to restrictions of capacity due to their easy reproducibility and the fact that there are only low constant marginal costs with rising production quantities. With the increase in production, the average costs decrease. At a very large quantity level the average costs even reach the marginal costs level (Shapiro et al. 1998, p. 21).

The supply of network effect goods as part of public goods or quasi-public goods could only be efficiently organized by means of the market if the production and consumption met the following conditions valid for private goods. If one or more preconditions are broken, then one of the other types of goods described in Table 2 is given. Although the structure of the Table suggests a possibly clear distinction between the different goods categories, most goods properties are fluent and therefore only mixed forms or real types of goods can be found in real world scenarios.

Thus in Table 2 more ideal types are provided as postulated by Max Weber's classification concept (von Schelting 1922). Nevertheless, the Table seems to be helpful in discussing why traditional price and market models are not useful to analyze the diffusion of network effect goods.

Pure private goods are—according to neoclassical assumptions—character-ized by perfect competition in all product and factor markets, perfect informa-tion (complete, accurate, and freely available) on the relevant prices and char-acteristics of products and factors, and perfect mobility of all resources. Fur-thermore, and in a direct distinction to public goods, pure private goods must not have any kind of externalities (positive or negative) in the production and consumption of goods or any other interdependence in consumption between consumers. In order to guarantee a functioning market, private goods must al-ways have an excludability property, meaning that everyone but the buyer of the good is excluded from its benefits. Some goods have the characteristics partly of private goods (no effects or spillovers on third parties in the case of a pure private good) and partly of public goods at the same time. It is possible for the market to produce such club goods to a limited extent (Buchanan 1965), but not at an appropriately satisfying level for all market participants.

Table 2: Extended Classification of Private, Public, and Network Goods

		Non-excludable or non-proprietary	
	Excludable or pro-prietary	Limited scope, multiple regional clusters	Unlimited scope, single supra-regional cluster
Collective consumption impos-sible (rival)	**Private Goods**	Local Common Goods	Global Common Goods
Collective consumption (non-rival) → Possible →Necessary	Club Goods / Sponsored Network Goods	**Public Goods** / Local Network Goods	Global Public Goods / **Network Goods**

In particular, if potential transaction costs for enforcing property rights are high, it might be unattractive for private markets to supply such goods (Coase 1960). Private markets can be established only for goods for which property rights can be guaranteed and easily exchanged. If there are open communica-tion standards or pure network goods that market participants desire to have but which have large coordination and transactions costs, these goods are unlikely to be supplied in a sufficient amount by the market. If one of the above-mentioned conditions does not hold, then a market failure condition exists.

In summary, non-proprietary digital communication standards tend—due to their easy reproducibility—to be non-rivalry in consumption, and therefore can be assigned to the group of public goods. Nevertheless, communication standards can also be rivalry in consumption, e.g., if the given underlying infrastructure has capacity restrictions such as a server which can provide only a certain capacity. If too many users try to access this server, then the download time increases. Another problem for privately supplied digital goods can occur if the usage cannot be restricted to customers paying for the information or service. Non-rivalry in this case and the difficulty of excluding unauthorized customers can lead to undersupply of markets with digital goods if free riders have access. Since it is assumed in this contribution that unsponsored communication standards as an ideal type belong to the group of public goods, their successful diffusion among potential participants cannot be coordinated by common market instruments developed for private goods. Because communication standards are necessary for networked economies to realize potential reductions in coordination and transaction costs, the diffusion of standards that constitute a virtual infrastructure remains a difficult task.

2.5 Infrastructure and Networks as part of Public Goods

In traditional economic literature, the importance of distributed standards with network effect properties are discussed in the context of infrastructure theory while the term "network effect" does not appear there. The economic effects of infrastructure can be divided into household-related and enterprise-related effects, as well as into time horizon effects in the phase of infrastructure creation and long-term effects in the phase of infrastructure power output. The long-term power output effects of the installed infrastructure are multilayered, so that it cannot be assigned continuously to a single sector. Therefore, the effects must be subdivided further on into tendentially one-sided and double-sided effects. Table 3 provides the most important effects based on the existence of infrastructure.

Household-related infrastructure covers all systems and standards which are used mainly by households, as well as by all educational, social, cultural and leisure facilities. Although it is mainly households that use traffic and communication facilities, they are usually assigned to the enterprise-related infrastructure.

During the development phase, the infrastructure affects the incomes of the households and employment directly and indirectly. The direct effect arises because of the employment of work and capital during the construction of "bricks-and-mortar" facilities, leading to direct labor factor incomes. These incomes again produce multiplier effects, which likewise have a positive impact on incomes and employment. The phase of power output begins after the production of household-related infrastructure. If it is made publicly available, then the prices for its use are more favorable than the use prices of private market goods. In extreme cases where the state makes infrastructure facilities available free of charge, e.g., with schools, universities, or roads, households and enterprises have in general utilization costs of zero. Thus the consumption and use-possibilities increase (Momberg 2000).

Table 3: Systematic of Infrastructure Effects

Time horizon		Household-related effects	Enterprise-related effects
Short-term effects during infrastructure creation		Income and employment effects	Production effects
Long-term effects during infrastructure power output	→ tendentially one-sided	- Direct consumption effect	- Direct productivity and growth effects - Direct cost effects - External agglomeration effect - Regional and inter-sectoral discrimination effects - Inter-regional trade effect
	→ tendentially double-sided	- Inter-temporal allocation effect - Inter-regional allocation and mobility effects	

Source: (Momberg 2000, p. 37).

Enterprise-related infrastructure comprises the areas traffic, energy, communication, water supply, and water disposal and can be regarded as a factor of production. Therefore, investments in infrastructure may increase the production capabilities of enterprises. The production effect results on the one hand from the investments in infrastructure, on the other hand on additional consumer expenditures from the multiplier effect. Thus, productivity and growth effects are partly based on infrastructure as an input factor of production. If one utilizes an extended Cobb-Douglas production function, in which infrastructure represents an own factor of production, then increasing the input factor infrastructure leads to increasing output (Biehl 1986, pp. 87-100). With ceteris paribus employment of the other factors of production their productivity also rises (Biehl 1995; Biehl et al. 1980).

The direct cost effect results from the free or low-priced supply of infrastructure facilities used by households and enterprises, such as traffic routes and network connections provided by the state. An external agglomeration effect may emerge resulting from an increased number of industrial settlements caused by the cost effective availability of infrastructure facilities. Through the spatial concentration of customers and suppliers, the supply and communication paths shorten, resulting in further cost reduction. Subsequently, a regional and inter-sector discrimination effect occurs due to the lack of equally distributed infrastructure facilities in all regions and sectors, based on budget restrictions in the public finances. Therefore, the infrastructure in place can be used only by enterprises which need a certain infrastructure as a factor of production and are regionally close to it (Biehl et al. 1980). Consequently, such public goods have only a regional influence on enterprises located in this area (local network good, see Table 2).

The inter-regional trade effect is a consequence of the differences in infrastructure provision between different regions. Investments in the infrastructure change the factor of productivity itself and the rate of factor utilization in a region. These changed production conditions lead to a regional specialization of production. With the structure of production, the commercial stream also changes. The impact of a certain infrastructure can often not be assigned exclusively to a single sector. Among these effects are the inter-temporal allocation effect and the inter-regional allocation and mobility effect (Biehl 1995).

The inter-temporal allocation effect results from the financial need for infrastructure investments. The associated demand for capital changes the capital market interest rate, and as a result, the short and medium-term saving and investment decisions of the households and/or enterprises are affected. The productivity costs, discrimination and agglomeration effects lead to changing factors of production, resulting in a movement and rearrangement of work and capital.

The convergence of different infrastructure standards together with the afore-mentioned amalgam of infrastructure and private work force and capital leads to unpredictable implications for technological innovation, national regulation, and legal systems. Consequently, implications such as mix-and-match usage of network infrastructure have to be taken into account when a new infrastructure setup or an upgrade of an old one is planned. Gaining the full potential of an infrastructure as potential factor depends—similar to benefiting from network effects—on broad coverage. Thus interconnecting formerly unconnected or not standardized networks is a critical task for policy makers (Biesheuvel-Roosenburg 2001).

This section illustrated the important role of standards which constitute networks or infrastructure. The economic implications of communication standards are changing all processes and production parameters in a globally networked economy. Therefore, it is very important to understand the adoption and diffusion dynamics of network effect goods.

2.6 Diffusion Approaches in the Information Systems Discipline

While innovation diffusion theory is an interdisciplinary research area describing various forms of adoption and diffusion behaviors in a more general way, there are two widely recognized diffusion specification frameworks in the information systems research area, aimed at describing the diffusion of IT technologies, applications and software from a information systems point of view. Diffusion theory in conjunction with network effect theory supports the observed phenomena very well, as analyzed in more detail in chapter 1. However, for the diffusion of new technologies or innovative applications such as those discussed in chapters 1 and 1, where two applications are introduced to increase the compatibility in communication and automation between business partners, these two more specific and IT-oriented approaches are more helpful in discussing the diffusion of new technologies. Therefore, the technology acceptance model and the technology-organization-environment model are introduced briefly in the following sections.

2.6.1   Technology Acceptance Model (TAM)

Although information technology has doubtless made major progress accompanied by considerable changes in various business processes in recent decades, the question of how to measure the technological impact on efficiency and overall business value remains open. As Carr formulated it in his controversial article "IT Doesn't Matter" (Carr 2003), the contribution of IT to productivity is debatable. In order to throw light on the barely visible transmission process from the first gathering of information about an innovative IT solution up to the perceived usefulness of IT adoption Davis, Bagozzi and Warshaw have developed the Technology Acceptance Model (TAM) (Davis et al. 1989) as an extension of Aizen and Fishbein's theory of reasoned action. The base assumption of both approaches is that a potential adopter can behave and decide independently without being restricted by any environmental or organizational constraints. Consequently, although individuals might have good reasons for adopting a technology or not, their decision might not always be the result of a clearly formulated intention (Davis 1989; Davis et al. 1989).

In their often-cited contribution, they examined the acceptance or rejection decision for or against the adoption of IT in long-term surveys before and after an adoption. The model is constituted by two constructs determining the potential adopters' behavior and intention in terms of whether or not to adopt a new technology: the "perceived usefulness" and the "perceived ease of use" (Davis 1989). A refined version proposed by Davis considers the pre-implementation belief about the usefulness and ease of use, as well as the post-implementation beliefs (Szajna 1996).

The perceived usefulness describes the anticipations a potential adopter associates with a new technology or system that is promising to enhance the performance of the business processes affected. According to Davis, potential adopters want to be rewarded when they worry about improvements in working performance, and such a system is supposed to have a positive influence on the use-performance relationship (Davis 1989). Initially, interested adopters have to gather information about the regarded innovation in order to examine its features and to create an image of its perceived usefulness. The perceived usefulness could contain the promise, e.g., of increasing the production quality or improving the quality management. Another reason might be the promise of increasing work productivity or lowering workforce costs. In general, if a job can be done easier, cheaper, or faster than before then an innovation might perceived as useful (Davis 1989).

Furthermore, the perceived usefulness depends on the perceived ease of use or in other words, its usability. If an innovation fails to be regarded as usable, it can hardly be perceived as useful. The perceived ease of use is the degree to which a potential adopter believes that implementing a new technology will be free from effort. An application considered as easy to use is more likely to be adopted than another one. Nevertheless, for attracting new adopters the perceived usefulness seems to be more important (Davis 1989).

Because of its robust predictions of user acceptance, tested in several empirical surveys, several extensions of the model have been developed since David introduced his model in order to explain the perceived usefulness and usage intentions in the context of social influences and cognitive instrumental processes.

2.6.2   Technology Organization Environment Model (TOE)

The Technology Organization Environment or TOE framework was developed by Tornatzky and Fleischer in 1990 and examines the decision making process of adopting new technologies (Tornatzky et al. 1990). The focus of the TOE approach is on the analysis of the evaluating process until an adoption decision and implementation is made. According to Tornatzky and Fleischer, three important factors influence this decision-making process, namely technology, organization, and environment as already mentioned in the name of the framework.

The technological context comprises the internal and external technology or IT infrastructure relevant for a firm. As a result of path dependencies and affiliation to a certain industry, firms have different needs for and different environments of information technologies. Furthermore, firms do not need every available innovation, nor can they capitalize on new technology in the same way compared to other firms. Because of this, the TOE framework takes into account the technologies a firm already uses and analyzes the benefits accompanying the new technology that is under evaluation for adoption at the same time (Tornatzky et al. 1990).

The organizational context defines several descriptive measures such as the kind of organization (e.g., central or decentral managed organization), the degree of formalization and standardization of business processes, the quality of the human resources, or the available amount of "slack" resources. Anything inside a firm (staff, business processes, IT infrastructure in place, etc.) and managed by the firm belongs to the organization category. While the processes inside a firm can be subdivided into formal and informal, the structure of a firm can be distinguished into organic and mechanical (Tornatzky et al. 1990, p. 41).

The environmental context also influences the decision-making process and comprises all kinds of business environmental drivers and inhibitors, such as the decisions of business partners, of competitors, or of the government (including legal issues or potentially available subsidies). The (business) environment includes various factors such as the availability of skilled labor, changes in market demand, market pressure from innovative competitors, or the customer-supplier relationship, to mention only a few examples (Tornatzky et al. 1990, p. 153).

Several information systems researchers have used and adjusted the TOE framework to analyze empirically the adoption decision-making process for different technologies, industries, and countries. For example, Zhu et al. analyze the value of e-business technologies and have identified six factors influencing this value based on an empirical survey and testing (Zhu et al. 2004).

While the adoption and diffusion process for stand-alone usable private goods can be described properly by applying one of the aforementioned models, the situation changes when the diffusion of public goods or more precisely communication standards is to be analyzed. As illustrated in the sections 2.4 and 2.5, communication standards as part of public goods have external effects on other market and network participants. Consequently, the diffusion and infrastructure theory has to be expanded by introducing network effect theory in chapter 1 as a complement in order to understand the nature of communication standards. By the application of all three theories, diffusion, infrastructure, and network effect theory, we will be able to analyze the ergodic paths of communication standards diffusion in the subsequent chapters.

3 Network Effect Theory

There are several definitions for network effects in the economic literature which are more or less detailed or specific. Katz and Shapiro (Katz et al. 1985, p. 424) describe the source of positive consumption externalities as the "utility that a user derives from consumption of goods" which "increases with the number of other agents consuming the (same) good". Another definition also provided by Katz and Shapiro defines network effects as "the value of (a) membership to one user (which) is positively affected when another user joins and enlarges the network" (Katz et al. 1994, p. 94). Church, Gandal and Krause (Church et al. 2002, p. 1) emphasize that "network effect exists if consumption benefits depend positively on the total number of consumers who purchase compatible products". Economides introduces the term "network industries" where external effects in vertical industries play a crucial role (Economides 1996a). According to these definitions, it is easy to come up with many examples such as computer or telecommunication networks, but also automated teller machines (ATM), credit cards, VHS video systems, QWERTY keyboards and more. Such wide definitions would also include newspaper subscriptions, golf club memberships, or customer loyalty programs. Literally all kinds of consumption with positive feedbacks on the supply side, as well as on the consumer side could be subsumed under the terms of network effects and network externalities. Obviously, such a broad definition is not helpful to describe the unique constellation in communication networks, where each adopter is a "consumer" and (willingly or not) a "supplier" of an adopted standard at the same time. These network externalities should therefore be the core of any definition of network effects.

3.1 Network Effect Goods

Liebowitz and Margolis have refocused the academic discussion on this point in many articles criticizing the widespread use of the term and suggestion that all kinds of economic phenomena are network effects. They define network externalities as a constitutive element of specific kinds of network effects "in which the equilibrium exhibits unexploited gains from trade regarding network participants" (Liebowitz et al. 1994b, p. 135). In the following, this work is oriented on the later definition, regarding only network effects in horizontal (direct) and vertical (indirect), two-sided networks of adopters where each new adopter adds to the value of the network for the existing network members.

Such a limited and more focused view of network effects allows the identification, isolation and analysis of phenomena which occur in adopter networks more precisely while still being able to emphasize the public goods properties of communication standards as a research object.

A simple illustration of an adopter network is a system of objects (agents or participants) and (physical or virtual) connections between these objects. If the connections and objects are represented in physical form, as with telecommunications or road system infrastructures, then one speaks of material, tangible or physical networks. Immaterial or virtual networks, however, are characterized by the fact that the connections exist not physically, but in the form of contracts or by application of the same standards, e.g., when adopters of the same software can exchange files, then they are in the same virtual network (Shapiro et al. 1998, p. 230).

The expression "goods" can be divided into private and public goods, as already described above. A further possible classification is provided by classification into stand-alone goods, network effect goods and system goods. While stand-alone goods provide a stand-alone benefit by themselves in consumption (e.g., a desk or a bookshelf, etc.), network effect goods additionally offer benefits by the diffusion of compatible components which create derivative benefits (e.g., software for PCs, or games for video game consoles). Thus, in contrast to stand-alone goods, the benefit of network effect goods depend on the creation of positive network effects, network externalities (Katz et al. 1986b, p. 823), while demand-side economies of scale (Shapiro et al. 1998, p. 180), or increasing-returns technologies (Arthur 1989) are the source of benefits and a primary property of network effect goods.

System goods generate solely derivative or pure network benefits, e.g., telephones or EDI-converters, which inherently have no stand-alone benefit and consequently are useless if further market participants do not possess the same technology or standard. However, if the number of adopters increases, then the derivative benefit increases likewise, since the participants now have more possible communication partners. Thus, the individual purchase decision affects the purchase behavior of others. In economic literature such interdependencies are characterized as bandwagon-, herd-, avalanche-, and Veblen-effects (Ceci et al. 1982; Choi 1997; Leibenstein 1950).

From an economic point of view, information and communication technology (ICT) standards belong to the group of public goods due to the possibility of simultaneous use (non-rivalry) and open access (non-excludable). A lack of rivalry in consumption in particular is a constitutive element of communication standards. Even more such network-effects-generating standards call for a large number of users or adopters in order to benefit from them. Accordingly, existing standard users have an interest in an increasing number of adopters to benefit from likewise increasing network benefits.

Apart from these similarities between public and network goods, there are differences in the creation phase and exploitation or utilization phase of both goods categories. While physical public goods such as an infrastructure for highways normally produce high setup and investment costs in the creation phase, the costs for creating a communication standard can be relatively low in comparison to establishing a communication network with its recurrent individual setup-cost for each new adopter over the lifetime of a communication standard. Since the individual adoption costs may vary for each adopter, it is extremely difficult to predict the diffusion path of a particular communication standard (especially in pure network markets).

Katz und Shapiro (Katz et al. 1985) have introduced a differentiation between direct and indirect network effects. Accordingly, direct network effects describe an immediate connection between the number of users and the value of the regarded network effect good ("direct physical effect" (Katz et al. 1985, p. 424) such as in the case of the telephone. In contrast, indirect network effects are based on the interdependencies of consuming complementary goods or services. Examples are the hardware-software paradigm (Gandal et al. 2000), consulting services for standard software packages, or operating systems and application programs. Markets, which are strongly influenced by inter-cooperability or compatibility, can also be regarded as markets with strong network effects, since compatibility or standardization in general can only be achieved in cooperation with others. Kindleberger (Kindleberger 1983) proceeds from the public good property of standards (network externalities) to the fee-rider problem in the creation phase of standards, based on the economic difficulty of getting the funding when the standard can be used for free afterwards. Arthur (Arthur 1983; Arthur 1989) points out that the diffusion process of goods with increasing returns or network effect property can lead to multiple market equilibria. The diffusion process tends to monopolistic markets with lock-in effects in a certain standard or good. Furthermore, the diffusion process of standards is influenced by small, erratic incidences, especially in the case of unsponsored or open standards. In other words, the diffusion is not necessarily following a uniquely predictable path. The most frequently mentioned example in this context is the video recorder battle between VHS versus Beta (Arthur 1990; Dranove et al. 2003; Greenstein 1994) where the final market outcome remained indistinct while both standards competed to become the quasi-standard.

Analogous to the previous example, Besen und Farrell (Besen et al. 1994) illustrate that most networks are not robust once installed. As the video recorder example has shown, different incompatible standards can hardly coexist in network effect markets, at least not for a long time. In fact, even participants in apparently locked markets can switch almost completely from one to another standard (tippy networks), as the Netscape Navigator example as former market leader for Internet browsers has shown. It will be an interesting research area to analyze the ongoing adoption process of open source browsers such as Mozilla Firefox or Opera and their potential to tip the market again.

Having this in mind, the difficulty is to predict the market outcome or even the result of the individual decision-making process in terms of whether or not to adopt a certain communication standard. The discrepancy between the privately perceived benefit and the overall collective benefit can obviously result in Pareto-inferior market results or market failure. An ex post analysis could reveal that the wrong standard was chosen or too many (excess momentum) or too few users (excess inertia) have adopted a standard. Typically, the high risk for early adopters of a new standard is to adopt a standard with too little network potential or even to adopt the wrong standard. Avoiding the risk of stranding in a small network is therefore a pivotal issue for both adopters as well as suppliers of standards, especially in pure network markets. Assuming rational behavior and incomplete information, the above-mentioned stranding or start-up dilemma of an innovation or communication standard can impede its successful diffusion even when all prospective adopters are willing to adopt. This phenomenon is also known as "aggressive waiting" inside enterprises, where each department is "sitting out" the version changes for new software solutions (Weitzel et al. 2001, p. 192).

3.1.1   The Concept of Network Effects

Related literature in this area commonly differentiates network effects into direct and indirect ones. The distinction depends primarily on the source and availability of network effects. In the case of direct network effects, the external benefit component of an adopted standard or good depends on the number of additional adopters of the same standard. In the case of indirect network effects, the benefit is of a mediated nature based on the availability of complementary or additional services or goods for the adopted standard. If horizontal (vertical) complementarity between the considered goods is present, then one speaks of direct (indirect) positive network effects. Metcalfe's law describes direct network effects as the relation between the use of a network and the number of participants. From the viewpoint of an individual adopter the value of a network rises proportionally with the number of adopters, from a social welfare point of view the total benefit of a network however increases superproportionally with $n(n-1)$ (Shapiro et al. 1998, p. 184).

The term network externality is often used as a synonym for positive network effects and implies that positive network effects can cause—as is the case for public goods—external effects. This circumstance can be regarded as the reason why the size of a network is so important and why—from an economic point of view—most networks are only of suboptimal size (Liebowitz et al. 1994b, pp. 135-136). Since "bigger is better", problems occur when the network size is too small in the context of communication networks, because consequently the incentive for potential new adopters to join the network decreases. Such a prospective new adopter would increase the value and thereby the benefit of a network for already existing adopters inside the network without getting any compensation. In consequence, communication networks would not develop at all if there were no initial "critical mass" of adopters. The following example might illustrate the dilemma: the low numbers of only a few telephone network users in the early phase of telecommunication did not justify the huge investments necessary to develop the underlying network infrastructure. Hoping for more network users in the future, these potential adopters hardly had an interest to follow since they could only benefit from a small installed base and because they were not compensated for the additional positive network effect they created with their adoption of the telephone (Economides et al. 1995a). Investors in such networks apply a long-term calculation and hope (or more precisely bet) for enough users in the future. For potential users, this start-up problem is equivalent to the hen-and-egg problem: if there is no installed base of users already deploying a standard, nobody will join in (Beck et al. 2003c).

Network effects are part of economic externalities, but not every externality is a network effect. Liebowitz and Margolis (Liebowitz et al. 1994b; Liebowitz et al. 1995b) have emphasized that network effects are often used as a synonym for externalities. However, external economic effects are only externalities if they cannot be internalized. Market mechanisms such as contracts may be used to internalize network effects that occur by side-payment agreements. Furthermore, network effects may be pecuniary and efficiency may change while the network increases. Under perfect competition, the price for a product may decrease adding additional benefit to customers with an opposite effect on the provider side. An overall welfare accounting might not completely cover such effects because competitive decreasing costs are often based on upstream efficiency increases, independently of the market. With simple modification this also applies to pecuniary indirect network effects, for instance in the case of a complementary good for which the terms of trade have changed.

Nevertheless, despite the criticism of Liebowitz and Margolis, non-pecuniary direct and indirect network effects exist (Economides et al. 1998; Farrell et al. 2001). In this contribution, the terms externalities or positive external feedback effects are used to describe positive network effects within the boundaries defined by Liebowitz and Margolis.

External effects are analyzed in detail, especially in the context of allocation theory and the efficient and Pareto-optimal supply of network effect goods in central and decentral standardization models (Buxmann et al. 1999b; Weitzel 2004). In general, a Pareto-optimal allocation can only be achieved under the exclusion of external effects in decentralized standardization models. Thus, external effects can cause market failure and serve as justification for governmental interference in a market. However, governmental interference does not necessarily imply that the Pareto-optimum will be achieved afterwards (Shy 2001, p. 6).

A good overview of different existing approaches in the field of network effect theory is given by Weitzel (Weitzel 2004). Kleinemeyer (Kleinemeyer 1998), or

Yang (Yang 1997) provide different perspectives on analyzing network effects. Empirical approaches try to prove the existence and degree of network effects by regression analyses and estimate hedonic price functions for network effect goods (Economides et al. 1995a; Gandal 1994; Gröhn 1999; Harhoff et al. 1995; Hartmann et al. 1990). More analytically oriented research focusses mainly on economic equilibria for the analysis of the start-up phenomena (Besen et al. 1994; Borowicz et al. 2001; Economides et al. 1995a; Economides et al. 1995b; Katz et al. 1985; Katz et al. 1994; Köster 1998; Oren et al. 1981; Rohlfs 1974; Rohlfs 2003; Wiese 1990), market failure (Farrell et al. 1985; Farrell et al. 1986; Gröhn 1999; Katz et al. 1986b; Katz et al. 1992; Katz et al. 1994; Köster 1998; Weitzel 2004), tippy networks (Arthur 1989; Arthur 1996; Besen et al. 1994; Farrell et al. 1985; Katz et al. 1994; Shapiro et al. 1998), as well as path dependencies in the diffusion process (Arthur 1989; Besen et al. 1994; David 1985; Katz et al. 1994; Liebowitz 2002; Liebowitz et al. 1995c).

Simulation-based approaches to analyzing the diffusion patterns of network effect goods on the micro- and macroeconomic levels have been conducted (e.g., (Köster 1998; Weitzel 2004)) to analyze the Pareto-optimal welfare equilibria. Both analyze the market from a network effect good provider's point of view and consequently focus on the impact of monopolies or oligopolies on welfare, such as in the case of communication or compatibility standards.

The dynamics of complex network developments are also part of research in other disciplines such as in physics, where, e.g., the linkage network between websites consisting of hypertext documents (nodes) and hyperlinks (edges) is analyzed (Bornholdt et al. 2001).

3.1.2 Direct Network Effects

Direct network effects are based on identical agreements and adoption decisions by agents using a product, standard or good whose value increases with the number of further adopters (Katz et al. 1985). This horizontal effect occurs when, e.g., a communication standard gains a widespread diffusion so that each single participant in the network can communicate with the *(n-1)* users of the same standard. Frequently cited examples are the telephone, mobile phones, e-mail accounts, but also electronic data interchange (EDI) networks (Beck et al. 2003a; Beck et al. 2003c).

While some network goods have a stand-alone utility, so that one can benefit from their use even without any other users of the same good, other network goods have strong increasing demand-side externalities, such as mobile phones or EDI converter software which are useful solely when they can be used to communicate with other adopters. Adopters of such "pure" network effect goods gain increasing benefits with each new adopter, according to Metcalfe's law at least theoretically quadratically with the number of adopters. Metcalfe's law indicates that the potential communication benefit increases with the number of additional adopters with $n(n-1)$ or n^2 for large networks (Shapiro et al. 1998, p. 184).

3.1.3   Indirect Network Effects

In comparison to direct network effects, indirect network effects occur not as horizontal externalities while using the same network effect good, but as vertical externalities, when using related goods or services. Therefore, adopters can benefit not only from a large installed base with high direct network effects but also from the availability of complementary, indirect network effects, such as in the hardware-software market with its two-way contingency between the demand for the hardware product and the supply of software (Church et al. 1996; Church et al. 2002; Gandal et al. 2000; Gupta et al. 1999; Katz et al. 1985) or learning curve effects (Schilling 1999). An installed base of complementary or indirectly useable goods and services can support the diffusion of a new standard. According to Church, Gandal and Krause (Church et al. 2002), what is required from network effects in terms of indirect network effects is threefold: (a) increasing returns on the production side, (b) free market entry or unsponsored networks, and (c) demand for a variety of complementary products. These requirements are based on the critique of Liebowitz and Margolis (Liebowitz 2002; Liebowitz et al. 1994b).

Although the hardware-software paradigm (Gandal 1995) is a suitable example of the impact of indirect network effects on the adoption decision, one should mention that the paradigm can also be explained without modeling indirect network externalities. As Economides (Economides 1989) notes, a system composed of two components each compatible to other competitors' systems results in higher prices and less competition in comparison to incompatible components composing incompatible systems (e.g., Beta vs. VHS). At the same time, in the compatibility scenario consumers can choose between different components (hardware or software) with different features according to their preferences instead of adopting one monolithic system.

The well known example of the battle between Beta and VHS video recorder systems (Ohashi 2001) revealed VHS as winner. Although DVDs have already made inroads into most households (Dranove et al. 2003), the VHS case is still a good example: a user of VHS recorders can exchange video tapes with her or his friend, thus benefiting from direct network effects. At the same time, she or he can borrow a great variety of further video tapes from the video store because all movie-producing firms are offering VHS tapes to serve the large network of VHS-using customers. So the VHS users can also benefit from the indirect effect of being part of this network. Further examples are ATM machines (Economides 1991b), the QWERTY keyboard (David 1985), and operating systems (Liebowitz et al. 1996). Indirect network effects or complementary products can also be used as a strategic element for standard providers to bind vertically related firms by licensing them to ensure that a broad supply of additional goods for their own standard are available (Besen et al. 1994).

Although direct and indirect network effects are discussed here separately, neither network effect excludes the other, quite the contrary is the case: they often appear at the same time when an adopter uses a network effect good.

3.2 The Diffusion of Network Effects Goods

If and to what extent positive network effects can be realized depends strongly on the underlying communication standard. Furthermore, network effects have a direct impact on the diffusion of communication standards with resulting market diffusion scenarios that are difficult to forecast, e.g., in comparison to stand-alone normal private goods. Agent-based computational economics approaches are used for simulations to give an idea of how diffusion could develop (Vriend 2000; Wendt et al. 2000). A potential adopter of a new standard would never adopt when she/he assumes that the standard will not be adopted by anyone else, even if she/he believes that this standard is worth adopting. Consequently, the diffusion depends on the estimates made by each adopter, depending on the probability that other potential adopters will also affiliate. These individual decisions on the microeconomic level whether or not to adopt can severely hamper the diffusion of a certain network effect good on the mac-roeconomic level, leading to market failure.

As soon as the number of adopters rises not only does the network effect good become more attractive for further potential network participants, but the prod-uct itself is also increasingly useful. This externality effect is similar to increas-ing economies of scope on the demand side (Economides et al. 1996). How-ever, this analogy to economies of scale on the production side does not fit completely. While economies of scale usually arise within an enterprise, the increasing benefits in a network are distributed to all network participants. With each new adopter, the positive external network effects of all existing network participants' increases. Consequently, the total sum of individual benefits is not identical with the overall social benefit or, in other direction, the costs of adop-tion.

Network effects do not increase boundlessly (Borowicz et al. 2001) and also do not automatically imply an optimal network size of 100% of the total popula-tion. An optimal number of network participants can already be achieved with fewer adopters, as the network structure model and the concept of closeness proposed by Wendt and Westarp shows (Wendt et al. 2000). This is due to the marginal private benefit from joining a network that is lower than the social benefit when the network market exhibits positive demand side externalities. The optimal aggregation size is also discussed in the infrastructure theory lit-erature (Biehl et al. 1980) when it comes to an optimal setting of public goods or, in this case, an optimal setting of network effect goods. So the network size in an equilibrium may be smaller than the socially optimal size (Yang 1997, p. 11). If the number of adopters' increases beyond that optimal agglomeration point, excessive demand can decrease the network effect benefit or negative network externalities can even occur. The bottleneck or "common land" effect is a good example of negative network effects, e.g., when too many users slow down the Internet connection delaying the IP-package transfer or when too many people try to use public land. The same proves true for the airline indus-try, when one airline adds more flights to its hub thereby increasing the risk of more delays for other airlines at the same time (Mayer et al. 2002). The exter-nality occurs because the packet-switched Internet network is a shared me-dium. Consequently, each extra package imposes costs on all network partici-pants because the resources blocked are not accessible for others at the same time so that congestion results (MacKie-Mason et al. 1994). Congestion pricing mechanisms may offer some relief to reduce Internet usage at peak-time (Crawford 1996).

Furthermore, negative network externalities can occur through the feedback when network participants leave. This can be the case if, as a result of the introduction of a new technology or innovation, the participants in the old network change to the new and technologically superior but incompatible network. Since the network effect benefit loss for the remaining participants of the old network is a negative external effect, the leaving adopter does not consider this effect when deciding to switch networks (Shapiro et al. 1998, p. 176).

However, to benefit from network effects a decision must first be made about which standard should be adopted or whether an existing network should be left in favor of a new, maybe improved network. This is a difficult decision, if the installed base of the new one is not yet as large as the former one. Therefore, a new adopter may be stranded in a new network or with a new standard, if the network benefits of the new network are not sufficient to attract further adopters since the benefit to participants of the previous network is still high (Katz et al. 1985).

Thus, the individual decision to adopt a new network effect good decides on success or failure, depending on which network is able to overcome the critical mass necessary to establish itself (Picot et al. 2002; Shapiro 1999). Therefore, the "market outcome" is hard to predict (Arthur 1989). If several competing standards are available at the same time, then multiple equilibriums of coexisting networks may occur (Köster 1998; Weitzel 2004). This statement is still appropriate even when regarding the "tippiness" of standard networks, when, e.g., different world regions or markets with stable but incompatible standards are taken into account, e.g., when considering the different television standards in Europe (PAL) and North America (NTSC) (Farrell et al. 1992b).

In the case of only one standard to chose, a polar equilibrium could appear where either all or no potential users adopt the new standard (Shy 2001). However, such a scenario is more of theoretical importance, since firstly a complete adoption by all potential users is very unrealistic and secondly such a standard network might not be a stable situation because it attracts further standard providers trying to enter the market with their own one (Economides 1998; Greenstein 1992).

Both market equilibriums are rational results for the market participants because they demonstrate the highest net present value while simultaneously considering the adoption decision of further adopters. If all participants are in possession of perfect information about the benefits of each available standard, then they will select the one promising the highest net present value (Katz et al. 1986b). In a more realistic scenario, with imperfect information and uncertainty about the preferences of other participants, so-called opinion leaders may provide a market signal by deciding either for or against a new standard. This form of signaling corresponds to sponsoring or penetration pricing and does not lead inevitably to a welfare-optimal market result (Farrell et al. 1985).

The announcement of a new standard in the near future can also have a similar market-manipulating effect when potential users are now waiting to decide about their adoption (Dranove et al. 2003). But Katz and Shapiro (Katz et al. 1986b) suggest that in "sponsored networks" (individual participants hold rights and can exclude others from their use) the market can be over-promoted with a single standard (excess momentum) by subsidizing early adopters to benefit from higher producer surplus in the future when later adopters want to use the now more valuable standard. In the case of perfect information and symmetrical preferences concerning the advantages of a certain standard, a bandwagon process starts when early adopters with high stand-alone benefit start the domino effect, thus solving the coordination problem.

However, it remains unclear which elements or components are responsible for the stand-alone benefit. The stand-alone benefit of a pure network effect good such as communication standards cannot be the reason for the adoption decision because this type enfolds its benefits solely in the interaction with other adopters and consequently has no stand-alone benefit. Farrell and Saloner (Farrell et al. 1986) show that due to strategic behavior and heterogeneous preferences even perfect communication cannot reliably solve the diffusion dilemmas of excess inertia or momentum.

In the case of proprietary or sponsored networks there is in principle the possibility of internalizing indirect network effects in the owners net present value calculation, if they are pecuniarily measurable (Liebowitz 2002; Liebowitz et al. 1995b). Providers of such a proprietary network have an incentive to solve the start-up problem by inter-temporal price discrimination or sponsoring of early adopters. Monopolistic behavior by proprietary network providers does per se produce natural monopolies and therefore might be a sub-optimal, Pareto-inferior solution from a neoclassical point of view (Weitzel et al. 2003b). As a result, the lack of stand-alone benefits from communication standards, as well as the marketing strategies of providers (Postrel 1990), may hamper the market coordination of network effect standards (Economides 1998; Köster 1998).

For the evaluation and calculation of the net present value of a decision to adopt a new standard with network effect characteristics, it is important to consider the potential size of the new standard network (expected installed base). Common tools to forecast the potential return on investment in, for example, a communication standard, are the prolongation of previous data of diffusion behaviors with an auto-regression approach, which systematically underestimates, however, the potential of innovations. The neoclassical net-present value approach assumes a homo oeconomicus with perfect information at the time when a decision is made. Both approaches have their strengths and weaknesses.

The prolongation of historical diffusion paths systematically underestimates the benefit of new and presumably dominant standards. Furthermore, necessary data can often not be observed directly, in particular in the case of the direct and indirect network effects realized by other market participants. In order to supply a complete picture of past diffusions, this data has to consider the changing structure of incentives over the life cycle of the network effect good (the changing relation between direct and indirect network effects). In addition, the upcoming adoption decision is limited by path dependencies such as the business environment and the existing IT infrastructure, which doubtlessly has an influence on the adoption decision and thus diffusion. Beyond these difficulties of data gathering, a regression analysis cannot consider changing parameters in the case of groundbreaking innovations (one could hardly forecast the diffusion of the Internet based on the analysis of the diffusion of computers or fax machines).

Assuming rational behavior, expectation is based on the assumption of perfect information about all variables relevant to the adoption decision process. This idealized assumption corresponds to the neoclassical view of a homo oeconomicus, which, however, does not correspond to observable real world conditions. Often, potential adopters have only imperfect and incomplete information about both the quality of the network effect good and the expectations of further market participants. These reasons make a successful prognosis of the possible diffusion of standards very difficult.

An approach offered by Choi tries to eliminate the uncertainties about the quality of a network effect good by introducing an experimentation phase (Choi 1996). However, this suggestion seems not to be applicable, due to the coordinated effort necessary among all network participants at the same time.

A possible solution in between the aforementioned regression analyses and net present value approaches to predicting and thus determining the success or failure of a standard might be offered by the network effect helix approach presented in chapter 1. By considering probable environmental conditions (analogous to the regression analysis) and by including information about the quality of a standard at the time of the adoption—while considering the behavior of other market participants—(analogous to the rational behavior analysis), the diffusion of, e.g., communication standards can be determined as a function of direct and indirect network effects.

In the following sections, the aspects of the network effect theory relevant to the later introduced network effect helix approach for determining the diffusion process, in particular under consideration of the so-called start-up problem and critical mass, are discussed in more detail.

3.2.1   Standards and Compatibility

The ever-shorter cycles of newly developed and emerging standards in the IT area and the need for fast diffusions of those standards in order to capture increasing network returns and commercial success raises the level of uncertainty of market participants regarding which standard to chose. Facing this adoption dilemma of potential users, providers increasingly join coalitions and committees before the rollout of a new standard. Such signaling may help to convince adopters by delivering an open standard or at least the possibility of using it with other (older) technologies or adopters of the same standard. But this example also illustrates that compatibility is not only a characteristic of a standard, but also an important success factor in the diffusion (Cowan 1992).

Consequently, goods are compatible when their design is coordinated in some way, enabling them to work together (Farrell et al. 1985). Compatibility can also be realized by the deployment of converters after the standardization process is finished, in order to realize at least one-way compatibility (Farrell et al. 1992a). Farrell and Saloner also differentiate between three types of compatibility:

- *Physical compatibility* (interfaces are a physical unit of a good, such as railway connections)

- *Communication compatibility* (interfaces between goods enable them to communicate by applying the same transmission protocol)

- *Compatibility by convention* (the usability of an interface is guaranteed by contract or convention, such as time or currency, etc.)

Compatible standards or interfaces within networks can be both more material and immaterial. Telecommunication standards without appropriate end devices are just as worthless in mobile phone communication as CDs without compatible playing equipment. Therefore, complementary products must be equipped with the same standard in order to guarantee that they can cooperate successfully together (Shy 2001). The same is true for the transmission network linking the different end-devices together.

The network infrastructure of a compatible network is determined by the nodes (adopters or users of a standard) and the edges (the type of compatibility or standard) (Westarp et al. 1999). If the compatibility is determined by equality of the nodes or objects, then one speaks of horizontal networks. Vertical networks however are characterized by complementarity of the different objects or services available in addition to the network. The case of the typewriter keyboard (David 1985; David 1986) represents a "horizontal" network, since the users are connected to a network by the same knowledge of how to use it, whereas a PC with associated software or Internet access is part of vertical networks (Haj Bakry et al. 1999). If vertical and horizontal networks arise at the same time, one speaks of complex networks (Economides et al. 1992).

In order to realize network effect benefits, full compatibility (Economides 1998; Economides et al. 1996; Farrell et al. 1985) or at least partial compatibility (Economides 1991a; Economides 1991b) among network participants within a system is mandatory (Gilbert 1992). Durable goods such as communication standards with strong externalities benefit from possible compatibilities which help them to enter a monopoly market with an existing standard (Economides 2000). Therefore, uniform languages have to define the syntax, characteristics and rules of a compatibility standard (Buxmann et al. 1999a) so that adopters and providers can benefit from it (Katz et al. 1985), e.g., by selling additional products through bundling (Matutes et al. 1992). Compatibility standards can also enable the communication between systems which are actually not compatible, e.g., between Apple Macintosh and Windows PC computers over standardized interfaces. Thus hardware interfaces or gateways such as USB or Firewire and related protocols are like adapters or converters (Farrell et al. 1992a), allowing interconnectivity to realize electronic data transfer between incompatible systems.

Apart from the classification of networks into physical and virtual, technical and functional, as well as horizontal and vertical networks, one can also divide them into one-way and two-way networks. Examples of one-way virtual networks are radio and television broadcasts. Here the information flows from the sender to the receiver, but not vice versa (vertical complementarity). In horizontal complementary communication and transportation networks information can be transmitted or transported in both directions (Economides et al. 1996).

Standards can also be classified with regard to their openness, analogous to purely public goods and club goods. If market participants cannot be excluded from the use of a standard, then one speaks of an open standard. The widespread adoption of the Internet is regarded, due to its openness, as a successful example of a non-proprietary standard network (Hawkins et al. 1999, p. 11). If property rights to a standard belong to a single provider who charges licensing fees for its use, then one speaks of a proprietary standard (Schilling 1999). These kinds of standards correspond in their characteristics to club goods and lead—from the view of the market participants—to a market undersupply with a monopolistic price and quantity setting.

The diffusion success of an open or proprietary compatibility standard is not independent of the emergence, development, and choice of market strategy (Ehrhardt 2004). Several policies and strategies for suppliers of standards are possible (Gandal 2002). One can generally distinguish three forms of establishing a standard (David et al. 1990):

- *De facto standard*: if a standard has been successful in competition with others and remains as the dominant standard generally used and accepted by a broad majority then one refers to it as a de-facto or market-based standard. The standard can be an open, as well as a proprietary one. Famous examples are the QWERTY keyboard (David 1986), the microcomputer (Gandal et al. 1995), or spreadsheet software (Shurmer et al. 1995). For the role of intellectual property rights in the standardization process see (Farrell 1995; Warren-Boulton et al. 1995).

- *Committee standard*: if an open standard is introduced in the context of a negotiation process between different groups of interests within a standardization committee, then the framework developed can be regarded as a committee-based solution or standard. As an example, the Internet architecture and its underlying standards are maintained by the Internet Engineering Task Force (IETF) committee (Crocker 1993). The disadvantages of committee standardization are the long time delays and the need for consensus among the committee members, which does not necessarily lead to optimal results (Farrell 1993).

- *De jure standard*: if the standard is set by an official organization or national instance it is always an open standard, which is obligatorily fixed and thus not part of any market-based diffusion coordination. That does not automatically imply that the best standard is always established or that the process is efficient (Molka 1992; Toth 1996).

Increasingly, firms utilize a hybrid model that combines elements of market and committee-based processes (Keil 2002). Despite the fact that these two standard-setting approaches bear the inherent threat of suboptimal diffusion results, formal de jure standardization "solves" the standardization dilemma for adopters. Since such a governmental standard setting is not regarded as the first-best solution for communication standards, the adoption and diffusion problem discussed in the following is focused on market coordinated, informal standards that are de facto, committee, or hybrid forms of standardization.

3.2.2   Externalities and Positive Feedback-Effect

The phenomenon of externalities is not new in economic literature. They are assumed to be the underlying reason when markets cannot be established or fail to solve the supply and demand problem properly on markets (Arrow 1977). Thus externalities are often excluded by definition from economic analyses because they influence the market results in an unpredictable way or may even be the reason for market failure. Traditionally, a solution is offered by introducing governmental market regulations in form of property rights granted to a provider (natural monopoly) or even by supplying themselves with these goods in the form of public goods such as road or water conduit infrastructure. In contrast to such merit goods with externalities, demerit goods are more of concern in economic literature (Musgrave 1959, p. 14). Since these externalities are regarded as poison for competitive markets and often only mentioned in the context of market failure in charging plants for polluting the air for free, the positive aspects of externalities as surplus as in the case of network effect theory is slightly incompatible with neoclassical Cobb-Douglas production functions. By introducing property rights, two parties can bargain to overcome external costs in the absence of transaction costs, as Coase argued (Coase 1937; Coase 1960) with the goal of getting rid of negative external effects (assuming transaction costs are zero!). Recently positive feedback effects or externalities have been more intensively discussed in the context of network effects and the benefits of common standards.

The diffusion of network effect standards is more influenced by positive feedback effects or increasing returns (Arthur 1990; Arthur 1996; David 1994; Farrell et al. 1986) than any other goods categories. Positive externalities are part of the adoption of a standard that generates benefits for further members of the network without monetary compensation. Alternatively, new adopters can realize positive returns from positive externalities generated by other members of the network. Positive feedback is the source of externalities such as direct and indirect network effects and stimulates the diffusion rate superproportionally with each new adopter, at least after reaching the critical mass. It is also responsible for the strength of path dependencies. Path dependence models emphasize that small initial advantages may determine which one of possibly several competing standards is chosen by the market participants (David 1994). Path dependence has several roots: historically grown mutually consistent expectations, "sunk" investment costs in communication standards, or positive externalities (Loch et al. 1999). Positive externalities can be ana-lyzed as a global phenomenon in the whole network but also as local ones in sub-clusters of a network (Cowan et al. 1998; Wendt et al. 2000). Furthermore, positive externalities are also responsible for the so called bandwagon effect or herd behavior (Choi 1997; Leibenstein 1950; Rohlfs 2003) described in more detail in section 3.2.4.

Positive feedback effects are closely related to network effects. They are re-lated to the size of a network that combines demand and supply side econo-mies of scale. With increasing network size, not only the potential network benefits increase, but also the willingness of new adopters to pay higher prices to join it (Cabral et al. 1999; Csorba 2002).

The positive feedback effect leads to increasing market shares and declining marginal cost per unit of the network effect good. This is especially the case for information goods such as software or encyclopedias. While the production of the first version is highly expensive, copies can be produced with marginal cost per unit near to zero. The costs for the first sample of information good can be extremely high: the Brothers Grimm, famous for their fairy-tales, started to write the first complete volume of the German language dictionary in 1838, but it took 123 years until the work was completed in 1961. Today one can get all the information on the Internet for free (Christmann 2001). The external positive feedbacks of a native tongue such as German as a network of per-sons using the same communication standard can be regarded as a huge as-set. An interesting question is if a unified world language such as Esperanto or more likely English may establish itself someday. According to (Church et al. 1993) it is a minority who are likely to become multilingual rather than the ma-jority. Maybe Chinese as most spoken living language will be the standard in the future. However, for the moment, English is the predominant language spoken around the world: as long as sunk costs for learning a language and switching costs for adopting a new one exist, they will impede the fast spread of another language. Even a slight modification of a standard can provoke huge learning costs, as the change towards a new orthography in Germany demonstrates.

Such as languages, competing standards battle acrimoniously on the market to reach a critical mass in order to take over the market (Beck et al. 2003a). Once established, a dominant standard becomes even stronger due to positive feedback effects while the "outgunned" standards lose even more market share. In extreme cases, a monopoly can be established, also known as "the winner takes it all" in increasing returns networks (Arthur 1996). Despite strong positive feedback effects accelerating the diffusion of dominating standards, stable equilibriums with several coexisting standards can also emerge (Köster 1998; Weitzel 2004; Westarp 2003). A prominent example of a stable oligopoly is the operating system software market for computers with Microsoft Windows as the dominant standard and Linux, as well as Mac OS for Apple Macintosh as sturdy clusters. Although Microsoft extended the positive feedback effects of its standard by adding complementary applications (e.g., by integrating Windows Internet Explorer), it was not able to displace its competitors completely. The former example indicates that standards on network effect markets can tend to lead to natural monopolies.

Positive feedbacks does not always stem from network effects and can emerge simply on prospering markets such as that for cars: selling cars attracts customers, which thereby attract more suppliers with more varieties of cars, which in return attract more customers. Such two-sided market relations are not characterized by externalities or direct interactions within the adopter network. Unfortunately, the confusion is pre-assigned if even in network effect theory literature authors' confuse common economy of scale and growing demand driven positive feedbacks with network effect externalities.

This is the case, e.g., for Rysman's work on the market for yellow pages. The phenomenon he is describing is a simple vertical network based on a telecommunication network for yellow pages. The availability of yellow pages is an indirect network benefit, but not an independent network of publishers and customers (Rysman 2004). It is an internalized indirect network effect, but not an externality (Liebowitz et al. 1995d). According to Economides and White (Economides et al. 1996), such one-way networks are indirect networks lacking the reciprocal characteristic of direct networks and are produced for the

anonymous market, where nodes cannot be identified. Therefore, it is not possible to use positive loops and network effect-based positive feedback as
synonyms. Another example can be found in the diffusion of payment systems
or ATM machines. While the individually perceived value of electronic micro
payment networks such as PayPal increases with each new adopter
(Gowrisankaran et al. 2004), the rising value of ATM networks for bank customers is not based on direct network effects. Some literature on ATM machines misleadingly assumes network effects with each new location in the
network (Saloner et al. 1995). Such a wide definition of network effects including all kinds of networks disregards the critique formulated by Liebowitz and
Margolis. Nevertheless, the economic synergy effects might result in increasing positive customer feedback due to the larger availability of ATM machines
in such a one-way network.

3.2.3   Start-up Problem and Critical Mass

In this section, the start-up problem (Besen et al. 1994; Economides et al.
1995a; Farrell et al. 1986; Grilli 2002; Katz et al. 1985; Oren et al. 1981; Rohlfs
1974; Weitzel 2003; Wiese 1990) and critical mass phenomenon (Economides
et al. 1995a; Economides et al. 1995b; Mauboussin et al. 2000) are described
and their influence on the diffusion of network effect goods is analyzed. Since
network effect goods—in contrast to stand-alone usable goods—draw a majority of their value from their joint use with other adopters, the diffusion of such
goods can be retarded or even omitted completely. This can be the case due
to incomplete information about the good at the point of adoption decision,
heterogeneous preferences among potential adopters, as well as due to uncertainties about the adoption decision of the other market participants. Another reason might be that from the social welfare point of view it is dominant
strategy to wait instead of choosing a standard too early since a potential consequence could be an inferior decision compared to a later adoption (Choi
1994). As in the case of public goods, a dilemma exists where no adopter
wants to be solely responsible for the creation of the good or network, although a joint interest exists.

IS-related approaches analyzing the start-up and diffusion of standards with
network effect properties are based on reflections of social science concepts
such as social coherence or closeness. Relational closeness in a social sys-

tem is analyzed by using neural networks simulating a population of agents (Plouraboue et al. 1998), or stochastic simulation models (Wendt et al. 2000) to analyze the patterns of diffusion for standards. Where communication between the agents or experiencing a standard is important for gathering information to learn about the features of a new standard in a group, the so-called first-mover-advantage astonishingly diminishes (the first-mover concept is regarded as important in entering new markets (Hawkins et al. 1999, p. 84), or to establish an installed base due to network effects (Katz et al. 1985)). Plouraboue, Steyer, and Zimmermann argue that an early innovation can start a learning process but not necessarily an adoption process (Plouraboue et al. 1998). The learning process is a by-product of individual experience (Arrow 1962). After a certain time, depending on the structure of the network (the number of relations and the intensity of communication), another standard or second-mover might take over the market. Accordingly, intrinsic utility in addition to a cumulative interaction-based utility can only emerge after the network of agents has gathered information and made their decisions. Consequently, the diffusion of a network standard does not depend necessarily on a group of early innovators or opinion leaders, but on the experienced maturity or benefit accompanying with the adoption of a new technology recognized by a larger group of market participants.

Thus a group of network subscribers or adopters must be induced to join simultaneously (or at least with the same anticipation of further adopters joining in) to overcome the start-up problem. If the group of early adopters is large enough the diffusion will progress self-propelled by positive feedback effects when the critical mass of adopters is reached or passed (Oren et al. 1981). Thus, in order to start the diffusion process, the start-up problem has to be solved first by addressing the different social behavior patterns of market participants, e.g., by using the results of an agent-based computational economics model. Such an approach may reveal the interdependencies among important characteristics of diffusion-relevant factors for network effect goods to start the adoption in social networks.

Emerging problems during the start-up phase of the market introduction of a new standard have to be overcome, such as switching costs for users of existing standards (Farrell et al. 2001; Grilli 2002; Klemperer 1987; Rohlfs 1974) when they change to a new but incompatible communication standard, or even additional costs during the very early phase of diffusion due to the lack of an installed base and the necessity of using both standards at the same time. To solve the start-up coordination problem, monopolistic providers may solve the dilemma by offering side-payments to the first adopters or subsidize the price until the critical mass is reached (Greenstein 1992). Unfortunately, a monopolist sponsoring a future technology can also delay the overall diffusion process of standards, e.g., by licensing such a standard for a fixed price today as a binding commitment in the future when the provider will introduce the sponsored technology (Choi et al. 1998). Such scenarios or solutions do not emerge in the case of open standards with pure network effect properties. Thus, the problem is not a market oversupply with a standard but the risk of a market undersupply (excess inertia) (Besen et al. 1994; Economides et al. 1995a; Katz et al. 1985; Katz et al. 1994; Wiese 1990). From a centralistic point of view, a possible solution may be offered by the introduction of a market intermediary or central network manager who coordinates the diffusion (Korilis et al. 1997).

To understand the emerging dynamics based on network effects in the early phase of diffusion for both participants in the network as well as anticipated adopters, it is important to analyze the structure of the realizable, network-based benefits in more detail. The diffusion of communication standards seems to be particularly difficult due to the purely network-based benefits. Therefore, early adopters bear an above average risk when adopting a new standard that has not already been established as de facto standard so far. The individual decision whether or not to adopt is based on heterogeneous preferences and personal behavior. Nevertheless, the incentive for early adopters to join a standard must be different or at least higher than for other market participants and has consequently to be analyzed in more detail.

Closely related to the start-up problem is the critical mass phenomenon. If the number of adopters is not sufficient, then a standard cannot reach the critical mass and therefore cannot be established on the market. The diffusion of network effect goods follows an S-shaped diffusion path similar to the diffusion of a contagious disease, an innovation diffusion cascade (Bikhchandani et al. 1992), or information cascade (Watts 2002): after the critical mass is reached, market participants follow the adoption decision of former adopters like lemmings. That is the reason why the critical mass is so important for the successful diffusion of standards. A good example of a standard that never reached the necessary threshold of adopters is SGML, which was regarded as a sophisticated but too complex solution (Adler 1992) to attract a wider audience.

The concepts of critical mass and path dependency are not undisputed due to the lack of empirical evidence and also because of the implied inevitable success of standards once the initial start-up problem is solved (Borowicz et al. 2001; Liebowitz et al. 1995b). Indeed, it appears unlikely that an established standard can reach complete diffusion with such strong lock-in effects that it cannot be removed anymore. Equilibrium analyses prove that even monopolistic network markets can be tippy and another standard can take over the market. Furthermore, the penetration of an entire market is implausible even with strong network effects as the S-shaped contagious disease diffusion or the existence of stable Linux and Mac OS clusters in a Windows-dominated market illustrate.

3.2.4   Bandwagon Effect

Bandwagon effects are consumption sided externalities that emerge if the demand for a certain good increases when market participants are consuming the same good (Leibenstein 1950; Rohlfs 1974; Rohlfs 2003). Bandwagon effects are not restricted to network effect goods and can also be observed with normal stand-alone goods such as in the case of customized license plates (Biddle 1991). While the bandwagon, domino, avalanche, or snowball effect or herd behavior has been known for a long time in economics, the phenomenon is of pivotal importance for the successful diffusion of network effect goods.

The speed of diffusion in a growing network of standard users can be accelerated by offering additional compatible standard goods and services. The basic idea is to find other providers following the same standard to increase the available design palette and product variety for customers. This can be done by licensing, as Economides suggests (Economides 1996b) in order to invite further providers into a sponsored network, or by the attractiveness of a growing network of an unsponsored standard after the critical mass is passed. Providers can jump onto the rolling bandwagon by copying the properties of a standard or good in order to catch a share of the market, e.g., in the case of the software market for ERP systems. A good example of a successful bandwagon-based standardization process is the personal computer market with

PC clones compatible with the ones IBM manufactures. While the network of IBM personal computer users rose quickly due to the huge diversity of PCs provided, Apple Macintosh was following another strategy by serving the market demands for Mac computers alone (Wade 1995). Another example of a bandwagon-based diffusion which has not yet gained momentum or even failed to establish itself as standard is Bluetooth, although more than 2000 IT hardware manufacturers are members of the standardization committee (Keil 2002).

The bandwagon effect also describes a sequential adoption process over time, where market participants do not enter the network simultaneously but according to their individual threshold (Granovetter 1978). A provider has to consider this important issue when hoping for a bandwagon effect because it offers another perspective on the critical mass phenomenon. Due to individual preferences and thresholds, critical mass cannot be defined as a single determinable number of adopters, but as a kind of floating critical area of network size varying around a point which can analytically be described as critical mass. Given a normal distribution of the thresholds, the expanding network has the potential to accelerate the speed of diffusion as described in an S-shaped diffusion function. Such a bandwagon diffusion can be observed in the spread of epidemic diseases where the likelihood of falling ill can also be normally distributed among the potential victims (Gavious et al. 2001).

The increasing number of adopters triggers not only the bandwagon to attract new adopters but also attracts new providers of complementary services or products, amplifying the spiraling adoption circle by adding positive indirect network effects to the network. The increasing number of goods and services together with competition inside a chosen standard increase the adopters benefit (Brynjolfsson et al. 1996b).

However, the bandwagon effect also suffers from the general problem of how to estimate the standard benefits and network growth. Therefore, the bandwagon coordination mechanism does not necessarily result in an optimal standard diffusion (Greenstein 1992) in the end, as, e.g., the existence of three incompatible color television systems demonstrates. While the diffusion might be faster in the bandwagon case after an opinion leader has adopted or the critical mass is reached, the standard diffusion process might be more likely when standardization alliances or committees set a consensus standard (Farrell et al. 1988b).

3.2.5   Installed Base, Lock-in and Switching Costs

After the successful establishment of a growing standard network as installed base with increasing positive externalities, participants become more and more reluctant to change to another standard, even when a potential new standard promises a higher network benefit. Willingly or not, adopting a durable standard also means being bound to this decision for some time. Once made costly investments to a standard together with positive experience reduce the likelihood of switching soon into another, incompatible network. This lock-in effect phenomenon is not uniquely network effect specific and occurs in manifold situations but especially for participants of an existing network the reluctance to switch to a new incompatible good or standard is extremely high due to the network effects and the switching costs (Arthur 1989; Farrell et al. 1985; Farrell et al. 1986; Katz et al. 1992). While a tight binding to an unsatisfactory contract or product might be annoying and expensive enough for an individual, the overall effects on the network in case of a lock-in in a standard holds even more problems.

If the adoption of a new durable standard or good is associated with high setup costs where the costs and the benefits do not emerge at the same time, then one is locked into the decision once made until the return on investment is reached and the sunk costs have amortized. This again is a common characteristic of infrastructure or public goods with high setup and fixed costs on the one hand and positive adopter-sided network externalities on the other hand (Keppler 1998). But switching goods is more difficult in the case of network effect goods or standards compared to switching car brands after the vehicle has broken down (Varian et al. 2004). Especially when using compatible or communication standards, the conversion to a new one can be expensive and risky, e.g., in the case of customized software with high development, installation, and training costs.

Switching costs and lock-in have been intensively studied, e.g., in two period consumer games with unfavorable outcomes for consumers when confronted with high switching costs (Farrell et al. 2001; Farrell et al. 1988c; Farrell et al. 1989; Klemperer 1987; Klemperer 1989). Shapiro and Varian have drawn possible provider strategies implicated by switching costs and lock-in (Shapiro et al. 1998). Empirical evidence for lock-in effects is analyzed by Greenstein (Greenstein 1993) in the area of incumbent contractors for computer procurement or in the case of nuclear power reactors by Cowan (Cowan 1990).

Further famous examples of lock-in are the QWERTY keyboard (David 1985; David 1986) as a lock-in into a possibly inferior keyboard design. Liebowitz and Margolis later criticized that they have not found any evidence for a market failure (Liebowitz et al. 1990; Liebowitz et al. 1994b; Liebowitz et al. 1995b; Liebowitz et al. 1995c; Liebowitz et al. 1996), e.g., as discussed for nuclear power plants or for co-evolutionary lock-in into two standards in separate markets (David et al. 1996a; David et al. 1996b).

Lock-in can be achieved by early market entrance to "corner the market" locking out other standards or technologies from the market. However, such an early adoption bears the risk that market participants will be locked into an inferior standard in the long run (Arthur 1983; Arthur 1989). The lock-in effect is independent of the market structure at the beginning of the diffusion although it can generate a monopolistic dominance in favor of a single standard after the diffusion process. Therefore, in the first place even unsponsored standards have the potential to become a de facto standard in the end. But what is more likely and more predictable for providers is to lock a market by sponsoring a certain good until the critical mass is reached and a de facto standard is established, as in the case of Microsoft DOS in the early eighties. After the DOS/IBM standard cornered the market, IBM and even more Microsoft were able to benefit from the installed base by enjoying high margins while the diffusion of DOS/IBM was ongoing due to increasing returns, although the IBM PC itself nowadays again belongs to the bulk processing world of decreasing returns (Arthur 1996). To dislodge a locked-in standard, a new one must be twice or three times better than the old one that is installed (Arthur 1996). This seems to be especially true for communication standards. The duel of UMTS with the installed GSM standards has just started, while the next generation of communication standards has already appeared on the horizon with an already huge installed base of access points for PCs. Wireless local area networks (WLAN) or the fourth generation of mobile telecommunication have already kept a larger piece of the wireless world, promising significantly more features for lower prices than GSM or even UMTS.

Lock-in effects can emerge for various reasons. Shapiro and Varian (Shapiro et al. 1998) have formulated five different forms of lock-in effects:

- *Lock-in due to contractual costs* (Farrell 1987; Farrell et al. 1989; Klemperer 1987): signing a long-term contract with a service provider means a customer cannot easily swap to another one without paying at least a contractual penalty for canceling the contract.

- *Lock-in by learning costs* (Klemperer 1987): learning required in order to use a standard or technology may not be transferable to other ones even if they are functionally identical. Consequently, new skills are required reducing productivity until the new knowledge is acquired.

- *Lock-in due to conversion costs*: swapping data standards means changing into a new syntax or even semantic. Data can be lost or even converted into a totally different meaning.

- *Lock-in due to transaction costs* (Klemperer 1987): two standards may offer identical functions but finding and switching from one to another is associated with additional transaction costs.

- *Lock-in due to brand loyalty* (Farrell et al. 1988c): loyalty programs such as those for frequent flyers bind customers to a product or company. Therefore, switching to another product is equivalent to losing the cumulated additional benefits of the old program.

While lock-in by long-term contracts are artificial lock-in effects, loyalty costs and high costs for searching for new solutions also occur, e.g., in the case of switching from one car brand to another, and are therefore not only restricted to goods with increasing returns. In contrast, training costs and the costs of data conversion are indeed critical in the area of network effect goods. Even without being bound by contract or loyalty, the user of an ERP-system might not migrate to a competitor or even a new version of the same provider if the training costs are high and the data conversion is risky. As the year-2000 problem showed, many firms were reluctant to switch their legacy systems or had a hard time migrating their literally outdated solutions to new ones by spending up to several million dollars. They were trapped in a really expensive lock-in of old standards and therefore some risked the computer crash on New Year's Eve rather than implement year-2000 bug-free hard- and software.

Although lock-in effects are strong mechanisms trapping market participants into a specific standard, users are still free to adopt another standard if the new one is more promising (or if the change is unavoidable as in the Y2K case). Independent of the reasons, agents are confronted with switching costs which weaken the negotiation position of new standard providers and strengthen the old provider at the same time (Farrell et al. 1989). In unsponsored networks, suppliers can hardly offer discounts or side-payments to new adopters. Therefore, only the quality of the new standard can convince new adopters (such as in the WLAN case, if one disregards possible sponsoring by bundling WLAN hardware together with a DSL access). In sponsored networks, providers can subsidize new standards in addition to possibly superior features of an innovative standard to reduce the frictions of adopters (providers try to break the GSM lock-in by offering penetration prices to new adopters of UMTS).

The previous examples introduces us to the broad area of provider strategies accompanied with network effects offering solutions, firstly to establish an installed base, and secondly to break up the installed-base of a competing standard, technology, or provider (Katz et al. 1992). For the latter strategy, overcoming the lock-in by reducing the switching costs threshold is decisive for success. The question of how to initiate the entry of a new, incompatible standard in sponsored and unsponsored network markets arises. In unsponsored networks, the expected network benefit of a communication standard resembles a large value for providers due to compatible goods and services which may possibly become available (Besen et al. 1994), such as in the case of Sun Microsystems's open system strategy (Garud et al. 1993) or W3C's XML. Locked markets in proprietary or sponsored standards cannot benefit from these indirect effects to the same degree, unless the standard owner offers licenses to invite other firms to develop compatible goods and services (Economides 1996b). This will increase the speed of adoption of unsponsored communication standards since additional network effects are available for adopters.

Starting diffusion and overcoming the start-up problem is again the issue addressed in chapter 1, where the network effect helix simulation model is introduced, offering new insights into develop market entrance and diffusion strategies.

3.2.6   Path Dependency

Goods and standards with network effects and increasing returns can not only lock a market temporarily into a certain standard, but also remain stable over time, determining further standards developments in the same direction in order to be compatible with an installed base of adopters. This can even be the case if a market participant realizes after the diffusion of and lock-in into a standard that the standard chosen is an inferior standard development path in comparison to alternative paths (Arthur 1989). This phenomenon of closely related standards and its successors over time is called path dependency.

Small initial events can lead to different diffusion and development paths of standards. Therefore the economic effects of path dependencies are difficult to forecast, because most often not all circumstances influencing the path of diffusion are known to the public, e.g., in the case of the light water reactors as a chosen standard. When the U.S. navy and the government decided in favor of the light water nuclear reactor technology, a de facto standard for all following reactor types was set (Arthur 1990). According to Arthur's explanations, markets seem to work poorly as a mechanism to coordinate and diffuse innovations when an installed base of incompatible or inferior standards is in place. If the network externalities are strong, the decentral market-coordinated diffusion path can occur discontinuously unlike traditional diffusion paths for goods without increasing returns in adoption (Agliardi 1995).

Such a discontinuous adoption process characterized by market uncertainties can be differentiated into three forms of path dependencies: In order to complete the traditional two forms of first- and second-degree path dependencies, Liebowitz and Margolis formulated a third-degree path dependence (Liebowitz et al. 1995c; Liebowitz et al. 1996; Margolis et al. 1998). The first-degree path dependence describes a situation with perfect information at the point of decision. That means that the right standard was chosen at that time and the decision once made was efficient ex post. Second-degree path dependence describes the case where information is imperfect at the point of decision and a path once chosen may appear ex post as inefficient. However, the inferiority of the chosen path was not known at the time of decision.

In contrast to the second-degree path dependence, the third-degree path dependence now describes a case of willingly choosing an inferior alternative, although better alternatives were in place at the time the decision was made. Consequently, the development path based on that decision was inefficient at the time the decision was made and remained inefficient in an ex post analysis.

A chosen path may appear ex post inferior, but empirical proof is difficult to undertake since, firstly, competing standards are not improved or developed any more after the market has been locked and, secondly, a market failure can only be taken into account if the market has willingly decided to adopt the inferior or wrong standard. Moreover, who will admit that she/he has willingly decided wrongly? Nevertheless, third degree-path dependencies take place, e.g., when considering the renewed adoption of gasoline-fueled cars when old ones are replaced. The automobile industry is continuously developing new combustion engines while it becomes more and more obvious that oil is a limited fossil resource and the so-called man-made greenhouse effect is not a fiction created by scientists.

According to Liebowitz and Margolis, choosing the wrong path was only avoidable in the third-degree path dependence (Liebowitz et al. 1995c). Therefore choosing a standard under limited information may be efficient when all available information and alternatives are evaluated before the adoption decision is made. However, especially for unsponsored standards, suppliers do not advertise or spread the information automatically, so that the information available is often limited to the features and quality characteristics of a standard as described in white papers published by of standardization committees or field reports by pilot users. Even if market prices exist for the standards an adopter is interested in, prices can change over time. They will most probably decrease as the unsponsored network grows, but they will probably increase in the case of sponsored networks. The decision for or against a standard should therefore primarily be based on the features offered and potential benefits. Thus, direct and indirect network effect benefits that emerge after the adoption of a standard are used to simulate likely diffusion paths in chapter 1.

3.3 Network Externalities: A Source of Market Failure?

Externalities in economic models are regarded as the reason for non-existing markets, imperfect allocation, or market failure. Consumption externalities between customers of stand-alone goods are uncommon due to the defined ownership of products on markets where supply and demand are clearing the market. This is different if the product considered belongs to the group of public goods such as in general information, software, or communication standards (Rohlfs 1974). As in the case of traditional public goods where opportunistic free-rider behavior can completely inhibit the supply of public goods, the diffusion of network-constituting standards with network externalities can also fail if the adoption cannot exceed a critical mass of users. Therefore, the existence of network effects seems to tend to lead to market failure, which is equivalent to network sizes smaller than the socially optimal one (Pareto inefficiencies) (Gröhn 1999; Yang 1997). Since market participants are unable to consistently consider the influence of their adoption decision on the additionally achievable utility of others, decentral market coordination seems to tend to lead to inferior market results due to network externalities. With positive consumption externalities, the marginal individual benefit of adopting a certain product or standard is smaller than the social benefit.

In spite of the extensive literature on network externalities and market failure, there are only a few empirical analyses of network effects, primarily due to the lack of data. Furthermore, it is nearly impossible to differentiate in time-series between network-effect-induced increasing benefits based on more network participants or simply due to technological progress and effects induced by decreasing prices (Dranove et al. 2003; Economides et al. 1995b; Gowrisankaran et al. 2004). Liebowitz and Margolis argue that so called market failures are mostly neither based on network externalities (Liebowitz 2002; Liebowitz et al. 1999) nor accurately empirically detectable (Liebowitz et al. 1995b).

Westarp (Westarp 2003) points out that although it is unlikely for an individual adopter to consider her/his positive network effect on other network participants, the same is not necessarily true for providers or vendors of the network underlying products or standards. The successful diffusion and therefore the market failure might be solvable by applying new marketing strategies, but only for proprietary standards or software products. However, single marketing strategies or penetration pricing are not appropriate methods to infiltrate a market if a communication standard is open and supported by a broad majority of providers. Therefore, they have only limited possibilities of jockeying for a leading position by applying only some marketing and advertising strategies in the early phase of diffusion to attract a critical mass of adopters and to overcome the start-up problem.

3.4 Diffusion Theory Revisited in the Light of Network Effects

Discussing the diffusion of network effects goods means primarily the integration and adoption of positive externalities and spillover effects as the most important characteristics of network effect goods into existing diffusion models. The widespread adoption and therefore diffusion of such goods accelerates the further speed of diffusion as the network size increases, stimulating the provision of complementary products or services at the same time. The difference from common diffusion literature here is the stronger emphasis on the importance of path and speed of adoption as pivotal elements of successful diffusion and the way adoption is related to the overall benefit of network effect goods such as communication standards (Loch et al. 1999).

3.4.1   Prosumers of Network Effect Goods

For the diffusion of network effect goods the differentiation into providers and consumers is not very expedient in the context of the network effect theory, since both standard providers and consumers have a common interest in a wide diffusion to benefit from high producer margins and high network externalities. Even more, the consumer of a communication standard provides the same standard at the same time to its business partners and can be seen consequently as provider and consumer ("prosumer") simultaneously.

However, from an allocation point of view, this does not hold absolutely true if a market-dominant supplier or monopolist demands monopoly prices thereby artificially shrinking the optimal network size. This is not the case for pure network effect goods such as open communication standards where product sponsoring is not a dominant strategy because other suppliers would also benefit (free-rider problem) since they cannot be excluded from the market. In the traditional diffusion theory, the diffusion of innovations is mostly oriented on the consumer side, disregarding the potentially occurring externality effects for suppliers. Consequently, for the diffusion of network effect goods it is possible and necessary to analyze the supplier and consumer side simultaneously.

The term diffusion is generally defined as "the process by which an innovation is communicated through certain channels over time among the members of a social system" (Rogers 2003, p. 5). The traditional economic analysis of diffusion focuses on describing and forecasting the adoption of products in markets. In particular, identifying the factors that influence the speed and specific course of diffusion processes is of focal concern (Weiber 1992). Generally, the number of new adopters in a certain period is modeled as the proportion of the group of market participants that have not yet adopted the innovation. New adopters have to be informed or have to be aware of an innovation. Based on the underlying information diffusion, network diffusion models can be subdivided into relational models and structural models. Relational models analyze how direct contacts between participants in networks influence the decision to adopt or reject an innovation. In contrast, structural models focus on the pattern of all relationships and show how the structural characteristics of a social system determine the diffusion process (Valente 1995, p. 4).

Most empirical studies on the diffusion of innovations in networks are focused on critical mass approaches, analyzing the diffusion rate of innovations, collective behavior, and public opinion (e.g., (Granovetter 1978; Marwell et al. 1988)). As a result, network analysis in this context is an instrument to uncover the pattern of interpersonal communication in a social network (for concepts of sociological network analysis, see, e.g., (Wigand 1988; Wigand et al. 1989)).

In opposition to the concept of opinion leaders or early innovators being responsible for the start of an innovation diffusion (exemplified in the form of the diffusion of new fertilizer among farmers or family planning in Korea (Rogers 2003; Valente 1995)), network simulation models for network effect goods suggest the stronger influence of learning effects among potential network participants as an important reason for the adoption (Beck et al. 2003c; Plouraboue et al. 1998; Wendt et al. 2000). Accordingly, individual relationships and information exchanges between agents on a market lead on the microeconomic level to common decision-making among innovation-friendly groups rather than to individually made decisions. The result of such an adoption decision is visible macro-economically as diffusion.

3.4.2   Networks as Virtual Infrastructure

The diffusion of network-constituting standards depends not only on the existing infrastructure determined by path dependency or critical mass, but also on the number of groups involved. Since communication standards require at least two adopters and a standard provider, a standard generally has first to be adopted by, e.g., telecommunication service providers and afterwards by their customers. Once attracted, customers have a certain market impact on their surrounding sphere like traveling salesmen for the adopted standard, having their own interest in a growing network, especially among neighbors, friends, and business partners (Valente 1995).

Consequently, cascading adoption at at least two levels (provider and adopter) can be observed in all kinds of settings, where two different and inhomogeneous groups with different preferences have to adopt a standard to benefit from network effects. This is the case for all kinds of EDI standards in vertical supply chains (large and small adopting firms), mobile data services (the mobile service provider and the customer), ATM machines (the banks and the banks' customers), credit cards (supplying banks and customers), VHS (manufacturers and customers) and many more. While all market participants benefit from large networks, not all can benefit from the network externalities which are available inside the adopter networks of communication standards. Suppliers of products supporting a certain standard can benefit from increasing demand, but network effects in the form of direct and indirect network benefits can only be skimmed by the adopters or users themselves, who thus benefit from network externalities. This is the case for all network participants of a communication standard, but not for the manufacturers or providers, as described above.

Nevertheless, the creation of a network with network effects depends on the adoption of such standards by providers or manufacturers, which are not necessarily part of the later network (that is the case when providers are not at the same time consumers of their own standard). If one does not distinguish between these two forms of networks, the network infrastructure providers from the network infrastructure users, then misleading conceptions can occur, as in the case of ATM machines (Saloner et al. 1995) or yellow pages (Rysman 2004). In both cases, the adoption and diffusion of network infrastructure is described in a way that leads to the incorrect assumption that simply providing

ATM machines or yellow pages would be similar to adopting a network with positive externalities.

The traditional diffusion theory does not differentiate into multi stage diffusions, where the adoption or the infection of one group leads to the adoption or infection of another group. In terms of traditional diffusion theory, this is equivalent to a pandemic, e.g., where the contagion of bird flu would also infect humans. While this infection scenario seems seldom to appear in nature, the diffusion of standards quite often follows such a cascading diffusion model over several disjunctive stages: nuts and bolts fit together because the manufacturers follow the same standardized sizes when producing them. Different television programs can be received on the same set and people can talk to each other even without subscribing to the telephone service from the same provider. This is the advent of standardization, where compatible or standardized products can be used together because the manufacturers or providers have used the same standard (Farrell et al. 1985). The Internet, e.g., is based on different but dependent standardized communication and transmission layers and protocols that are nested into each other. After such corresponding standards have been developed as a virtual infrastructure or network, its diffusion among market participants can start.

While traditional diffusion models generally focus on a diffusion process in a certain market or group, the spillover of social norms and standards constituting networks with other groups or even countries are often disregarded. Since the international diffusion across national boundaries is impeded by different national standard settings and path dependencies, the building of a common market with common laws and standards in order to increase the installed base and overall benefit is difficult. Even the standard setting process by governmental decision or de jure standardization often cannot solve this standardization problem, although the social network benefit would increase (Adams 1996). Relevant literature in this context related to the adoption of new technologies or standards explain this phenomenon with the primary focus on the reduction in fixed costs of adopting a new standard rather than on marginal costs or because network effects are not considered at all (Brancheu et al. 1990; Fudenberg et al. 1985; Katz et al. 1987).

Although the aforementioned theories are capable of explaining the process of diffusion, in general they fail in the area of explaining the impact of innovation on existing organizational structures or the measuring of improvements. However, positive results in the form of increased efficiency might not be visible when the adopted innovation is used insufficiently or the existing accounting or measuring systems are not able to measure utilities that occur. If the increased usage of innovations has an impact on intermediary goods which cannot be measured directly then the impact should be visible at least on the output side. But even measuring these spillover effects seems to be difficult (Goolsbee et al. 2000), although PCs and the Internet have doubtlessly created additional consumer surplus (Gordon 2000). Furthermore, these models do not explain the real-world phenomena of different adoption decisions by, e.g., SMEs and large enterprises at the same time, nor do they give any information about the role of "gun-to-the-head" adoption pressures by large business partners on small enterprises.

3.4.3   Analogies of Public and Network Goods

Due to the free-rider-problem as an external effect, individuals only have a low incentive to reveal their willingness to pay for the supply of public goods, resulting in a low or even no supply at all. Such opportunistic behavior is comprehensible but leads to overall welfare losses. The same rational but opportunistic behavior is responsible for the diffusion dilemma of communication standards or network effect goods, as long as these frameworks or agreements are not established as standards on the market (Farrell 1996). The Lindahl equilibrium shows that a welfare-optimal supply can be ensured by public goods only by perfect price discrimination as a market mechanism, but this market condition is not achievable due to the free-rider problem. From a supply-theoretical view, the Clarke-Groves-mechanism, for instance, provides the necessary incentives for users of public goods to contribute to the financing. However, a first best solution is still difficult to realize. Second best approaches, such as second and third degree price discrimination are not able to reach a Pareto optimal solution, but guarantee at least that more market participants are willing to contribute in order to finance public goods even if they have heterogeneous preferences.

Communication networks can also be considered as public goods with an increasing value with each new subscriber or adopter (Artle et al. 1973), e.g., telephone networks (for a dynamic model of telephone subscriber networks based on Artle and Averous see (von Rabenau et al. 1974)). The contribution of Artle and Averous is one of the first papers that inductively analyzes the additional system gains with each new entrant and the optimal size of a network from the view of public goods theory. Inspired by Samuelson (Samuelson 1954) and his belief in a large world of public goods flavored domains with consumption externalities, research like that of Artle and Averous is nothing less than the public goods property roots of network effect theory. They also proved that the often used but theoretically seldom derived S-shaped logistic function in more descriptive studies is capable of describing the diffusion of public goods such as telephone networks. In doing so, they confirm the existence of a critical mass, a contagious exponential phase of growth, and finally a phase of market saturation.

Analogous to network effect goods where early adopters can reduce their risks of stranding with a certain good or standard by using the right adoption strategy, users of public goods can be given incentives to contribute financially, even when free-riders can benefit due to spillover effects. Since network effect goods such as digital goods or communication standards in general possess public good properties, appropriate diffusion strategies have to be developed taking the special phenomena of such goods into account. In this context, the models developed in chapter 1 allow for emerging effects in network economies, while the network effect helix model in chapter 1 explicitly analyzes the two network effect types and their role for a successful diffusion in more detail.

In the following chapter 1 the diffusion and implementation of e-business and communication standards is discussed, in order to be able to analyze the path of diffusion of communication standards and their impact on adopters. In the light of a networked economy, it is important to understand the business environment, drivers, and inhibitors of standards adoption, which are closely related to social interactions during the adoption process.

4 Diffusion of E-Business Standards: Empirical Results

Advances in information and communication technologies and standards offer new ways of interacting between humans and machines and machine-to-machine communication, thereby inducing intended and unintended business process changes in many areas. Consequently, new networked coordination forms utilizing these information infrastructures influence spatial and temporal restrictions and, e.g., make it increasingly difficult to identify an enterprise's regional, temporal, and organizational boundaries. For example, the automation of inter- and intra-enterprise business processes is supposed to influence economic and social reality. Many phenomena witnessed in globally networked markets cannot sufficiently be explained since large parts of the underlying dynamics are not yet well understood. The challenges of a globally networked economy are to understand the governing dynamics in networks better and to conceive and implement strategies in order to take advantage of these new possibilities. A combination of a more positivistic approach towards information systems and network analysis and normativistic research into prototyping and simulation may offer a valuable path towards an improved understanding of the basic principles underlying networks. This dual mode of research may support the network diffusion theory in understanding the dynamics behind emerging network standards and adoption behavior, as well as the overall benefit or impact of e-business standards on the industry and the national level (Beck et al. 2005b).

4.1 Research Framework

The globalization or internationalization of markets and the networked economic world, as well as their impact on business process efficiency has become a subject of research in recent years (Beck et al. 2005a). The research focus is whether all industries and countries have adopted a standardized way of internal and external business processes, or if industrial and national diversities will lead to path-dependent standardization solutions resistant to any kind of global convergence. The emergence of the Internet as a common communication standard has intensified the diffusion of further applications, offering the potential to remove geographical, as well as firm- and nation-size obstacles. A related concern is that the disruptive diffusion of e-business will create a new digital divide between large and small firms, as well as among countries. After the early phase of the Internet diffusion, there are already significant country differences observable in terms of Internet and e-business adoption. These differences may be attributed to national factors such as quality and cost of telecommunications, regulatory and legal environments, business environments, consumer preferences, and social and cultural attitudes. In addition, such environmental factors can shape the impacts of the Internet and e-business on national economies and social systems (Castells 1999).

The individual adoption of e-business standards is dependent on the adoption behavior of other consumer decisions. Networked markets such as the market for e-business applications and standards have inherent consumer sided economies of scale. In this context, the compatibility concept is important for the usage of e-business in a networked economy. Due to the openness of international standards such as Internet-related ones members can benefit from communication networks to exchange software, data, and documents. Standards together with compatibility have strategic relevance to being competitive and successful on a global level (Besen et al. 1994). Although e-business existed before the Internet era, e.g., in the form of traditional EDI, e-business applications have spread more rapidly over the Internet due to the openness, low costs, ubiquitous availability, and large network effects in comparison to proprietary networks.

The research results presented in this chapter are based on a survey conducted together with the Center for Research on Information Technology and Organizations (CRITO) at the University of California at Irvine, in conjunction with International Data Corporation (IDC). Apart from Germany, the survey includes Brazil, China, Denmark, France, Japan, Mexico, Singapore, Taiwan, and the United States. The focus of the research is to identify the degree of e-business standards diffusion and usage in each of these countries together with the impact of e-business on business processes. The different diffusion paths are closely related to path dependencies in the studied industries and seem to be closely connected with the extent of e-business communication standards adopted over time, but also with differences in national mentalities such as openness to innovative technologies, general adoption behavior or consumer preferences. While the manufacturing, as well as the banking and insurance, sectors have traditionally used EDI-systems to interchange data electronically, the retail and wholesale sector started implementing and using such e-business standards later.

The implementation of e-business standards is not an end in itself but is used to reduce costs, to improve internal and external business processes and/or to enter new markets. It may be used as a substitute for existing standard processes or technologies but can also be deployed as a complementary way to communicate and process data. Knowledge about different ways of e-business diffusion together with the intensity of integration may help to analyze the impact of e-business standards on the competitiveness of firms and countries on an international level. The primary objective of the empirical research results described in this section is to develop new knowledge about the global diffusion of socio-technical systems such as the Internet and e-business, the influence of national environments and the impacts of global standards on networked economies.

The survey was conducted in ten countries (Brazil, Denmark, China, Germany, France, Japan, Mexico, Singapore, Taiwan, and the United States) with altogether 2,100 establishments during the period of February 18, 2002 to April 5, 2002. An establishment is defined as the physical location of a firm. The sampling was a stratified random sample classified by size (large firms with 250 or more employees, and small firms with between 25 and 249 employees) and by industry (manufacturing, wholesale/retail distribution, and banking/insurance). The questionnaire comprised 50 questions on different topics such as globalization of enterprises, implementation of e-commerce technologies, as well as the use of these technologies, drivers and inhibitors of e-commerce implementation and use, impacts on business processes and efficiency and e-commerce implementation strategies. The questionnaire is provided in the appendix of this thesis.

In Germany, 202 establishments were investigated, subdivided into 68 from the manufacturing industry, 66 from the wholesale/retail industry and 68 from the banking and insurance industry. In total, 102 of the establishments interviewed belong to the class of small and medium-sized enterprises, while 100 belong to the class of large establishments. The survey included only establishments which used the Internet to buy, sell or support products or services.

4.2 Diffusion of E-Business Standards

Aside from the overall availability of e-business applications at the national level, the use of e-business solutions at industry levels is also entering an advanced stage after the completion of the experimentation phase. The overall e-business readiness in the German industry is high as can be seen from the figures in Table 4. However, it should be kept in mind that this survey only represents advanced users, rather than a sample of all German firms. It is worth noting that the observed readiness is not only present among large firms, but also among SMEs. While the existence of a "digital divide" or "digital gap" is between large and small firms or developed and developing countries assumed (Pohjola 2002; Wong 2002), only slight differences remain between SMEs and large firms in this survey in Germany. Differences still exist in the application of extranets and the use of call centers, which are defined as a part of e-business customer service. Depending on the chosen definition, extranets connect additional establishments of the same firm as wide area networks and additionally offer access to business partners such as suppliers and customers. Given that most SMEs have only one establishment, the low diffusion of extranet solutions might be a consequence of the lack of any necessity to connect other establishments over wide area networks. Interestingly, electronic funds transfer (EFT) is more often used among SMEs than among large establishments. This might reflect the use of online banking by SMEs that one may regard as a type of EFT, while large establishments more often use automatic EDI-based transactions, which are less personnel-intensive, to transfer money. A still existing gap in the diffusion of e-business applications can be found in the availability of call centers.

Table 4: E-Business Readiness by Size of Firm and Industry in Germany

Percent using:	Total[a]	Establishment Size[a]		Industry[a]		
		Small[b]	Large[c]	Manufacturing	Retail/ Wholesale	Banking/ Insurance
E-mail	100.0	100.0	100.0	100.0	100.0	100.0
Website	91.8	91.7	100.0	90.5	92.0	94.5
Intranet	84.4	84.4	84.4	77.8	85.9	88.8
Extranet	22.3	21.7	51.5	38.8	15.9	36.6
... accessible by suppliers	14.0	13.6	32.6	27.4	8.5	28.5
... accessible by customers	11.8	11.4	28.7	23.1	8.4	13.7
EDI	67.7	67.7	70.2	56.6	71.1	65.4
Electronic funds transfer	86.6	86.9	71.9	94.9	85.2	77.2
Call center	30.3	29.8	55.7	26.4	29.3	50.6

Notes: [a] Results are weighted by the total number of establishments in an industry by size of firm.
[b] Small firms are defined as firms with 25 to 250 employees.
[c] Large firms are defined as firms with more than 250 employees.

4.2.1 Drivers of and Barriers to E-Business

After more mature e-business applications have shown their potential to expand markets or to improve the quality of business processes, they are no longer only of interest to innovation-friendly or IT-related firms but also to the majority of firms. While e-business is able to support all kinds of internal and external business processes, the diffusion still follows path dependencies based on sector-specific industry traditions and history. This seems also to be true at the national level when compared with other countries in the survey.

As Table 5 indicates, competition is a significant factor for online activities. Nearly 43% of establishments in the three sectors consider major competitors going online as a significant trigger for also using e-business. While only 29.8% in the manufacturing industry viewed this reason as significant, high competition is a significant pressure for distributors (45.5%) and even more for firms in the financial service sector (53.7%). Surprisingly, pressure exercised by customers (24.8%) or suppliers (8.3%) to use the Internet is a rather low-rated reason for the adoption decision among German firms, compared to the global sample. One explanation may be the widespread use of EDI standards to transmit business messages in Germany.

The most important driver supporting the implementation and use of the Internet is the strategic need to expand markets for products and services by going online (57.9%). This reason seems to be less important for German bank and insurance institutions (45.2%) due to their mostly national market focus. Banks and insurance companies mainly use branches or traveling salespeople to distribute their products, offering online banking as a customer service as part of their multi-channel market penetration. The increasing number of online accounts reduces the necessity to be physically present with branches in each city or village. On the other hand, banks are not able to close their branches because there are customers who are unwilling or unable to use the Internet. For manufacturers (51.0%) and especially for retailers and wholesalers (61.3%), e-business is a door opener not only to improve their existing services like after-sales customer support, but also to use it as a further direct sales channel in the B2B and B2C area. While these two latter sectors have managed to gain benefits from e-commerce applications, the banking/insurance sector has to cope with strong competition, declining service

prices, and free online services, such as online banking and brokerage services.

Table 5: Drivers of Internet Use

Percent indicating a significant factor ...	Manufacturing[a]		Wholesale/Retail Distribution[a]		Banking/ Insurance[a]		Total[a]	
	GER	Global[b]	GER	Global[b]	GER	Global[b]	GER	Global[b]
Customer demanded it	32.6	35.4	22.2	37.6	27.8	36.7	24.8	36.9
Major competitors were online	29.8	31.2	45.5	29.2	53.7	47.6	42.9	31.3
Suppliers required it	32.3	26.5	2.3	21.3	0.2	12.6	8.3	22.3
To reduce costs	32.5	42.8	16.3	32.3	24.8	34.3	20.3	35.7
To expand market for existing product/services	51.0	51.0	61.3	45.6	45.2	53.0	57.9	47.9
To enter new businesses or markets	39.3	39.2	49.6	44.4	27.5	35.6	45.7	42.0
To improve coordination with customers and suppliers	59.0	50.8	37.9	40.5	35.2	39.9	42.1	43.7
Required for government procurement	7.6	19.1	0.1	13.7	5.8	11.4	2.1	15.2
Government provided incentives	8.6	10.5	0.0	7.4	2.3	6.7	2.0	8.3

Notes: [a] Responses were weighted based on the total number of establishments by
         employee size within the sector for each country.
         [b] Consists of weighted survey responses in 10 countries combined: United
         States, Mexico, Brazil, Germany, France, Denmark, Singapore, Taiwan,
         China and Japan.

In addition to the strategic goal of expanding already existing markets, 45.7%
of German firms' intend to use e-business to enter new markets, which is
higher than the global sample average. While this seems to be less important
for the manufacturing industry already active on international markets (39.3%)
and not an important factor for the more national-oriented banking and insurance sector (27.5%), the retail and wholesale industry regards its online and e-
business activities (49.6%) as a highly important factor in order to enter new
markets. The last important economic driver for Internet use in the three industry sectors studied is the opportunity to improve the supply chain with customers and suppliers. Fifty-nine percent of establishments in the manufacturing
industry expect side coordination benefits from using the Internet, while only
37.9% in the wholesale and retail industry and 35.2% in the banking and insurance industry, respectively, do so.

Extremely unimportant are government-related reasons, which may positively
influence the adoption decision and can do so. Consequently, they cannot be
regarded as drivers for the use of Internet standards at all. Although govern-
ments and business associations have recognized the significance of e-
business standards for businesses and public administration, the perceived
impact on the adoption decision is very low. Institutional initiatives aimed at

supporting the diffusion of IT-standards among businesses and public agencies have been established but have had only little influence so far (Andersen et al. 2005; Andersen et al. 2003; Damsgaard et al. 2001). Neither governmental demand for online procurement capability (2.1%), nor direct governmental incentives or subsidies (2.0%) are reported as significant drivers for adopting e-business standard solutions. On the contrary, the results suggest that a lack of e-business knowledge and projects inside the government is, and will become even more an impediment not only today but also in the near future. While nowadays most business transactions are processed electronically and conducted online, firms have furthermore to prepare paper-based and therefore inefficient documents and processes in parallel to deal with the public administration.

While Table 5 demonstrates that it is impossible to identify the most important driver or "killer-application" supporting the diffusion of e-business applications, Table 6 deals with the most important barriers impeding the use of e-business. In comparison to the global average, most reported barriers are less important or restrictive for German firms, e.g., the need for face-to-face customer interaction (11.9% in Germany in comparison to 33.8% in the global sample). Concerns about privacy, personal data, or even security issues are no longer important obstacles in Germany (only 24.9% selected this issue as an important barrier) in contrast to the global sample (44.2%). This might be a good indicator of the level of maturity of the better skilled market participants, but it is also a sign of more sophisticated online services and security applications. Most Germans must have had positive experiences in the use of the Internet in the past and have lost most of their former resistance to using it. Further rather unimportant impeding reasons are Internet access costs due to the open and competitive telecommunications market (an obstacle only for 1.6%), the inadequate support of business laws (only 5.2% agree), and the taxation of online sales (only 1.5%), which is the same as for traditional businesses in Germany and Europe. While the latter factors are unimportant barriers in Germany not really hampering the diffusion e-business applications in contrast to the global sample, German establishments have to cope with other important problems. Finding qualified and experienced e-business-skilled staff is a major problem in Germany (41.2%) more than anywhere else (26.5%). The lack of IT specialists is especially critical in the retail and wholesale industry, where nearly 50% of the respondents mentioned this as a significant barrier.

Table 6: Barriers and Obstacles to doing Business on the Internet

Percentage indicating statement is a significant obstacle...	Manufacturing[a]		Wholesale/Retail Distribution[a]		Banking/ Insurance[a]		Total[a]	
	GER	Global[b]	GER	Global[b]	GER	Global[b]	GER	Global[b]
Need for face-to-face customer interaction	22.0	31.5	8.8	34.2	11.6	40.1	11.9	33.8
Concern about privacy of data or security issues	20.9	47.1	21.5	40.4	65.1	62.0	24.9	44.2
Customers do not use the technology	26.4	30.3	24.3	33.1	18.0	23.2	24.2	31.4
Finding staff with e-commerce expertise	28.2	23.8	47.7	28.8	13.5	19.9	41.2	26.5
Prevalence of credit card use in the country	17.3	22.4	23.0	19.9	19.7	15.4	21.6	20.3
Costs of implementing an e-commerce site	22.5	32.6	37.2	34.9	14.0	27.6	32.3	33.6
Making needed organizational changes	26.9	23.8	34.2	24.8	9.3	17.5	30.7	23.9
Level of ability to use the Internet as part of business strategy	14.6	28.0	14.1	23.7	14.7	20.8	14.3	24.8
Cost of internet access	4.6	13.5	0.0	16.3	8.8	12.7	1.6	15.1
Business laws do not support e-commerce	17.0	27.6	0.0	22.6	21.6	23.3	5.2	24.2
Taxation of internet sales	7.0	14.0	0.0	18.8	1.2	8.2	1.5	16.5
Inadequate legal protection for Internet purchases	13.3	37.3	22.2	33.6	26.2	26.0	20.8	34.1

Notes: [a]Responses were weighted based on the total number of establishments by employee size within the sector for each country.
           [b]Consists of weighted survey responses in 10 countries combined: United States, Mexico, Brazil, Germany, France, Denmark, Singapore, Taiwan, China and Japan.

As expected, the low diffusion of credit cards in Germany is an important barrier in the B2C area (21.6%), too. In fact, it is more common to use debit cards for payment at stores or gas stations instead of using credit cards. Although the number of credit card owners' is increasing, the corresponding possibility of online credit card abuse is rising too. This consequently prompts most online customers be reluctant to use their credit cards for online transactions. Another important barrier for industries in Germany is the necessity of structural business process changes in order to make them ready for e-business. More than 30% of German establishments are worried about or not able to accomplish the necessary organizational changes. This problem is especially salient in the retail and wholesale industry (34.2%), where the necessary prerequisites such as ERP-system or any kind of IT infrastructure is often absent in comparison to other sectors. In order to gain full benefits from e-business, the effort and changes required to make legacy systems e-business capable are therefore greater in the manufacturing or banking industries, while the retail and wholesale sector has to establish an IT infrastructure nearly from scratch.

Finally, policy and environmental issues are as unimportant obstacles as they are unimportant reasons for doing business online. Sufficient legal protection together with definite taxation and business laws, e.g., the long distance distribution law that covers traditional catalog sellers, as well as online retailers are regarded more as drivers rather than barriers to doing business online in Germany.

4.2.2 Diffusion and Use of E-Business Standards

As Table 7 depicts, the diffusion of rudimentary or basic e-business standard technologies seems to be complete to a great extent in all industry sectors in Germany. The existence of e-mail, websites, or intranets is quite common among the companies surveyed, with diffusion rates above the global sample at 84.4% to 100%. Nevertheless, the use of extranet technologies is far below the level of the global sample. While the manufacturing or banking and insurance industries use extranets extensively, the retail and wholesale sector is far behind.

Table 7: Use of E-Business Standard Technologies

Percentage using...	Manufacturing[a]		Wholesale/Retail Distribution[a]		Banking/ Insurance[a]		Total[a]	
	GER	Global[b]	GER	Global[b]	GER	Global[b]	GER	Global[b]
E-mail	100.0	95.5	100.0	99.9	100.0	99.2	100.0	98.5
Web-site	90.5	80.5	92.0	69.9	94.5	81.5	91.8	74.1
Intranet	77.8	63.5	85.9	63.3	88.8	66.5	84.4	63.6
Extranet	38.8	31.4	15.9	33.4	36.6	32.4	22.3	32.7
accessible by suppliers[c]	27.4	18.7	8.5	21.8	28.5	21.7	14.0	20.9
accessible by customers[c]	23.1	18.5	8.4	17.0	13.7	20.8	11.8	17.8
EDI	56.6	43.0	71.1	45.2	65.4	42.2	67.7	44.3
EDI over private networks[c]	20.3	14.2	34.0	22.8	27.6	13.4	30.8	19.4
Internet-based EDI[c]	16.3	12.3	8.1	6.1	12.5	10.7	10.1	8.4
both[c]	20.0	15.5	28.9	15.9	22.3	17.0	26.6	15.9
EFT	94.9	40.7	85.2	42.1	77.2	62.3	86.6	43.4
Call center	26.4	32.6	29.3	31.3	50.6	38.6	30.3	32.3

Notes: [a] Responses were weighted based on the total number of establishments by employee size within the sector for each country.
[b] Consists of weighted survey responses in 10 countries combined: United States, Mexico, Brazil, Germany, France, Denmark, Singapore, Taiwan, China and Japan.
[c] Percentage based on total sample.

Innovative forms of electronic data interchange, such as Internet-based EDI, are not yet very far-reaching. Only 10.1% of German industry uses Internet-based EDI, with the lowest percentage (8.1%) again in the retail and wholesale industry. This may be due to the long tradition and broad diffusion of traditional

EDI, resulting in a lower urgency to connect with business partners in other ways. It is only in the manufacturing sector where Internet-based WebEDI front-end systems are popular to integrate small business partners into existing supply chains. Call centers are not common in Germany, with the exception of the banking and insurance industry where call centers are used to adjust insurance cases or assist in telephone banking.

Figure 4: Diffusion of EDI-Standards

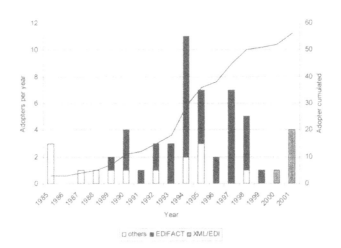

Further insight into German IT adoption behavior can be provided by considering the diffusion of EDI standards (Figure 4) per adopter per year. In Germany, the diffusion of innovations such as EDI is strongly driven by the advent of UN/EDIFACT. After a period with rather low adoption rates until 1994, a period with high adoption rates followed between 1994 and 1998. In 2000 and 2001, no further EDIFACT implementation was reported. Instead of EDIFACT, the adoption of XML/EDI frameworks appeared in 2000 and increased in 2001. Earlier EDI frameworks in the finance (SWIFT) and automotive (VDA) sector were also mentioned. XML/EDI frameworks are becoming increasingly important to connect business partners with no EDI-converter software systems over the Internet. Most of these business partners are SMEs (Beck 2002). In spite of the increasing rate of XML/EDI implementations, the ratio of messages sent and received is rather low (Figure 5). The use of further e-business-related innovations like Internet-EDI or WebEDI is slightly higher. The diffusion of these standards is still in its infancy in Germany, although these technologies are not new.

More important than the potential availability of e-business is the de facto use of these technologies (Beck 2002). In 2002, firms using EDI were asked about the ratio of electronic messaging in comparison to paper-based, manual messaging. The results are provided in Figure 5. Although 100% of the respondents are EDI-using firms, less than one-third of all messages are processed electronically via traditional EDI-systems, with an additional 10% via innovative EDI-solutions such as WebEDI, Internet-EDI, or XML/EDI. The survey shows that the hypothetical availability of e-business communication standards is not sufficient to draw conclusions about readiness or efficient use, since many standards have been adopted but are hardly used.

Figure 5: Messages by Communication Channel in Percent

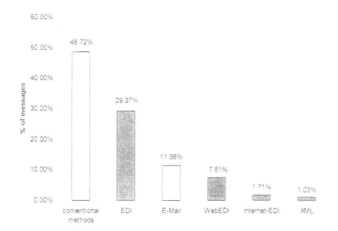

The diffusion of e-business standards among SMEs and large firms in Germany (G) differs only in comparison to other nations such as France (F), Denmark (DK), or the US. Figure 6 depicts the use of EDI and electronic funds transfer (EFT) in these four countries, divided into SMEs (S) and large establishments (L).

While a size-dependent difference is observable between large and small firms in the use of EDI for French firms, German firms use EDI and EFT nearly equally independent of size. As expected, large establishments in Denmark or France are leading in the use of EDI but on the other hand, SMEs in these countries are far behind. Even US establishments do not use EDI or EFT as often as Danish or German establishments. Surprisingly, German SMEs take the overall leading position with regard to EFT and are close to the percentage of EDI use reported by large firms in Germany. Therefore, the often-quoted "electronic gap" between large firms and SMEs cannot be verified by this empirical study.

Figure 6: Use of EDI and Electronic Funds Transfer at the National Level by Firm Size

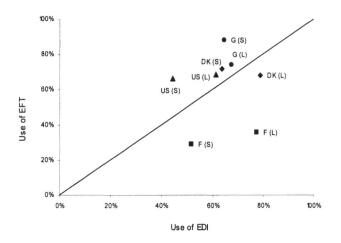

In terms of the percentage of establishments doing online sales and online purchasing or procurement, German firms take only a midfield position (Figure 7). Nevertheless, German SMEs seem to utilize online services more often than large firms do. Comparing this with the leading countries, large US establishments do more online sales and purchasing than US SMEs, while French firms report the lowest percentage of all countries. Interestingly, all countries and establishments conduct more online purchasing than online sales. While online sales are not as complex to integrate into existing ERP-systems, firms in this study do more online procurement. This may be due to the fact that online sales are too complex for the manufacturing industry with its heterogeneous and complex products, while the retail and wholesale and banking and insurance industry use online sales more extensively. Another explanation for the higher use of online procurement instead of online sales is that most establishments have not integrated automatic replenishment systems or interlinked their ERP-systems with the Internet, but order manually at web front-ends. This is, of course, the easiest way to use e-business standards as a first step, but holds no additional positive network effects for users such as storage and processing of operational data in in-house systems. The use of these technologies is therefore not applicable to making assumptions about the e-business readiness of an industry.

Figure 7: Use of Online Purchasing and Sales at the National Level by Firm Size

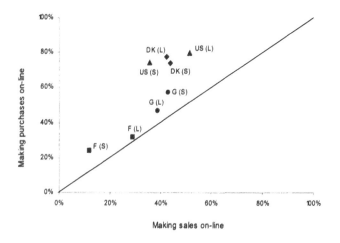

Making sales on-line

In the area of more advanced and sophisticated e-business solutions, the overall penetration is lower in all countries and dominated by large establishments (Figure 8).

Approximately 60% of large US firms use operational data exchange with their suppliers and approximately 70% of them conduct operational data exchange with their customers. In comparison to German SMEs and large establishments, who use these two e-business categories only up to 50% each, the differences between SMEs and large firms are considerably larger in other countries. French firms, as well as small and large Danish firms, have higher use rates of supplier-oriented supply chain management. At the same time, French and US SMEs use less of the last-mentioned technology in comparison to German firms. SMEs in these countries do not use the two e-business solutions as often as German SMEs, which are again not far from the position of large firms.

Figure 8: ICT based Supply Chain Management at the National Level by Firm Size

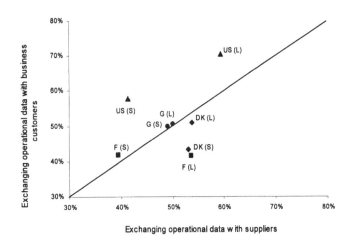

A more detailed view of e-business use at the industry level is provided in Table 8. Industry differences are evident, as significantly more retail and wholesale firms use e-business for online sales and purchasing, as well as data exchange with suppliers and formal integration of the same business process, than firms in the other two sectors do.

Table 8: Use of the E-Business

	Manufacturing[a]		Wholesale/Retail Distribution[a]		Banking/ Insurance[a]		Total[a]	
	GER	Global[b]	GER	Global[b]	GER	Global[b]	GER	Global[b]
Advertising and marketing purposes	75.4	55.8	79.3	57.1	77.8	68.3	78.4	57.6
Making sales online	29.0	25.1	68.1	31.9	37.8	33.0	57.8	29.9
After sales customer service and support	46.1	48.4	55.5	40.7	58.1	48.3	53.8	43.7
Making purchases online	51.3	43.4	65.1	47.8	45.3	52.2	60.7	46.8
Exchanging operational data with suppliers	49.5	49.9	65.1	48.0	42.8	41.9	60.2	48.1
Exchanging operational data with customers	57.9	53.4	50.4	49.0	56.4	52.5	52.4	50.7
Formally integrating the same business processes with suppliers/partners	23.6	26.8	55.5	37.5	37.2	33.5	47.7	33.9

Notes: [a] Responses were weighted based on the total number of establishments by employee size within the sector for each country.

         [b] Consists of weighted survey responses in 10 countries combined: United States, Mexico, Brazil, Germany, France, Denmark, Singapore, Taiwan, China and Japan.

The extent of integration of Internet applications with internal databases or ERP-systems is as low in Germany (55.2% reporting "little to no integration") as in the global sample (52.5%). The same low extent of integration can be observed in the area of electronic integration of customers and suppliers, where 72.2% of the German sample reported little to no integration, on a par with 72.1% of the global sample. Regarding the percentage of firms reporting a great deal of back-end integration, more German firms are able to benefit from it. Fully 26.9% (Germany) compared to 23.9% of the global sample estimate that they actively use such integration solutions, while the percentage with only some integration is below the global sample. Most German firms seem to wait until they can benefit from Internet application integration, but they integrate completely if they see any advantage in doing so.

The electronic integration of customers and suppliers follows similar rules: "do it or forget it," especially in the retail and wholesale sector. Nearly double the percentage of German firms as in the global sample, i.e. 17.1% in comparison to 9.6%, respectively; have integrated their business partners electronically.

Nevertheless, at the industry level different degrees of implementation are observable. In the banking and insurance industry, only 23.1% of German firms have achieved a great deal of back-end integration, compared to 40% of the firms in the global sample. This may be explained by the prevailing concerns about security issues accompanying the integration of open networks with their back-end systems, but it may also be an expression of the current economic slowdown in this sector. Most network effects benefits occur on the customer side while, conversely, banks are not able to reduce costs by using Internet technology.

4.3 Globalization and Diffusion of E-Business Standards

The diffusion and use of e-business applications and standards has been of research interest from a technological (Angeles et al. 2001), as well as an organizational point of view (e.g., (Mackay et al. 1996; Massetti et al. 1996; Rose et al. 1999)). While the main attention has focused on the adoption and implementation of e-commerce in large enterprises (e.g., (Hausman et al. 2003; Karahanna et al. 1999; Saloner et al. 1995)), e-business-driven changes and improvements are also observable at the level of SMEs, such as in the case of EDI adoption (Chau et al. 2001; Fink 1998; Iacovou et al. 1995; Powell et al. 2000).

This section does not analyze the whole data sample of the global study, but only a subset of these data for three European countries: Denmark, France,

Germany and the US. The impact and efficiency of e-business implementations is analyzed by conducting a Data Envelopment Analysis (DEA) (Charnes et al. 1978) for each industry sector and national market.

The impacts of the adopted e-business standards on process improvements are observable not only within large firms (König et al. 2003) but also among strong and innovation-friendly SMEs. In fact, SMEs in particular can benefit from the full potential of automation by adopting and implementing e-business carefully (Beck et al. 2003d). While the size of an enterprise seems to be more and more negligible as a variable determining the success of e-business implementation, the affiliation to a certain industry has still a positive or negative impact on overall e-business readiness. Some industrial sectors have done better in adopting e-business standards, e.g., computer-based electronic data processing and transmission. The automotive industry has successfully developed EDI-standards and delivery processes resulting in considerable savings of time and money (Hoppen et al. 2002; Wigand 1994). In comparison to the manufacturing sector with its sophisticated e-business processing, the retail and wholesale sector is much more fragmented and only a few best-practice cases such as in the former sector are known (Fearon et al. 1999).

During the last few years a rapid rate of diffusion and use of e-business solutions has been observable not only in the so-called "new economy" sector but also inside traditional industries (Dutta et al. 1998; Hawkins et al. 1999). E-business-driven changes and innovative improvements led to substantial efficiency increases (Cantwell 2001) in globally active, as well as nationally-oriented firms (Jalava et al. 2002; Kiiski et al. 2002). The impact of e-business diffusion is observable not only in firms focused on local or national markets but especially among internationally active corporations. In fact, e-business solutions are an important prerequisite of globalization for enterprises which are active worldwide to benefit from the advent of efficient communication and co-operation processes. Therefore, *Proposition 1* in this context is that the competitive pressure on the global level is positively related to the diffusion of e-business applications and standards.

Gaining the full potential and benefits from e-business technologies depends—apart from the degree of globalization of a firm—even more on their consistent integration and implementation in business processes while these processes must be adjusted at the same time. Consequently, *Proposition 2* assumes that the impact of e-business on business processes is positively related to the extent and number to which e-business applications are deployed.

Strongly export-oriented nations (as a percentage of GDP) such as Denmark or Germany have to be more competitive not only in their own market segment but also in the employment of e-business solutions on an international level. As a result, the need for cost-oriented and efficient production and distribution processes has a long tradition in those countries. Nevertheless, because of national differences such as available IT knowledge, ICT infrastructure or business laws but also mentality based variations such as concern about privacy or security, the importance of different e-business drivers varies among countries. Thus, *Proposition 3* is that the existence of national e-business drivers has a positive impact on the diffusion of Internet technologies and e-business applications.

Firms acting on an international level have a higher demand to adopt e-business applications to protect or expand markets or improve their business processes. Competitive pressure is an important reason for IT adoption, especially in the case of EDI (Angeles et al. 2001; Raymond et al. 1997; Vijayasarathy et al. 1997). Analogously, the same competitive pressure should also drive the diffusion and adoption of e-business applications.

The purpose of this section is to identify the determinants of efficient e-business standards using industries acting in national or international markets. More specifically, this paper examines the relative influence of e-business drivers by analyzing a sub-data sample of the empirical survey with 903 firms (or 903 data sets) altogether from Denmark, France, Germany and the US.

Globalization in this context may be defined as the growing interconnections through cross-border flows of information, capital and people (Held et al. 1999) resembling a network economy. It represents a challenging task for firms operating internationally while being competitive on both national, as well as global markets. The adoption of e-business applications may lower transaction and coordination costs and may enable firms to enter new markets or to penetrate existing markets efficiently (Steinfield et al. 1999). Therefore, creating and sustaining competitive advantage is mandatory for successful enterprises and is typically achieved by reducing transaction costs and the deployment of innovative and efficient e-business standards at the same time (Gordon 2000). From a macroeconomic view, there is evidence that highly export-oriented countries and/or industry sectors which are open to foreign trade and invest- ment exhibit a higher level of e-business implementation (Caselli et al. 2001; Shih et al. 2000). At the same time, due to higher competitive pressure, global enterprises use e-business applications more holistically than nationally or lo- cally oriented ones. Accordingly, this section investigates the relationship be- tween globalization and the efficient usage of diffused e-business applications and standards at industry and national levels. Focusing on the economic im- pact, globalization in this paper is measured in terms of the competitive pres- sure at international level. Furthermore, the impact of several e-business driv- ers on the deployment of e-business applications is analyzed and national variations among drivers are identified.

4.3.1   Globalization and the Usage of E-Business

The following paragraph addresses *Proposition 1* and analyzes the relation- ship between the usage of e-business applications and competitive pressure from abroad as an indicator for the degree of globalization of a firm. Are glob- ally active companies indeed leaders in the area of e-business usage and can this proposition also be validated for the data sample at hand, as well as for the various countries?

Doubtlessly, an important driver of the diffusion and usage of e-business ap- plications is the strong international competition or globalization of markets, especially in export-oriented countries such as Germany. The manifold inter- national trade connections increase the speed of diffusion of standardized electronic transactions. However, the German industry sectors surveyed are not focused exclusively on foreign trade, in fact, they are closely intercon- nected with their own foreign branches or headquarters (cf. Table 9).

Compared to the global average, Germany is above average, with exception of the total sales from abroad. The international diversification enables and in- creases the number of foreign business contacts, which is also measurable when focusing on the percentage of procurement from abroad, which is equal to or above the global average with the exception of the banking/insurance sector in Germany. In spite of strong international competition, the German in- dustry sectors surveyed seem to be well positioned in the global sample, especially in the manufacturing and banking and insurance industry, where the intensity or impact of international competition is reported to be below average.

Table 9: Indicators of Globalization

	Manufactur-ing		Retail/ Wholesale		Banking/ Insurance		Total	
	GER	DK, F, USA	GER	DK, F, USA	GER	DK, F, USA	GER	DK, F, USA
% with establishments abroad	57.4	53.1	45.5	42.2	32.4	30.2	45.0	41.9
% with headquarters abroad	23.5	17.4	18.2	11.1	14.7	10.4	18.8	13.0
% of total sales from abroad	23.0	28.7	13.4	13.3	6.2	8.9	14.1	17.2
% of total procurement from abroad	26.1	22.8	26.2	23.1	1.4	4.6	16.4	16.4
Affected by competitors from abroad (in %):								
Low	42.2	38.9	57.4	67.5	82.3	81.8	60.5	62.3
Moderate	21.9	21.2	14.8	13.7	11.3	9.7	16.0	15.0
High	36.0	39.9	27.9	18.7	6.4	8.6	25.5	22.7

Note: 4 countries: (DK) Denmark, (F) France, (GER) Germany, and the USA (USA)

The impact of global competition on the diffusion of e-business applications is analyzed by using the data of Table 9 and Table 10. While the perceived competitive pressure from abroad is shown in Table 9, the degree of deployed e-business applications is calculated as the total number of solutions deployed shown in Table 10 for every firm.

Proposition 1 suggests a positive relation between the perceived competitive pressure on the global level and the number of e-business applications and underlying Internet technologies implemented (Table 10).

Table 10: Implementation of E-Business Applications

	Manufacturing		Retail/ Wholesale		Banking/ Insurance		Total	
	GER	DK, F, USA	GER	DK, F, USA	GER	DK, F, USA	GER	DK, F, USA
Advertising and marketing purposes in %	73.5	64.5	81.8	69.7	92.6	79.3	82.7	71.1
Making sales online	26.5	23.1	48.5	47.0	48.5	43.3	41.1	37.7
After sales customer service and support in %	44.8	43.9	43.9	49.0	68.2	58.1	52.3	50.3
Making purchases online in %	55.4	62.5	59.4	58.9	41.2	58.6	51.8	60.0
Exchanging operational data with suppliers in %	51.5	52.2	66.2	51.9	31.3	45.2	49.5	49.8
Exchanging operational data with customers in %	54.5	58.0	51.5	45.3	44.8	53.2	50.3	52.2
Integrating same business processes with business partners in %	28.1	32.6	46.2	38.2	29.7	37.6	34.7	36.1

Note: 4 countries: (DK) Denmark, (F) France, (GER) Germany, and the USA (USA)

Spearman's correlation coefficient between the competitive pressures from abroad (see Table 9 for reported affection rates) and the number of e-business applications in place (Table 10) reveals a positive correlation (significant at the 0.01 level) of 0.142 for the global sample and the French sub-Sample (0.256). There is no significant correlation in the German, Danish and US sub-sample between competitive pressure and the number of e-business applications deployed. Therefore, *Proposition 1*, which suggests that global acting companies are extensive users of e-business technologies, is only supported for the French sub-sample. Only French enterprises that feel highly affected by competitors from abroad tend to be extensive users of e-business applications.

4.3.2   Enterprise Application Strategy and Impact of E-Business

The following paragraph addresses *Proposition 2* and analyzes the impact of e-business applications on different internal, as well as external business processes. First, the extent of electronic integration and implementation of e-business applications in Germany and the global sample is compared (see Table 11). Then, the correlation between the number of e-business applications deployed and their perceived impact on business processes is investigated.

Table 11: Enterprise Application Strategy

Extent to which Internet applications are electronically integrated with...	Manufacturing		Retail/ Wholesale		Banking/ Insurance		Total	
	GER	DK, F, USA	GER	DK, F, USA	GER	DK, F, USA	GER	DK, F, USA
internal databases and information systems:								
% little to none	53.1	55.1	44.4	39.8	37.3	32.4	44.8	42.5
% some	26.6	22.4	22.2	24.0	34.3	24.8	27.8	23.7
% a great deal	20.3	22.5	33.4	36.2	28.3	42.7	27.3	33.7
those of suppliers and business customers:								
% little to none	76.7	73.9	63.9	66.5	78.3	66.5	72.9	69.1
% some	20.0	16.0	14.8	19.7	11.7	16.9	15.5	17.5
% a great deal	3.4	10.1	21.3	10.7	10.0	16.5	11.6	13.5

Note: 4 countries: (DK) Denmark, (F) France, (GER) Germany, and the USA (USA)

The extent of integration of Internet applications with internal databases or ERP-systems is as low in Germany (44.8% responded with "little to no integration") as in the global survey (42.5%) (see Table 11). The same low extent of integration can be observed in the area of electronic integration of customers and suppliers, where German industry responded with a non-integration rate of 72.9%, even higher than the global sample rate of 69.1%. Regarding the percentage of firms responding that integration is "a great deal", only 11.6% of German firms are able to benefit from it. According to the survey, most Ger-

man firms seem to be waiting until they can benefit from Internet application integration. The electronic integration of customers and suppliers on the industry
level seems to follow similar rules, especially in the banking and insurance industry, where 78.3% reported "little to no" integration.

Although the low levels of integration of external business partners in Germany, but also in the global samples, is an important hindrance to the
achievement of the full potential of e-business-based automation. The positive
impact is nevertheless measurable. As the correlation analysis for *Proposition
2* suggests, there is a strong interconnection between the number of e-
business applications deployed and their impact on these perceived business
process.

Table 12: Impacts of Doing Business Online (percent indicating impact is above average)

	Manufactur-ing		Retail/Wholesale		Banking/Insurance		Total	
	GER	DK, F, USA	GER	DK, F, USA	GER	DK, F, USA	GER	DK, F, USA
Internal processes more efficient in %	29.2	33.7	25.3	31.6	26.9	32.8	27.2	32.7
Staff productivity increased in %	15.6	21.5	18.2	24.7	15.4	22.1	16.4	22.8
Sales increased in %	8.1	15.6	18.1	20.3	19.4	18.1	15.3	17.9
Sales area widened in %	13.9	24.0	23.0	26.3	16.6	23.8	17.7	24.6
Customer service improved in %	27.7	35.4	30.1	34.6	51.6	44.6	36.6	38.3
International sales increased in %	12.5	12.6	11.9	9.4	3.2	4.8	9.2	9.1
Procurement costs decreased in %	9.4	15.1	17.7	16.0	6.4	11.8	11.2	14.4
Inventory costs decreased in %	6.5	8.1	6.5	10.2	11.7	10.7	8.2	9.6
Coordination with suppliers improved in %	33.3	31.8	21.5	30.5	21.0	26.4	25.2	29.6
Competitive position improved in %	25.0	26.5	21.9	27.6	37.5	33.4	28.1	29.2

Note: 4 countries: (DK) Denmark, (F) France, (GER) Germany, and the USA (USA)

For the test of *Proposition 2*, the impact of business applications on business
processes (see Table 12) is correlated with the diffusion of e-business applications deployed (provided in Table 10). Business process improvements were
aggregated to a single index by adding up all potential improvements. Spearman's correlation coefficient between e-business applications deployed and
the overall business process improvements index reveals a positive correlation
of 0.207 (significant at the 0.01 level) in the global sample and 0.212 (significant at the 0.01 level) in the German sub-sample. Both data sets exhibit similar correlations between the number of e-business applications deployed and
their impact on business processes. Therefore, a higher number of e-business
applications in place do indeed have a strong positive impact on the perceived
improvements on all kinds of business processes, resulting in higher productiv-

ity, lower costs, or even efficiency increases. A broad deployment of e-business applications significantly improves all kinds of business processes.

As already discussed in the preceding paragraphs, some differences exist between the German sub-sample and the global sample. The purpose of the following paragraph is to identify the significant deviations, as well as to discuss *Proposition 3* identifying possible relations between national drivers of e-business and the diffusion of Internet technologies and e-business applications.

Table 13: How Establishments Use the Internet to Sell Products and Services

	Manufacturing		Whole-sale/Retail Distribution		Banking/ Insurance		Total	
	GER	DK, F, USA	GER	DK, F, USA	GER	DK, F, USA	GER	DK, F, USA
Addresses new markets only in %	0.0	10.1	12.1	12.0	2.5	10.5	5.3	11.0
Addresses traditional distribution channels only in %	90.9	56.2	78.8	51.9	77.5	45.2	81.1	50.6
Competes directly with traditional distribution channels in %	9.1	24.7	9.1	26.3	15.0	36.3	11.6	29.5
Replaces traditional distribution channels in %	0.0	9.0	0.0	9.8	5.0	8.1	2.1	9.0

Note: 4 countries: (DK) Denmark, (F) France, (GER) Germany, and the USA (USA)

Consequently, following a multi-channel strategy, the Internet does not compete directly with other distribution channels (only 11.6% of German firms think it does) in comparison to other countries (see Table 13).

Table 14: Drivers of E-Business

Percent indicating a significant factor ...	Manufacturing		Retail/ Wholesale		Banking/ Insurance		Total	
	GER	DK, F, USA	GER	DK, F, USA	GER	DK, F, USA	GER	DK, F, USA
Customer demanded it	33.8	34.1	25.8	32.4	25.8	42.8	35.0	36.5
Major competitors were online	33.3	29.0	36.0	34.7	36.0	53.8	45.4	39.2
Suppliers required it	22.0	21.6	15.4	14.1	15.4	10.0	13.7	15.4
To reduce costs	23.5	32.7	22.7	34.4	22.7	35.7	24.2	24.3
To expand market for existing product/services	38.2	39.5	37.9	41.7	37.9	47.3	37.8	42.8
To enter new businesses or markets	36.7	34.9	44.0	37.0	44.0	35.9	38.2	35.9
To improve coordination with customers and suppliers	60.0	50.3	57.6	59.5	57.6	45.1	48.2	48.3
Required for government procurement	9.1	11.7	7.7	10.7	7.7	8.1	7.6	10.2
Government provided incentives	4.5	3.4	1.6	4.8	1.6	4.8	4.1	4.4

Note: 4 countries: (DK) Denmark, (F) France, (GER) Germany, and the USA (USA)

As Table 14 indicates, competition is a significant factor for online activities. 39.2% of establishments in the three sectors consider major competitors going online as a significant incentive for e-commerce use. While only 29.0% of the manufacturing industry viewed this factor as significant, a high level of competition is a significant pressure for distributors (34.7%) and even more for financial firms (53.8%). Pressure by customers (36.5%) or suppliers (15.4%) to use the Internet is rather low in the global sample. Administrative issues (required for government procurement, government provided incentives) only play minor roles (10.2%, 4.4%), neglecting the impact of B2A.

Proposition 3 suggests that the existence of national e-business drivers has a positive impact on the diffusion of Internet technologies and e-business applications. To test this thesis, Spearman's correlation coefficient between drivers of e-business diffusion and the number of e-business applications deployed is calculated (Table 15 shows the results) for all countries.

Table 15: Correlation of E-Business Diffusion Drivers and Deployed E-Business Applications

Drivers	E-business applications deployed				
	Germany	France	Denmark	USA	Total
Customer demanded it	0.108	0.137	0.015	0.250**	0.174**
Major competitors were online	0.181*	0.130	0.160*	0.204**	0.186**
Suppliers required it	0.088	0.101	0.092	0.104	0.098**
To reduce costs	0.178*	0.148	0.048	0.309**	0.226**
To expand market	0.096	0.216**	0.014	0.160*	0.129**
To enter new businesses or markets	0.223**	0.144	0.118	0.216**	0.211**
To improve coordination	0.096	0.063	0.143*	0.278**	0.183**
Required for government procurement	0.083	0.033	0.056	0.007	0.005
Government provided incentives	0.054	0.012	0.069	0.013	0.015

Note: **significant to 0.01; *significant to 0.05

In the global sample, all drivers except B2A-related ones are correlated with the number of e-business applications deployed. Reducing costs and having the opportunity to enter new businesses or markets appear to be the most important drivers for the deployment of e-business applications. National variation of important e-business drivers can be observed when comparing the correlation weights. The main drivers for German firms are cost reduction, the opportunity to enter new markets, and the fact that major competitors are also online. In France, the only significant driver is the expansion of markets for existing products and services. The main drivers of Danish firms are that competitors are online, as well as supplier coordination-related issues. Cost reduction and new business opportunities are the most important drivers for firms in the US. As this suggests, there are indeed strong national differences. Nevertheless, B2A related drivers do not play an important role in any of the countries investigated.

In contrast to other countries, German firms do not use and understand the Internet and related e-business applications as a substitute to traditional markets or distribution channels. German firms use the Internet as a complementary instrument to complete and support the already sophisticated market penetration (cf., Table 13). Consequently, the goal of addressing only new markets is not perceived as that important because national and international markets were the object of market penetration strategies even before the Internet emerged (only 5.3% affirm). As a result, 81.1% of German industry responded describing the use of Internet capabilities only to serve and support existing distribution channels while only 2.1% responded mentioning the reduction or replacement of traditional distribution channels. Consequently, because they follow a multi-channel strategy, the Internet does not compete directly with other distribution channels (only 11.6% of German firms think it does) in comparison to other countries.

The diffusion of e-business applications and solutions in German industry seems to have reached a high level of saturation. Large firms, as well as SMEs in the studied industries utilize more or less the same high level of e-business applications. Competitive pressure from abroad is often cited as a strong driver of e-business diffusion to strengthen and defend competitive advantage by extensive usage of information systems. This empirical survey does not reveal a significant relationship between competitive pressure and the number of e-business applications deployed. Only the French sub-sample reveals a strong positive correlation between perceived competitive pressure and applications deployed, whilst competitive pressure from abroad seems not to be an important factor for German, Danish or US firms. A positive correlation between the impact on business processes and the number and extent of e-business applications deployed is supported for the global sample and the German sub-sample. Both correlation indices suggest a strong correlation between the number of applications deployed and their positive impact on distinct business processes.

The impact of several national drivers on the deployment of e-business applications is also analyzed. As a correlation analysis has revealed, there are distinct national drivers which encourage the diffusion of e-business applications. The two foremost important drivers in the global sample and the German sub-sample are cost reduction and the opportunity to expand markets or businesses by applying communication standards and information technology. B2A-related drivers have proved to be irrelevant in all samples. In contrast to the global survey, German firms regard e-business less often as an enabler to increase markets on the international level. Given the existing global market orientation, German firms were competitive on international markets even in the pre-e-business era.

To recapitulate, many of those firms implementing e-business in a consistent way benefit from process improvements and increasing efficiencies. The e-business diffusion race has reached a stage of maturity, which seems to be an excellent base for further developments such as mobile commerce or towards a network economy in the future.

4.4 Diffusion and Impact of E-Business Standards among SMEs

Gaining the full potential and benefits from e-business depends on the consistent integration and implementation of all kinds of e-business technologies into existing business processes, while at the same time these processes have to be adjusted (see section 4.3). Thus, there is a strong possibility that a strategy of selective use of single applications with insufficient interfaces will fail. Therefore, purposeful implementation is especially important for SMEs in strongly export-oriented nations in order to be competitive on an international level. Due to national differences such as available IT knowledge, ICT infrastructure or business laws, different paths of e-business diffusion are observable. Such differences are based on reported variances of e-business drivers and inhibitors among the countries investigated. One major methodological problem is certainly the measuring of increased productivity or efficiency improvements directly attributable to e-business. A common problem is the lack of data, weak definitions, and a lack of applicable methods. If it has not been possible to measure the impact of the increased use of IT directly so far, it follows that an impact should at least be visible on the output side. Nevertheless, even measuring these spillover effects seems to be difficult, although PCs and the Internet have doubtlessly created additional consumer benefit.

This section focuses on the analysis of the diffusion of e-business on the one hand and the resulting efficiency improvements or perceived satisfaction among SMEs on the other hand. The introduction of a satisfaction factor is not new in information systems research: the transmission process relating the information systems utilization to perceived user satisfaction has already been analyzed by Bailey and Pearson (Bailey et al. 1983) or Ives et al. (Ives et al. 1983). An assessment of existing user satisfaction concepts is provided by Melone (Melone 1990).

Different sets of e-business standards and technologies among countries and industry sectors may be explained as national and sectoral differences (such as available IT knowledge or ICT infrastructure). Consequently, the number of efficient e-business-using firms should be correlated with the business environments investigated, based on the underlying empirical survey. Efficient firms should value drivers of e-business significantly more highly (and vice versa obstacles lower) than the rest of the firms investigated.

Although the mere existence of different e-business standard technologies at firm level might be a good estimator for the diffusion of IT knowledge and use of new standards, this information still allows only limited insights into the de facto intensity of use or the productivity improvements related to the implementation. Obviously, efficient and consistent use is more important than the mere existence of such technologies. Therefore, the efficient use of e-business standards should be positively related to the number of e-business solutions used.

The number of employed e-business-based applications together with the perceived impacts of e-business are used in the following to identify the relation between the total number of e-business solutions and efficiency per sector.

4.4.1   Data Sample and Methodological Background

For the analysis of the impact on SMEs, only a sub-sample of the overall data is used in this section with altogether 458 SMEs responding from Denmark, Germany, France, and the United States. 152 SMEs in the manufacturing sector are surveyed from Denmark (35), Germany (33), France (34), and the United States (50). In the retail/wholesale sector, the survey was conducted among 151 SMEs from Denmark (33), Germany (34), France (31), and the United States (53). In the banking and insurances sector, the survey was conducted among 155 SMEs from Denmark (32), Germany (36), France (35), and the United States (52).

Denmark, France and Germany differ in the intensity of demand drivers (industry structure, information infrastructure, financial and human resources, and social and cultural factors) but are experiencing the same increasing productivity gap based on a time-lag in e-business readiness and diffusion (Kraemer et al. 2000) in comparison to the US. Due to these national and industrial path dependencies in the diffusion of e-business, a comparison between e-business-leading countries such as Denmark and the US with the two largest economies in continental Europe (France and Germany) seems to be a promising way to identify differences in the ways e-business is used, as well as finding "best practice" cases or "leading" sectors or countries.

To analyze the relative efficiency of SMEs deploying e-business, a Data Envelopment Analysis (DEA) is conducted (Charnes et al. 1978). Since most SMEs cannot determine the benefits they derive from implementing innovative technologies in monetary units, the questionnaire asked for the set of e-business technologies adopted on the one hand and the individually perceived efficiency or satisfaction on the other hand.

The BCC (Banker, Charnes and Cooper) model of the DEA analysis used offers a distinction between technical efficiency and scale-efficiency (Golany et al. 1989) and evaluates solutions for non-increasing, decreasing, and variable returns of scale. The object of interest in a DEA model is the decision-making unit (DMU) which is similar to a firm. A DMU is a flexible unit responsible for the input and output variables. DEA only compares each DMU with the "most efficient" DMUs in the sample (Bala et al. 2003). Efficient combinations of input and output relations or efficient DMUs in a sample form the so-called 'efficient frontier line'. In an n-dimensional room, the efficient frontier is equivalent to an imaginary umbrella over the sample, covering the efficient DMUs and all theoretically possible combinations of efficient, virtual DMUs. The DEA model calculates the relative position inside the data sample for each DMU, based on its set of inputs and set of outputs (Parsons 1992). Using a linear programming procedure for the frontier analysis of inputs and outputs, DEA accordingly evaluates the "best practice" users of e-business. The basic idea of DEA is multi-input and multi-output-oriented efficiency evaluation without any further assumptions about structure (e.g., normal distribution) or side conditions. Unlike parametric methods, DEA can use all kinds of input and output data to analyze the production behavior. The DEA model used was non input- or output-oriented because neither an input minimizing (input-oriented) nor an output-maximizing (output-oriented) analysis was necessary to evaluate the actual observed input/output relation identified in the survey. Moreover, the model assumes returns of scale for each DMU depending on the size and a concave function of decreasing returns. The software used for the data analysis together with a detailed description is available from Scheel (Scheel 2000).

DEA was chosen due to the unique alternative way of analyzing a set of data in comparison to the best performing data sets. A regression analysis, for example, only describes the deviation of best performing data sets from the average. Unlike parametric approaches, DEA optimizes on each individual observation independent of any distribution assumptions. Different kinds of DEA models have been used in a large number of ways to measure the impacts of IT: e.g. in the banking industry (Barr et al. 2002; Beck et al. 2003b) or in the distribution (Beck et al. 2003e) and manufacturing (Beck et al. 2005c) industry.

In this thesis, the DEA model was adapted and used as follows: the input variables—aggregated to an Internet usage indicator—are the results of seven questions (concerning online advertising, online sales and procurement, online customer services, exchange of operational data with customers and suppliers, as well as formal integration of similar business processes along the supply chain) about which applications are actively used by the respondents. Variables are coded as 0 when an establishment uses the e-business application requested and 1 if it does not use it. The coding is equivalent to costs of input when e-business is not available or the other way round, i.e. firms using e-business gain benefits by reducing their processing costs.

Input variables (Internet usage indicator) = v (online advertising, online sales, online procurement, …, same formal business processes along supply chain)

$$s.t. \quad v_i \in \{0;1\}$$

The ten output variables—aggregated to an e-business satisfaction index—of the model are measured on a five-point scale with 1 ('no impact at all') to 5 ('a great deal') and comprise the results of the following questions: internal processes more efficient, staff productivity increased, sales and national/ international sales area increased, customer service improvement, procurement and inventory costs decreased, coordination with suppliers improved and competitive position improved.

Output variables (E-business satisfaction index) = u (internal process more efficient, staff productivity increased, ..., competitive position improved)

$s.t.$ $u_j \in \{1;2;3;4;5\}$

The basic formula of the model chosen is similar to the CCR model (Charnes, Cooper, Rhodes):

$$\max \theta = \frac{\sum_{j=1}^{s} u_j y_j}{\sum_{i=1}^{t} v_i x_i}$$

Equation 1: Charnes, Cooper and Rhodes maximization

Efficiency in this context is the relative benefit gained, based on the e-business application used improving efficiency or productivity. SMEs with a high satisfaction index based on the installed e-business infrastructure may be defined as efficient in comparison to other SMEs of the sample.

4.4.2   The Diffusion of E-Business in Three Industry Sectors

The diffusion of e-business applications or standards has received broad attention, especially in the business-to-business and interorganizational cooperation area together with the integration of heterogeneous partners such as SMEs (Ketler et al. 1997; Kiiski et al. 2002). One of the most challenging problems—not only inside industry sectors but also on a macroeconomic level—is the often insufficient electronic supply chain integration of SMEs, reflecting the physical stream of goods.

SMEs have to cope with a variety of problems which normally impede the successful integration of e-business applications, such as inadequate ERP systems, lack of IT know-how or not totally automated internal business processes, as a prerequisite to gaining benefits when exchanging business messages electronically (Beck et al. 2002). In the pre-e-business era, SMEs were forced by large business partners to integrate standards such as EDI—often not necessarily for economic reasons (Wigand 1994). Nevertheless, in comparison to large enterprises, SMEs have more difficulties in attracting IT specialists for their business and cannot usually benefit from economies of scale, nor do they have sophisticated distribution systems (König et al. 2003).

Therefore, the fast adoption of innovative applications and standards is a critical factor for all SMEs if they want to be successful and competitive. Through the internationalization of markets, manufacturers and their suppliers are increasingly being forced to intensify and improve their business relations in order to avoid losing competitive advantage. Consequently, a higher level of integration or cooperation is needed. The Internet and e-business-based supply chain integration into SMEs business processes implies more than just the exchange of business documents. Moreover, the planning, execution and control of supply chain activities requires the efficient use of e-business, as well as the organizational willingness to cooperate (Swaminathan et al. 1998). This involves the sharing of information and knowledge that used to be considered proprietary or even strategic. The sharing of business-critical information and Internet-based supply chain management is therefore inefficient as long as SMEs within value chains are not totally integrated. As a result, a preliminary step towards a soundly functioning supply chain is the availability of rudimentary e-business applications among SMEs.

The impact of e-business on accepted and traditional business processes and methods has especially influenced the retail and wholesale industry. No other industry has to cope as much with the changes in customer preferences to shop online instead of making sales at traditional brick-and-mortar shops. Internet customers are better informed and more price-sensitive than off-line customers are. The ability to compare prices directly on the Internet increases competition and provides greater transparency (e.g., (Wigand 2003)). On the other hand, SMEs are predicted to be flexible and innovative in using the new form of conducting business more flexibly than large retailers. In contrast, SMEs are often not able to compete with large competitors due to the high setup costs of web-enabled material management systems or web-based shopping systems.

In the banking and insurance sector, the products offered are mainly information goods which can easily be provided in digital form over the Internet. The underlying ICT-driven processes are subject to steady changes, due not least to new distribution channels such as online banking. Changing customer preferences together with decreasing loyalty are a new challenge banks have to cope with. The usage of the PC and the Internet has doubtlessly created consumer surpluses, especially with regard to online banking and brokerage services. However, the multi-channel distribution strategy holds no additional utility for banks if they cannot benefit from economies of scale by reducing the number of physical branches at the same time.

4.4.3   E-Business Readiness among SMEs

The overall diffusion and adoption of e-business applications has reached a high level in all the countries studied. As Table 16 indicates, Danish SMEs are at the forefront in the field of Internet-based services in comparison to most of the other countries and sectors investigated.

Table 16: SMEs E-Business Readiness per Nation and Sector (in Percent)

	Denmark			France			Germany			USA		
	M	R	B	M	R	B	M	R	B	M	R	B
E-mail	100.0	100.0	100.0	94.1	96.8	97.2	100.0	100.0	100.0	98.0	100.0	100.0
Website	91.4	97.0	100.0	61.8	51.6	61.1	90.9	91.2	97.1	84.0	73.6	86.5
Intranet	74.3	78.8	96.9	67.6	71.0	61.1	69.7	82.4	91.4	44.0	58.5	55.8
Extranet	40.0	39.4	46.9	38.2	9.7	27.8	36.4	26.5	40.0	26.0	28.3	26.9
EDI	48.6	66.7	75.0	64.7	41.9	41.7	51.5	76.5	60.0	54.0	37.7	34.6
EFT	82.9	57.6	75.0	23.5	29.0	30.6	90.9	85.3	85.7	50.0	56.6	80.8
Call Center	31.4	33.3	37.5	20.6	25.8	16.7	21.2	41.2	54.3	50.0	35.8	48.1

Note: M: Manufacturing, R: Retail/Wholesale, B: Banking/Insurance, SMEs: 25 to 249 employees

With 100% availability of e-mail and 91.4% to 100% diffusion of public websites, as well as in the deployment of Intranet (from 74.3% in the manufacturing industry to 96.9% in the banking and insurance industry) Danish SMEs lead in being equipped overall to use e-business. However, German SMEs are not far behind, i.e. they provide their own websites less often (90.9%), and they are nearly equal to Danish firms in the areas of Intranet usage (69.7%). German SMEs lead in the use of electronic funds transfer (EFT) (90.9%) ahead of all other countries in the sample. Apart from German and Danish SMEs in the manufacturing sector, French (with the exception of EDI) and US SMEs (with exception of call centre use) use one of these technologies less often.

Based on the large installed base of established e-business applications, e-business is used to improve many kinds of internal and external business processes (cf., Table 17). While in Table 16 Danish firms have on average reported the highest availability of e-business standards, in the area of e-business use US and German SMEs are leading on average, especially in the field of more sophisticated and complex applications such as EDI with customers or Internet-based supply chain management. While German SMEs use, at a level of 75.8%, online advertising more often than any other manufacturing sector, only 32.4% of French SMEs used this application at the same time. On average, SMEs in the US reported the highest usage rates of e-business applications in the manufacturing sector in the areas of after sales customer service (60.0%), online procurement (76.0%), EDI with customers (64.0%) and Internet based supply chain management (34.0%).

Table 17: SMEs E-Business Usage per Nation and Sector (in percent)

		Online advertising	Online Sales	After sales customer services	Online procurement	EDI with suppliers	EDI with customers	Internet based supply chain management
Denmark	M	65.7%	31.4%	45.7%	74.3%	54.3%	54.3%	25.7%
	R	93.9%	45.5%	48.5%	72.7%	45.5%	27.3%	39.4%
	B	90.6%	56.3%	62.5%	71.9%	56.3%	46.9%	37.5%
France	M	32.4%	8.8%	17.6%	20.6%	44.1%	52.9%	23.5%
	R	25.8%	9.7%	12.9%	22.6%	29.0%	29.0%	16.1%
	B	47.2%	16.7%	27.8%	27.8%	41.7%	38.9%	33.3%
Germany	M	75.8%	27.3%	42.4%	51.5%	51.5%	57.6%	21.2%
	R	82.4%	55.9%	41.2%	73.5%	67.6%	52.9%	44.1%
	B	85.7%	45.7%	65.7%	42.9%	28.6%	40.0%	25.7%
USA	M	72.0%	26.0%	60.0%	76.0%	44.0%	64.0%	34.0%
	R	54.7%	49.1%	52.8%	69.8%	41.5%	43.4%	35.8%
	B	80.8%	30.8%	50.0%	76.9%	38.5%	63.5%	32.7%

Note: M: Manufacturing, R: Retail/Wholesale, B: Banking/Insurance, SMEs: 25 to 249 employees

In the retail and wholesale industry, German SMEs are at the forefront, employing e-business applications such as online sales (55.9%), online procurement (73.5%), EDI with suppliers (67.6%), EDI with customers (52.9%) or Internet-based supply chain management (44.1%) more often. In the banking and insurance sector, Danish SMEs use on average any of the e-business applications requested more often than SMEs in other countries. They are leading in the areas of online sales (56.3%), EDI with suppliers (56.3%) and Internet-based supply chain management (37.5%).

French SMEs are unable to dominate either in a single industry sector or in the use of a specific e-business application. German and US SMEs seem to use sophisticated solutions such as EDI with customers or Internet-based supply chain management more often. As proposition two suggested, the implementation and use of more complex technologies should be positively related to the satisfaction resulting from the positive impact e-business applications have on the efficiency of SMEs.

4.4.4   E-Business Drivers and Barriers for SMEs

While section 4.4.3 provides a brief overview of the diffusion of e-business standards and the differences in each country and sector, this section provides some possible reasons for the diffusion pattern reported, based on different drivers and barriers that encourage or hinder diffusion in each sector and or country. Figure 9 depicts e-business drivers in the manufacturing industry, using a five-point scale, where 1 corresponds to 'not a driving factor at all' and 5 to 'a very significant factor'.

Figure 9: E-Business Drivers for SMEs in the Manufacturing Sector

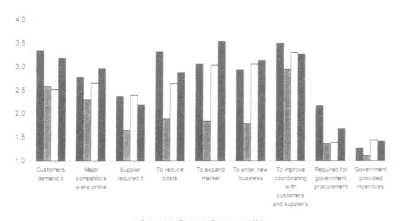

Important drivers for SMEs to adopt e-business applications are employed in all countries to improve coordination with customers and suppliers. The most important drivers in Denmark, Germany and in the US are the potential to reduce costs by implementing e-business solutions, the expansion of markets together with the ability to improve coordination with customers and suppliers. The latter reason is also of importance in France, while on average the overall lowest rated drivers were reported there as well. The governmental contribution to the diffusion of e-business seems to be rather unimportant in all countries surveyed. Apart from e-business drivers, the most important factors impeding doing business online in the manufacturing sector are also investigated (cf., Figure 10).

Analogous to Figure 9, a five-point scale was used, where 1 corresponds to 'not an obstacle' and 5 to 'a very significant obstacle'. Interestingly, SMEs in the US reported the highest obstacles scores on average. While the need for customer face-to-face interaction is not as important in Germany or France, American or Danish SMEs rate this obstacle as an important hindering factor. American SMEs, followed by Danish and French ones, regard security factors as important obstacles. While the obstacles in the field of technology support on the customer side or the bottleneck of e-business-skilled staff is more of a problem in France or the US, the prevalence of credit cards for online shopping is not seen as an important impeding factor in all countries, especially not in Denmark.

Figure 10: Factors Impeding E-Business for SMEs in the Manufacturing Sector

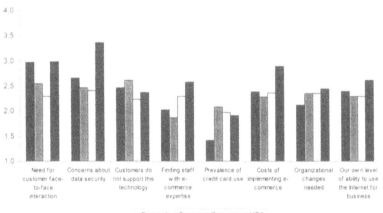

An often-mentioned barrier for SMEs is the costliness of integrating e-business solutions into an existing in-house IT infrastructure. US SMEs regard this as an important barrier. Mandatory organizational changes can be reported for US SMEs, followed by German and French ones, as the highest hindering factors. The level of ability to use the Internet for their own business is seen as critical in the US, followed by Danish SMEs. In general, US SMEs regard themselves as being confronted with more impeding factors than their European counterparts.

In the retail and wholesale sector, one of the least important drivers of e-business—for economic reasons—is the necessity to integrate e-business due to pressure from suppliers requiring e-business-ready business partners (cf., Figure 11).

Governmental contributions to the diffusion of e-business seem to be unimportant with the exception of France and Denmark, where online business with the government appears to require e-business applications to a certain degree. Overall, SMEs in the retail and wholesale sector do not regard the impact of the government as a driving factor for implementing or using e-business.

Figure 11: E-Business Drivers for SMEs in the Retail & Wholesale Sector

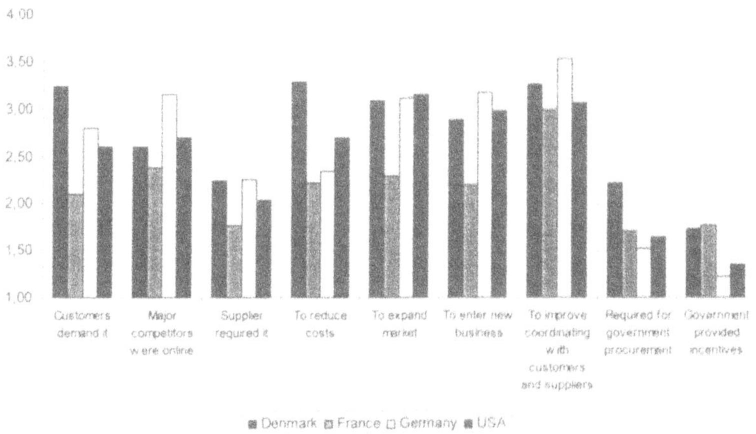

In comparison to other countries, US SMEs produce, on average, the highest level of obstacles in the retail and wholesale sector (cf., Figure 12). While the need for customer face-to-face interaction is not as important in Germany or Denmark, SMEs in the US or France rate this obstacle as an important hindering factor. US SMEs, followed by French and German ones, regard security factors as important obstacles. While the obstacles in the field of technology support on the customer side or the bottleneck of e-business-skilled staff is more a problem in the US, the prevalence of credit cards for online shopping is not seen as an important impeding factor in all countries, especially not in

Denmark. In general, it appears that US SMEs believe themselves to be confronted with more impeding factors than European ones.

Figure 12: Factors Impeding E-Business for SMEs in the Retail & Wholesale Sector

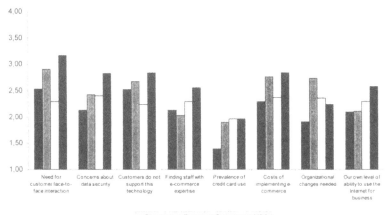

The reasons for implementing e-business applications also vary in the banking and insurance sector among the countries surveyed. While customer demand may be identified as an important driver in most countries, especially Denmark, the use of online banking seems not to be as widespread yet on the customer side in France (cf., Figure 13). The same seems to be true of online competition with major competitors. While the adoption of e-business is strongly driven by competition, especially in the US, in Denmark and again in France this factor seems to be less important in the banking sector. Due to the low degree of vertical fragmentation—in general, banks develop, create and distribute their products themselves—the need to integrate suppliers is not as important as, e.g., in the manufacturing industry. In Denmark, the US and even Germany, SMEs assess the benefits of e-business in the field of automation and increasing efficiency by exploiting economy of scale effects as an important driver of e-business investments. E-business as an enabler to expand markets, to enter new business areas or to improve the coordination with suppliers and customers is also seen as an important driver, especially for Danish and US SMEs. Government's contribution to the diffusion of e-business seems to be relatively unimportant in all countries surveyed.

Figure 13: E-Business Drivers for SMEs in the Banking & Insurance Sector

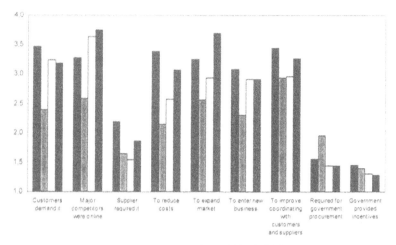

■ Denmark ▨ France ▢ Germany ▣ USA

Figure 14: Factors Impeding E-Business for SMEs in the Banking & Insurance Sector

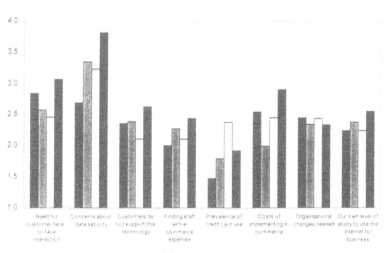

■ Denmark ▨ France ▢ Germany ▣ USA

With the exception of France, where online banking and insurance transactions with the government seem to require e-business standards, SMEs do not regard the impact of the government as a driving factor. Again, the highest obstacles impeding the use of e-business are reported by SMEs in the US (cf., Figure 14).

4.4.5   The Efficient Use of E-Business among SMEs

E-business output and, therefore, the impact of e-business on business processes or e-business satisfaction depend directly on the intensity and variety of applications implemented. To test this proposition, a DEA analysis was used as described in section 4.4.1. The chosen DEA model avails itself of the data sets from each industry sector, starting with 152 sets in the manufacturing industry. Afterwards, the results may be used to distinguish the efficient (marked by *) from the inefficient ones. The results of the DEA for the manufacturing sector are provided in Figure 15.

On average, efficient SMEs in the US use 67.5%, in Denmark 81.8%, in France 46.4% and in Germany 64.3% respectively of the seven e-business technologies asked for (i.e. use of: online advertising, online sales, after-sale customer service, online procurement, EDI with suppliers, EDI with customers, Internet-based supply chain management). The impact on business improvement is measured by the satisfaction index for Germany with an index of 3.0, France with 3.1, and 3.2 each for Denmark and the US.

Figure 15: Results of the DEA Analysis in the Manufacturing Sector

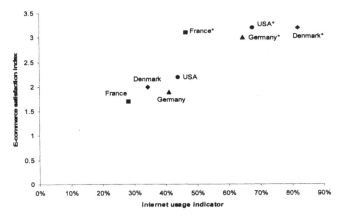

Note: DEA efficient firms per countries are marked by *

Interestingly, efficient French SMEs in the manufacturing sector derive a higher level of satisfaction from e-business than German ones with only 46.4% of all available e-business applications. One possible explanation might be the innovative character of e-business, which is embraced more enthusiastically in France. Another explanation might be the larger efficiency potentials of even fewer e-business standards in France than in Germany.

In the retail and wholesale industry, 151 data sets in total are used to calculate the relative efficiency of SMEs in the four countries by using DEA. The results are provided in Figure 16, where the relatively efficient SMEs are marked by *. On average, efficient SMEs in the US use 63.5%, in Denmark 42.9% and in Germany 64.3% of the seven e-business applications asked for and therefore significantly more than inefficient ones compared with both their national, as well as international efficient competitors. The impact on business improvement (measured as the satisfaction index) is therefore also significantly higher among efficient SMEs compared to their relatively inefficient counterparts. While inefficient German SMEs in the retail/wholesale sector use only 9.2% fewer e-business applications, the differences in Denmark, with 24.1%, or France, with 22.3%, are quite large. In Germany, the percentage of efficient firms is higher and the gap between efficient and inefficient SMEs is not as wide. This might be an indicator of a broader diffusion of advanced e-business solutions among the majority of the German retail and wholesale industry.

Figure 16: Results of the DEA Analysis in the Retail & Wholesale Sector

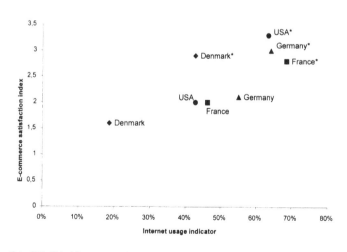

Note: DEA efficient firms per countries are marked by *

In the last industry sector investigated, the banking and insurance sector, the DEA uses 155 data sets as decision-making units (DMU) (cf., Figure 17). On average, efficient small and medium sized banks in the US use 74%, in Denmark 78% and in Germany 68% respectively of the seven e-business applications asked for. The impact on business improvement is measured as the satisfaction index for Denmark with 2.97, 3.03 for Germany, and 3.29 for the US. Although efficient finance institutes in France only use 43% of all available e-business solutions, the resulting output is, at 2.97, as high as in Denmark. As expected, relatively inefficient banks in the sample used fewer e-business solutions, resulting in a lower satisfaction rate.

Figure 17: Results of the DEA Analysis in the Banking & Insurance Sector

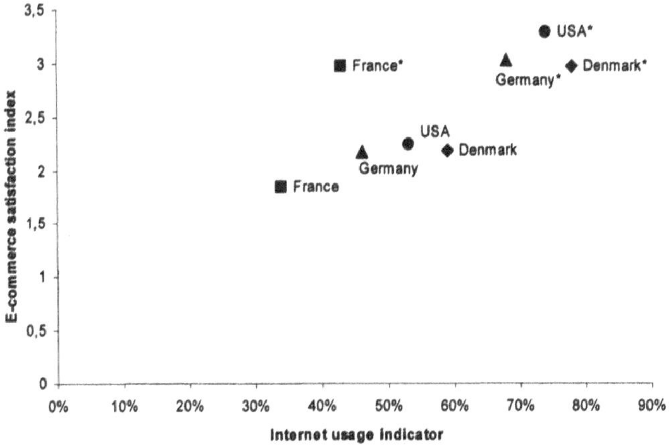

Note: DEA efficient firms per countries are marked by *

Based on the broad diffusion of e-business applications, Danish and US SMEs reported the highest level of business improvements provided by employing all kinds of e-business applications (cf., Table 18).

While Danish SMEs in the manufacturing sector reported the largest positive impacts on their business processes on average, US SMEs in the banking and insurance sector were able to gain higher benefits by using e-business in nearly every area asked for. While in France only SMEs in the retail and wholesale sector are at the forefront in the data sample in gaining the highest benefit from internal business improvements, German SMEs are at the forefront in the manufacturing sector (internal business improvement 36.4%) or in the retail and wholesale sector (international sales increased 14.7% and procurement costs decreased 20.6%).

Table 18: Impact of doing Business online, i.e. Percent indicating Impact is a Great Deal (4 or 5 on a five-point scale)

	Denmark			France			Germany			USA		
	M	R	B	M	R	B	M	R	B	M	R	B
Internal processes more efficient	31.4	38.7	31.3	26.5	27.3	22.2	36.4	29.4	28.6	32.0	24.5	36.5
Staff productivity increased	28.6	29.0	15.6	11.8	9.1	13.9	12.1	11.8	17.1	24.0	30.2	38.5
Sales increased	22.9	9.7	31.3	2.9	9.1	2.8	12.1	20.6	22.9	22.0	24.5	15.4
Sales area widened	20.0	16.1	25.0	8.8	12.1	16.7	18.2	26.5	22.9	40.0	35.8	30.8
Customer service improved	48.6	19.4	50.0	20.6	27.3	22.2	18.2	23.5	51.4	34.0	35.8	42.3
International sales increased	17.1	9.7	3.1	5.9	6.1	5.6	12.1	14.7	2.9	14.0	9.4	5.8
Procurement costs decreased	20.0	3.2	12.5	11.8	18.2	2.8	0.0	20.6	2.9	18.0	11.3	15.4
Inventory costs decreased	11.4	0.0	3.1	8.8	15.2	2.8	3.0	5.9	5.7	4.0	11.3	17.3
Suppliers coordination improved	28.6	16.1	18.8	23.5	30.2	19.4	27.3	17.6	14.3	28.0	28.3	28.8
Competitive position improved	28.6	12.9	31.3	2.9	21.2	8.3	18.2	23.5	37.1	34.0	32.1	28.8

Note: M: Manufacturing, R: Retail/Wholesale, B: Banking/Insurance, SMEs: 25 to 249 employees

As suggested above, e-business drivers have a significant positive impact on firms at the country level. Figure 18 provides the significant symmetric difference between DEA efficient firms and the rest of the data sample on average.

Figure 18: Significant Differences among Perceived Drivers between DEA-efficient Firms and the Rest of the Data Sample

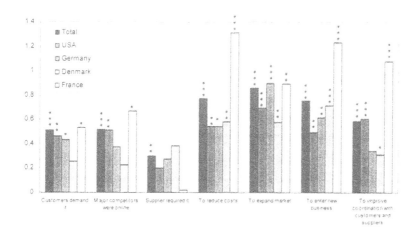

Note: *** p<.001, ** p<.01, * p<.05

Efficient firms always perceive higher impacts from drivers of e-business than DEA inefficient firms do. Government-related drivers, as provided earlier, are not taken into account because they are insignificant for all countries analyzed. On the other hand, there are no significant differences between DEA-efficient and -inefficient firms in relation to the obstacles requested (with exception of recruiting employees with IT expertise and the prevalence of credit cards). Drivers seem to bring forward efficient firms significantly better than inefficient ones, especially in France where the average gap between both types of firms is highest in most cases. A positive business environment seems therefore to have a significantly higher positive impact on firms applying e-business efficiently, whereas the obstacles tested are insignificant in terms of impeding efficient and inefficient firms.

Table 19 provides the correlations between the number of e-business applications used (e-business deployment) and the positive impact or efficient use on the industry level (impact of doing business online) based on a Spearman significance test. Therefore the correlations between the number of e-business applications used per firm in an industry in the rows (sum of used applications, see Table 17) and the efficiency increase, represented as positive impacts in the columns (see Table 18), are calculated.

Table 19: Number of E-Business Solutions deployed correlated with positive Impacts and efficiency Gains

	E-business deployment Manufacturing (N=152)	E-business deployment Retail/Wholesale (N=151)	E-business deployment Banking/Insurance (N=155)
Internal processes more efficient	.299**	.114	.273**
Staff productivity increased	.371**	.091	.319**
Sales increased	.263**	.397**	.486**
Sales area widened	.474**	.357**	.390**
Customer service improved	.378**	.251**	.321**
International sales increased	.381**	.095	.303**
Procurement costs decreased	.432**	.207*	.366**
Inventory costs decreased	.389**	.233**	.241**
Suppliers coordination improved	.424**	.300**	.414**
Competitive position improved	.469**	.211*	.449**

Note: ** $p<.01$, * $p<.05$

As we assumed, there is a significant but weak correlation between the number of e-business applications employed for the SMEs per industry and the perceived efficiency increases. The use of the rank order correlation coefficient reveals a monotonous relation among ordinally scaled data. While the results are very significant in the manufacturing and banking and insurance industry, in the retail and wholesale industry they are insignificant in terms of internal processes and staff being more efficient, as well as international sales being increased. Nevertheless, the efficient use of e-business applications seems to be positively correlated with the number of technologies deployed, as has already been revealed by the DEA analysis.

Within the four countries studied (Denmark, France, Germany, United States), the implementation of e-business has shown operational improvements and efficiency gains and thereby helped to decrease, e.g., procurement or inventory costs. Although the nature of e-business applications is more or less the same, each country is following its own diffusion pattern or path, based on national differences recognizable in competition, existing and emerging IT infrastructure, business concentration, governmental regulations or even national mentality.

Accordingly, the efficient use of e-business is indeed related significantly to positive national business environments. French firms have to cope with above average obstacles, resulting in low efficiency rates as the DEA analysis has shown. On the other hand, US firms seem to be confronted with high drivers and high inhibitors at the same time, gaining a huge efficiency position. SMEs in the three industries studied within the four countries utilize more or less the same high level of e-business applications. Although the de facto e-business readiness is clearly visible, in-depth statements about current usage behavior and intensity per se cannot be made based on the design and questions asked in the underlying survey. The overall diffusion of e-business applications may be described as high, but France especially is still lagging behind leading countries and sectors in terms of e-business applications diffusion. Whilst all industry sectors are more or less similarly well-equipped, industry-related differences remain. At the industry level, the e-business-based improvement of internal processes is highest in Germany, while the overall impact of e-business together with the installed set of e-business applications are highest in Denmark and the US. SMEs in the retail and wholesale sector benefit especially from the Internet-based possibilities of online sales and procurement. In this area, German SMEs lead in terms of e-business readiness with more e-business applications in place than anywhere else. Although US retailers reported a lower diffusion rate in comparison to German or French SMEs, the impact on efficiency was the highest, especially in the ability to increase sales or to improve customer services. A similar situation may be observed in the banking and insurance sector, where again Danish SMEs lead in terms of e-business application diffusion, but US SMEs benefit most, reporting the highest impact of e-business in nearly all areas investigated.

The results have shown that much more research is necessary in this under-researched area. Comparable data about SMEs and their e-business activities are still in short supply. In the following chapter 1, two EDI solutions will be discussed which have been developed to increase the diffusion and use of communication standards by incorporating the results of the empirical, as well as theoretical findings derived from the chapters elaborated so far.

5 Developing E-Business Standards

Apart from studying the empirical diffusion of existing e-business standards on an industry and a country level, the two following e-business application models contribute to possible future research directions aimed at solving problems occurring on the way to a network economy. While the need for interorganizational systems is widely agreed in the literature to be necessary in order to benefit from communication standards (Chau et al. 2001; Peffers et al. 1998), the following questions remain unanswered:

- how standardization settings should be designed (Beck et al. 2003d; Damsgaard et al. 2001; Gaynor et al. 2001),

- how the business process should be redesigned (Clark et al. 2000; Peffers et al. 1998) accompanied by the implementation of standards,

- and which components and features of an interorganizational system are the core benefit drivers and how can they be created by convincing SMEs, e.g., to adopt a standard.

While the first two questions are discussed in several information systems related contributions, the question of how to model and incorporate benefit drivers into standards in order to increase the degree of adoption is often disregarded. Since the realization of the full potential of communication standards such as EDI depends on the degree of internal integration and their wide adoption among related business partners, the provided solutions to the aforementioned questions remain critical for the successful diffusion. The importance of internal improvements and efficiency gains based on adopting e-business standards has been illustrated in chapter 1. As a result, it is not only the benefits that accrue and which are directly related to communication that are essential for the adoption, but also in particular the indirect, internal business process improvements among adopting firms. Therefore, the solutions presented in this chapter are two possible contributions to improving the usage and therefore benefits related to the adoption of communication standards by increasing the degree of process automation. By addressing the above stated pivotal questions, they may help to increase the network-based benefits of communication standards. By lowering the entrance barrier for firms which do not yet apply EDI and enhancing the benefits of automation, the interorganizational benefits will also increase, making the adoption and usage of communication standards more likely.

The first solution, i.e. introducing a WebConverter, presented in section 5.1 is developed to attract SMEs to the use of EDI. The second solution, i.e. the reputation-based customer complaints management solution in section 5.2 reduces necessary manual interaction to process claims by using reputation accounts.

5.1 Economics of Communication Standards: Integrating SMEs in EDI Supply Chains

Electronic data interchange (EDI) has been used for over 40 years to exchange business data (e.g. delivery notes, invoices) between two application systems in a standardized, automated form (Emmelhainz 1993). Firms use EDI-solutions in order to achieve efficient data and information management by reducing processing time and avoiding redundant data entry. In doing so, EDI has substantially contributed to integrating value chains across firm boundaries in a variety of industry sectors. For the benefits associated with traditional EDI, e.g., cost reductions induced by rationalization and automation, shorter order processing time, see (Emmelhainz 1993; Niggl 1994). Despite the alleged benefits, EDI is not as widespread as many would have expected. There are estimates that only 5% of all companies who could benefit from EDI actually use it (Segev et al. 1997). The information systems literature has provided a variety of instructive examples of this so-called EDI dilemma: one often used explanation argues that the considerably high costs of implementing EDI-systems are a serious obstacle, especially for small and medium sized enterprises (SMEs). Nevertheless, it is still assumed that even SMEs may benefit from the potential merits accompanying EDI when the EDI solution offered takes the requirements of SMEs into account.

It is assumed that for SMEs not only transaction volume but also a lack of technological readiness can be used to explain the SMEs' lagging behind the EDI evolution. Thus a necessary prerequisite for the advantages derived from traditional EDI is the existence of a material management system (MMS). To throw light on the true utility drivers and thus the underlying mechanisms of EDI standards adoption among SMEs, an empirical survey and economic analysis of different forms of EDI (traditional vs. WebEDI vs. the notorious fax machine) reveals that using fax machines can hardly be beaten for SMEs. Thus one first result is that one should not expect SMEs to actually profit from traditional forms of EDI, let alone WebEDI. This provides a strong explanation for the status quo of EDI usage among SMEs. Based on this fact, a requirements catalogue for SME EDI is derived and used to develop a technically viable and economically sound alternative EDI-solution within vertical industries. The solution developed appears to be somewhat useful, as it has been adopted in the German office supply industry where it has been in use by SMEs for more than four years now. The solution is a true alternative in the industry, not only compared to fax-based ordering but also with regard to traditional EDI. Accordingly, the solution has not only been adopted by SMEs that have not been prior EDI users but also by SMEs that had used traditional EDI before but with limited benefits.

5.1.1   The EDI Dilemma

In this section, the basic problem of the slow diffusion of communication standards among SMEs is illustrated in the case of EDI. A literature review shows that the adoption process is still not too well understood, and that there is a lack of cohesive models of EDI value creation for SMEs. It is proposed that technical readiness as a factor is often neglected in projections of EDI adoption that are made too optimistically. Subsequentially, an economic foundation for the SME's EDI business case is provided. Empirical data from the office supply industry supports the findings and reveals that most SMEs are better off using a fax instead of EDI. The information systems literature provides innumerable articles dealing with different aspects of EDI diffusion. Therefore the goal of this section is not to summarize all prior research in detail but rather to focus on pivotal aspects and major obstacles identified in the relationship between SMEs and EDI adoption and use.

Some research is concentrated primarily on the legal implications of EDI (Kilian et al. 1994) but greater attention is paid to the adoption and diffusion of EDI among firms (Chau et al. 2001; Iacovou et al. 1995; Ketler et al. 1997), in vertical industries, e.g., in the automotive industry (Fricke 2003; Mackay et al. 1996), the retail/wholesale and distribution industry (Beck et al. 2003e; Jimenez-Martinez et al. 1998; Vijayasarathy et al. 1997), or the pharmaceutical industry (Howells et al. 1995). Some studies focus on so-called "EDI-Champions" who try to learn from large corporations how to implement and use EDI to gain major benefits (Webster 1995). Furthermore, researchers have distinguished the impact of EDI, depending on the depth of integration into existing material management or enterprise resource planning systems (Fearon et al. 1999; Williams et al. 1998). Other research areas are more focused on the multi-dimensional integration levels (technologically on the protocol layer, as well as contractually on the organizational level), in connection with newer forms of EDI such as InternetEDI (Segev et al. 1997) or WebEDI (Beck et al. 2003d) and found a lack of EDI know-how to be an important entrance barrier (Muller 1998). From an enterprise point of view, the central EDI question is what degree of automation should be aimed at and is achievable (Swatman et al. 1991) and how partial or asymmetric compatibility (such as in the case of WebEDI) impacts on overall benefits and standard diffusion. Consequently, the question is not how to create the optimal EDI relationships in interorganizational systems, but the most satisfctory one in integrating even SMEs into an EDI value chain.

Literature on EDI adoption behaviour has focused on the utility of EDI for single firms related to communication cost savings by process automation or as resulting from pressure exerted by business partners (for an overview see (Saunders et al. 2002)). Unfortunately, the study mentioned has explicitly not considered contributions dealing with the importance of standardization and related impacts on adopters. Accordingly, current empirical research on EDI often fails to provide more than enumerations of EDI standards in place (for an example, see (Otto et al. 2002)). Such research, however, cannot help to explain SMEs' reasons for adopting EDI and the resulting diffusion patterns, which are crucial for the overall interorganizational system benefit.

Empirical studies have shown that the diffusion of EDI is influenced, among other factors, by competitive pressure and/or pressure by powerful business partners (Barua et al. 1997) or contrariwise by confidence and good business relations (Hart et al. 1997; Hart et al. 1998). Nevertheless, in general those solutions are designed to meet the demands of larger EDI-using initiators rather than having a more holistic solution in mind that also takes the technological and economical environment of SMEs into account. EDI is therefore more than just the exchange of electronic data (Kubicek et al. 1996) and strongly depends on firm size and super-ordinate business environment agreements or collective behavior respectively (Brousseau 1994). One can find a close relation between the size of a firm and the number of messages which can be

transferred electronically. Large EDI partners can often directly benefit mone-
tarily from electronic information exchange and in addition from internal process reengineering improvements based on just-in-time accurate data
(Mukhopadhyay et al. 1995). This is not necessarily the same on the SMEs'
side, since SMEs are not necessarily miniature versions of larger enterprises
(Chen et al. 1998). Therefore, an often-mentioned limiting argument against
the successful implementation and use of EDI is the number of potentially
electronically exchangeable orders, invoices, etc. (Beck et al. 2002; Chen et
al. 1998; Iacovou et al. 1995). In order to overcome this problem, a possible
solution discussed in the literature is the offer of subsidies for SMEs by larger
trading partners (e.g., (Beck et al. 2003d; Riggins et al. 1994)). However,
granting transaction volume-related subsidies requires additional managing
workforce for the EDI initiator, apart from simply giving the money to SMEs.

However, reaping benefits from an EDI-system also depends on the interfaces
available to connect the SMEs EDI-system with MMS or ERP systems, even if
a subsidy program for EDI is in place. This raises the question of how SMEs
can actually use the data received to improve their internal business processes. Astonishingly, reviewing prior research on EDI diffusion among SMEs
reveals that most work has not analyzed the MMS landscape on the SME side.
Even if an MMS system is in place to support the internal business process,
those systems are not necessarily capable of providing an EDI interface.

Apart from often-mentioned small transaction volumes, there are further drawbacks to SME integration. The empirical research shows that there are major
obstacles to integrating SMEs that are often neglected in the literature. If
SMEs do not deploy automated MMS systems and consequently cannot benefit from process automation potentials, one cannot expect any SME to adopt
EDI voluntarily. Thus, technical readiness is not solely a cost- but rather an
ability-related problem. In general, the following alternatives exist for SMEs
planning to participate in EDI networks (see Figure 19): according to some
publications (Muller 1998; Senn 1998), the maintenance costs of using traditional EDI may be reducible by introducing WebEDI for SMEs without MMS in
place (Kalakota et al. 1996). WebEDI applications use html as a presentation
layer to offer a web-front-end user interface for manual handling of EDI messages. Apart from adopting traditional EDI (for SMEs with MMS systems) or

WebEDI, SMEs can also outsource the applications to ASPs who will host the EDI-system or even the whole MMS system with EDI functionalities.

In addition, some hybrid forms of EDI exist, such as combinations of EDI and other available technologies that are not depicted in Figure 19. Examples are EDI hybrids like EDI-to-fax or EDI-to-e-mail and vice versa (Schmied 1998).

Figure 19: EDI alternatives for SMEs with and without MMS

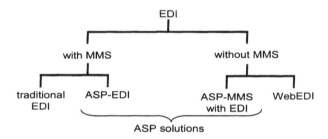

Similar to translators converting one language into another or adapters enabling the deployment of different norms and standards with each other, ASP-solutions can support SMEs in participating in vertical standard networks without adopting the underlying communication standard themselves. That might hamper the diffusion of a standard among all network participants as a first best solution, but allows at least the integration of non-EDI-adopting SMEs as a second best alternative in order to increase the number of vertical network participants.

Regardless of a firm's size, the automated processing of data is a necessary precondition for all kinds of electronic data exchange. All traditional EDI-converter-systems require at least an MMS system in order to process the data received or to gather data that is to be sent from an MMS system. It seems to be obvious that the integration of EDI into MMS systems is necessary in order to benefit from automation. However, it is essential to remember this when discussing the different forms and economic implications of EDI or B2B communication for SMEs. When starting a new EDI relationship, some problems emerge, especially in the context of how SMEs conduct their business. If MMSs are in place, then the often different and originally independently designed, operated, and optimized systems support only a limited number of interfaces, protocols, data formats, and business process designs, etc. Thus, EDI is more than a matter of connecting several MMS systems with the

ERP systems of suppliers. Very often, it is necessary to redesign existing systems to benefit from integration potentials. Thus, in many projects it is not the EDI installation itself that is the most expensive element, but the redesign of the existing IT applications and infrastructure. For an overview of the history of EDI diffusion and the necessary internal adaptation processes, see earlier and mostly empirical contributions to the literature such as those provided by (Deutsch 1994; Kilian et al. 1994; Niggl 1994).

Thus, at least an MMS is a necessary precondition for SMEs to generate and send EDI messages such as purchase orders or invoices, as well as an inventory administration system for an automatic delivery schedule, a dispatch handling system to produce a dispatch notification, a scanning system for physical access and exit control to handle the selling data, and an accounting and billing application to send the invoice to EDI partners. The implementation and use of such relatively mature technologies is a difficult venture for SMEs and often not sufficiently considered in EDI literature.

In addition to such MMS or ERP systems, SMEs have to apply an EDI-converter-system to communicate and interchange data. Depending on the depth of integration into the existing MMS infrastructure, the EDI converter can select data from the MMS to automatically address the receiver, convert data from an internal data format into an EDI standard language and also send it automatically by using the chosen communication layer, e.g., over the Internet.

Considering the two cases, MMS seems to be essential in order to generate further benefits, e.g., by automatic data handling and processing of the received EDI messages or to generate electronic orders. Subsequently, an economically useful EDI-system has to be connected to the local MMS system. Common WebEDI-solutions generally do not offer such an interface. Since automation benefits cannot accrue when WebEDI is used, this solution appears to be more a transitional, temporary phenomenon on the way to a totally integrated and networked vertical supply chain. With a similar manual effort required to use it, WebEDI is more comparable to deploying fax rather than using EDI.

In the following section, the history of establishing vertical standards in the German office supply industry is depicted in order to illustrate the different efforts made to standardize communication. Afterwards, the results of an empirical survey conducted among SMEs using the EDI-solution that was eventually successfully established within this sector are provided. In particular, the problems occurring during implementation and use, as well as the most important perceived factor hindering the use of EDI are discussed in more detail. Since WebEDI-solutions in general do not offer an interface to integrate them into an SME's MMS, and since traditional EDI-solutions are expensive and difficult to customize, the ASP-EDI (WebConverter) solution developed and presented in the section before last may help to close the EDI gap between SMEs and larger business partners, based on the empirical and theoretical findings.

5.1.2   Standardization History and Empirical Evidence from the German Office Supply Retailing Industry

An empirical survey within the German office supply industry and retailers was conducted in 2000 in order to discover the technical and economic determinants of EDI diffusion among SMEs. The German office supply industry is a relatively small part of the retail/wholesale and distribution industry in Germany. Its size and market structure with its large number of SMEs makes it an ideal case for analyzing the difficult but successful diffusion of EDI among SMEs.

5.1.2.1 EDI Standardization History

With SMEs accounting for more than 95% of all firms on the retail side, standardized electronic communication seems to be a difficult venture, as countless unsuccessful approaches in this industry have demonstrated:

As early as 1993, the German federation for office management (Bundesverband Bürowirtschaft) started an EDI standardization initiative called EDIoffice in order to develop a consortium-driven solution based on UN/EDIFACT for office equipment suppliers and retailers. A small group of suppliers with large trading volumes constituted the consortium. The goal was to customize and announce a smaller subset of EDIFACT as the de facto EDI standard in that industry. At that time, retailers were not involved in the project. Due to heterogeneous interests among the consortium members and the lack of strategic concepts of how to integrate retailers, the initiative failed. Suppliers competing in the same market segment as other consortium members were especially afraid of sharing sensitive customer-related data such as price agreements within a single data pool in the intermediary solution that was considered.

Therefore, the projected central solution of establishing an EDI clearing centre for all office equipment suppliers failed.

Another EDI initiative named EDI-Part also started in 1993, consisting of six major office equipment suppliers and an MMS software provider. Although this project did not even survive the planning phase, it provided for the first time definitions and frameworks containing the necessary EDI message types together with suggested implementation guidelines for MMS providers to develop EDI-interfaces in their software solutions. EDI-Part was based on an ASCII-oriented proprietary exchange standard and real-time point-to-point online connection between the communication partners, which added to the problems, resulting in marginal adoption rates. Consequently, and due to the low availability of MMS systems among SMEs, the benefits for SMEs were too low since again no EDI requirement analysis was conducted on the retail side.

Despite the setbacks of earlier initiatives, further efforts were made, resulting in a finally successful intermediary solution established by an office equipment supplier consortium named PBSeasy. Starting in 1996, two EDIFACT-based solutions have been offered for retailers: a traditional EDI version with stand-alone EDI-software, as well as a WebEDI-solution. The following survey results are based on SMEs' experiences with the two last mentioned EDI-solutions.

5.1.2.2 Results from the Retailer Survey

After the aforementioned attempts to establish EDI among SMEs in the office equipment retail sector in Germany in the nineties, an installed base of EDI-using SMEs was finally in existence in 2000. This circumstance made the office retail sector a highly interesting research area, since empirical data on the diffusion of vertical standards among SMEs were then, and are today, limited. In order to analyze the adoption behaviour empirically, as well as driving and limiting reasons for or against the adoption and use of EDI, a questionnaire was developed in cooperation with the EDI intermediary PBSeasy to get an improved understanding of the often disregarded problems and difficulties SMEs are facing when integrating and using EDI. To analyze the decision situation regarding whether or not and why to adopt an EDI-solution, a questionnaire was sent to 223 retailers (representing 2.5% of all office equipment retailers in Germany) with a response rate of 15.25% (n=34). The questionnaire was structured in four parts: existing application systems, drivers and reasons for or against EDI adoption, planned or de facto intensity of EDI usage, and economic impacts according to the EDI-solution deployed, if any. The questionnaires were mailed with prepaid reply envelopes. To get analyzable data, only retailers which had already adopted one of the EDI-solutions or were known to be in the decision making phase, based on statement of interest they made during road shows or at fairs and exhibitions, were asked.

One of the most important results of the survey was that the MMS systems used among SMEs were extremely heterogeneous, impeding an easy implementation of any kind of EDI converter software due to non-existent or non-standardized interfaces. More than 13 different software solutions were implemented among retailers with more or less equally distributed market shares. Of those MMS software installations, only 8 offered interfaces for the partial integration of EDI into stand-alone EDI PCs in order to transfer the messages manually between the MMS system and the EDI software. None of the installed systems offered full integration of EDI into the MMS software for application-to-application EDI. Ten SMEs, equivalent to more than 29% of all SMEs surveyed, had not even installed an MMS system using WebEDI instead of traditional EDI. The diversity of MMS systems installed was one of the most important obstacles to the implementation of a vertical EDI standard in this industry. The questionnaire also asked for the reasons for the EDI adoption decision. Interestingly, pressure from larger business partners was rated as an unimportant driver (not important: 57%). One of the reasons might be the low diffusion of EDI among the customers of SMEs on the downstream side of the retail value chain in this segment, where possible pressure could only be applied by industry partners on the upstream side.

In addition, the questionnaire asked for possible arguments against the implementation and use of EDI. One third of all survey participants responded that some forms of trading practices such as special deals and arrangements made directly with travelling salespersons are not possible when using EDI. Such special offers or arrangements comprise a large variety of agreements, ranging from special sales deal prices, individual supplier negotiations, unusual delivery arrangements, rebate in kind agreements, to changed compositions of complete sales product displays.

Furthermore, the success of an EDI-solution depends on the number of EDI-using business partners (or the number of potential EDI-messages) since the number of electronically conveyable and receivable business documents determines the savings possibly achievable by EDI on the communication level. On average, retailers participating in the survey had 147 industry business partners, while only an average of 14 of these industry partners offered an EDI-transfer at that time. Consequently, the reported average number of 3.56 EDI order messages per day sent by SMEs was very low in 2000, which was equivalent to only up to 10% of all orders for more than one third of all SMEs (for further survey results see also (Beck et al. 2002; Beck et al. 2003d)). As the economic sensitivity analysis in the next section reveals, the total number of orders and the fraction of electronic orders appeared to be too small to enable SMEs to benefit from the use of EDI.

5.1.2.3 Profitability Analysis of EDI for SMEs

Based on the findings from the survey, this section analyzes the different economic implications of EDI and WebEDI for SMEs in the office supply industry as compared to using a fax as the most common process of communication. To compare the three communication modes, first the related costs are described:

- **Fax**: in contrast to EDI, conventional ordering was done by fax for € 1.27 per order on average. These costs for a fax-based order include the printing of an order from a MMS system and the manual submission via a fax machine including the transmission fees for the telecom provider.

- **Traditional EDI**: the costs for traditional EDI include fixed and variable costs components: a base fee for the store-and-forward solution telebox 400 and the use has to be paid. Furthermore, variable costs depending on the time and amount of transmitted data occur. Adding all this up, the price for submitting and EDI message varies depending on the overall amount of messaging per year and is on average € 6.60 per message.

- **WebEDI**: For the comparison with WebEDI-based ordering it is assumed that a PC with Internet access is available and not used exclusively for the WebEDI application. Due to the low value and multiple possible applications, setup costs for hardware are considered to be marginal and are not taken into account. As in the case of fax-based ordering, WebEDI requires manual interactions, in this case for data gathering and input into the web-front-end. Without an MMS in place automating the order creation process, the manual data input induces an additional workload compared to using fax. Therefore, WebEDI is more time consuming than a fax transaction, resulting in higher personnel and communication costs adding up to € 2.37 per order on average.

Accordingly to the survey, the number of orders sent via EDI varies between 920 and 1,746 orders per year by the most active retailers. Therefore, the order numbers in Table 20 represent the reported numbers of orders by five SMEs and the resulting costs for the different order scenarios for SMEs are provided. The five are chosen to illustrate the range from the lowest number of orders to the highest number of orders responded to and the subsequently occurring costs for each communication channel.

Table 20: Fax vs. EDI vs. WebEDI

	Orders				
	920	1150	1380	1587	1746
Fax					
Material costs	56.45	70.56	84.67	97.37	107.11
Communication costs	169.34	211.68	254.01	290.48	321.38
Processing costs	940.78	1,175.97	1,411.17	1,622.84	1,785.43
Σ (€)	1,166.57	1,458.20	1,749.85	2,010.69	2,213.92
EDI					
Communication costs	244.60	305.75	366.90	421.94	464.21
System administration costs	4,600.00	4,600.00	4,600.00	4,600.00	4,600.00
Maintenance costs	299.10	299.10	299.10	299.10	299.10
Depreciation	414.15	414.15	414.15	414.15	414.15
Fees	521.52	521.52	521.52	521.52	521.52
Σ (€)	6,079.37	6,140.52	6,201.67	6,256.71	6,298.98
WebEDI					
Material costs	56.45	70.56	84.67	97.37	107.11
Communication costs	261.36	339.48	417.09	486.94	540.60
Processing costs	1,567.96	1,959.78	2,351.94	2,704.73	2,975.72
Fees	294.50	294.50	294.50	294.50	294.50
Σ (€)	2,180.27	2,664.32	3,148.20	3,582.54	3,917.93

As the calculations in Table 20 indicate, from the perspective of an SME with small numbers of EDI messages, using fax is always a dominant strategy. Figure 20 (left) visualizes the increasing costs curves in accordance with the increasing number of orders. The order curve reflects the number of orders (scaled on the second ordinate). On the left ordinate the total costs for each order transmission method are drawn. Analogous to the increasing number of

orders, the WebEDI and fax cost curves also increase while the cost development for EDI-based orders follows a more horizontal curve.

Figure 20: Fax vs. EDI vs. WebEDI Cost Development without (left) and with (right) Subsidies

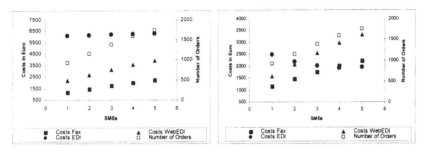

Since neither traditional EDI nor WebEDI seem to be able to reduce the communications costs for SMEs, the industry business partners started to offer two
different incentive models for the use of EDI and WebEDI. For using traditional
EDI, SMEs received bonus payments of € 5.- for each of the first 500 orders,
followed by € 2.50 for order number 501-1,000, and finally € 1.- for each order
number 1,001-1500. In the case of WebEDI, 1% of the order amount to a
maximum of € 50.-. awarded to the SME per month. Taking now the side payments offered by the industry partners into account, the situation changes. The
diagram on the right of Figure 20 illustrates the implications of the two bonus
models.

Although side payments are made, the compensation is still too small to make
WebEDI more desirable than using fax (mostly due to the limited refund of €
50.- per month), as the higher gradient of the WebEDI curve compared to the
order (and fax) curve illustrates. The curve is still steeper than the fax cost development curve. Thus, despite the existing incentive mechanism, fax is still
the favourite choice for SMEs. The subsidization model for traditional EDI is
more interesting in contrast to the WebEDI model and might be able to attract
SMEs with more than 1,475 orders per year. Above this threshold, using EDI is
less expensive than using fax.

These findings imply a substantial and possibly often neglected impact of the
underlying economics of vertical standards on EDI-diffusion, especially for
SMEs. For one thing, traditional EDI, and especially WebEDI, simply does not
make sense for SMEs with low transaction volumes. That is not a new insight
but contradicts many optimistic contributions from the first wave of e-

commerce, which often regarded WebEDI as a solution to the EDI-dilemma (Chau et al. 2001; Muller 1998; Segev et al. 1997). Moreover, in the survey the famous power argument (e.g., SME is forced to use EDI) turned out to be substantially less important than straightforward economic arguments, further supporting the significance of economically viable and technically feasible solutions. Finally, automation benefits accompanied by the use of EDI make the deployment of MMS systems mandatory. Therefore, the developed WebConverter ASP-solution described in the next section is oriented on SMEs using MMS systems.

5.1.3   From WebEDI to ASP-hosted EDI for SMEs

The theoretical and empirical findings so far suggest that transaction volume, e.g., measured in number of orders per day, is a cost-related obstacle and that technical readiness, e.g., measured as MMS deployment, is a process or potential-related obstacle to EDI-use by SMEs. Thus, two general requirements for successful SME integration can be proposed:

1. Economic condition: standardization should pay off individually. EDI profitability has mostly been a premise or uncritical expectation and should rather be considered as a precondition of industry standardization.

2. Technical condition: standardization should ideally be possible with the IT architecture deployed when standard diffusion is the goal. In the case analyzed, vertical standardization depends on the existence of an MMS system to gain the full economic potential from EDI.

What does this mean in terms of the efforts necessary to close the EDI gap? In the following, a solution is developed based on the technical possibilities of SMEs that is economically at least as advantageous using a fax machine (see Figure 20).

Motivated by the empirical findings, a WebConverter concept was developed that takes into account the technological and organizational environments of SMEs, thereby responding to the requirements necessary for successful bidirectional EDI. The WebConverter approach illustrates the way the economic disadvantages of EDI for SMEs can be reduced by adapting existing technologies in an innovative way. The solution enables SMEs to use standardized data in their MMS without the need for traditional EDI converter software. At the time of writing, it is being successfully applied in the office supply industry in Austria, Germany and Switzerland, reducing barriers to entry in the initial adoption phase and generating economic benefits in daily use.

The application itself was programmed by an EDI service provider for the office supply industry. It is based on the ASP-concept and minimizes the investment for a real bidirectional EDI-relation between SMEs with MMS systems and industrial business partners with EDI-converter-systems. The solution requires neither side payments like the incentive system described nor MMS adaptations and the implementation of an EDI-converter-system.

Figure 21: WebConverter Solution for SME with MMS

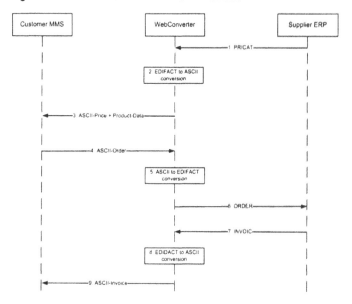

The functionality of WebConverter is very simple: the only further requirement (apart from a MMS system) is an e-mail program. The procedure can be described best by using an order process as example. After the MMS system has compiled the order, it generates an ASCII-based version of the order data, which is normally sent to a printer. The printed order is sent then manually using a fax machine. By using the WebConverter, the ASCII print spool is saved as a data file and transmitted as an attachment to a web server. The web server identifies the sender, opens the attachment and translates the ASCII-order into the appropriate EDI standard message, according to the mapping the SME has customized earlier. The mapping is no more than the linkage between the ASCII fields and the EDI message fields, which is supported by a graphic user interface. After an SME has made this setting once, the communication and translation is carried out automatically.

In the other direction, SMEs can receive EDI messages such as price and catalogue data or invoices, which are translated into an ASCII string code and sent as attachment to the SME. Analogous to the sending of orders, the SME now opens the e-mail, saves the data file and uses the import interface of its MMS system to update it. The only disadvantage is that a person still has to transfer the data manually between the MMS and e-mail system and consequently no real-time data sending and receiving is possible.

The use of the Internet as communication platform for a web-based converter reduces the entrance barrier for SMEs, while avoiding service and maintenance costs for expensive and complicated EDI-converter-systems at the same time. Figure 21 depicts the WebConverter solution schematically for EDIFACT-based messages. According to an interview with an SME retailer using the WebConverter solution in the office supply industry, the application is simple to use and enables SMEs to import and export data into and from the MMS very easily. Consequently, the retailer can not only communicate electronically, but also has accurate product-describing master data and related prices.

5.1.4   The Future of EDI for SMEs

As illustrated above, both technological readiness and economic profitability are important for EDI adoption among SMEs. The application of an EDI-solution does not benefit all users per se, especially not for SMEs. Even more, SMEs who are, for example, forced to deploy EDI by larger business partners might even face negative economic impacts. An empirical survey among German office supply retailers with its 95% share of SMEs revealed that contrary to large sections of the modern literature on vertical standards, WebEDI is in fact not a viable solution to the EDI-dilemma, as it neglects the dominant alternative fax while failing to provide additional benefits. This is not surprising, as most WebEDI approaches are nothing but html-based shopping systems: a person has to enter data by hand into web-based input fields using a web browser as communication interface. Consequently, there are no automation benefits and even more, media discontinuities are unavoidable because often no interfaces exist to enable the exchange of data between MMS systems and WebEDI front-ends.

Given the unfortunate situation of SMEs identified above, new solutions are necessary, firstly taking into account the limited IT resources and knowledge in comparison to large firms and secondly allowing SMEs to benefit economically from such a new solution. Providing such solutions, e.g., in the form of the WebConverter solution developed relying on simple but common ASCII code in combination with a web service approach, might be one imaginable way. So far, it has been used successfully in Germany, Austria, and Switzerland and has contributed to integrating SMEs into EDI networks. The solution developed is lowering the technological and economic entrance barrier for SMEs in EDI. It might not be the "optimal" solution, but for the moment a satisfactory one for SMEs.

The survey results and the WebConverter obviously mirror the experiences and findings of much other standards research: as long as the benefit of a communication standard depends on the size of a network, then a simple standard with a low entrance barrier (here: common technical denominator) will stand a higher chance of successful diffusion than a sophisticated but complex one. The use of the print spool file together with web services might be such a common denominator when trying to find a balance between simplicity on one hand and functionality on the other. The case of the office supply industry also suggests a prime role for vertical (industry) consortia, as they are possible areas of coordination which could reduce the system's interorganizational complexity.

Altogether, it was shown that there are technological and organizational drawbacks which inhibit SMEs from participating in EDI networks. Traditionally, EDI was adapted to the needs and capabilities of larger firms who can economize on costs by automating their business processes. In fact, EDI has proved to be a great source of efficiency for high transaction volume communication. Nevertheless, when trying to broaden the range of network participants it is important to take into account who actually benefits from such architectures.

On the one hand, the role of consortia or intermediaries in solving coordination problems and possibly in redistributing the costs and benefits of standardization, either directly through side payments or indirectly by providing services, know-how, and information, might still be underestimated. On the other hand, network effect theory and its extensions have provided important insights into the impact of direct network effects on EDI diffusion but mostly ignored possible indirect network effects. Both aspects are introduced into the network effect helix model introduced in chapter 6.

In the EDI case, that might imply that an important value source has largely been neglected in the literature so far: EDI standards for large enterprises have been designed primarily to accelerate and automate the exchange of data. Like large firms, SMEs can also benefit substantially from standardized master data as an indirect benefit of EDI. However, such indirect benefits related to EDI communication are only available if MMS systems can be integrated into the data exchange. Thus, it is not the originally intended active data transfer that is the sole source of vertical standardisation benefits, but the indirect benefits from the increased quality and availability of data.

5.2 Advancing Business Process Automation by Means of Customer Reputation Accounts

The continued demand for automated interorganizational business processes in order to reduce transaction costs inside supply chains has provided a strong incentive for the diffusion of Electronic Data Interchange (EDI). While there is general agreement about the potential benefits, most research and applications are focused only on a small proportion of possible EDI-use, i.e. mainly the exchange of orders and invoices. A consideration of the large number of 192 standardized UN/EDIFACT message types for various business transactions, many of which are still undeployed, provides an idea of possible automation benefits. A promising application area for the achievement of as yet unexploited automation benefits is the handling of customer complaints. While empirical research, and therefore data, are very limited in this area, two figures might provide an idea how much money could possibly be saved by an improved complaints handling process: Eastman Chemicals was able to save $ 2 million after improving the business processes associated with investigating and responding to complaints. They were able to cut expenses for waste removal and reworking caused by off-quality products or incorrect paperwork (Hallen et al. 2003). The second example provides a more accurate view of the de facto occurring costs of handling customer complaints manually: According to Schilling and Sobotta, a medium-sized enterprise with approx. € 5 million annual revenue calculated the average processing costs at € 837.47 for each complaint handling process in 1997 (Schilling et al. 1999).

A major impediment to increasing the degree of automation in this area is the need for human interaction and decision, e.g., to check complaints or to prevent opportunistic customer behavior. Since the handling of complaints is costly not only for suppliers but also for customers, only 5-10% of all dissatisfied customers decide to complain at all (Tax et al. 1998). But dissatisfied customers very likely switch their provider, with consequential revenue losses higher than the costs caused by complaints in the first place (Fornell et al. 1987). Therefore, suppliers have to cope with two dilemmas: Firstly, so far they have been unable to automate or standardize the complaint-handling process, since opportunistically acting customers might benefit from this and, secondly, they might never receive notice from a dissatisfied customer who has switched to another supplier because the manual complaint-handling is too expensive in comparison to the value of the defective or missing delivery.

This section proposes a model for establishing an automated complaint-handling solution based on existing EDI-messages and a reputation mechanism to not only benefit from a computer-based customer complaints management system, but also to prevent opportunistic behavior and customer losses. Furthermore, the environmental parameters under which this model can be applied successfully are analyzed. In the following paragraphs, a mechanism is provided which allows one to increase the degree to which business processes can be automated while avoiding possible incentives to opportunistic behavior at the same time.

In the following sections, the existing process for dealing with defective products or customer complaints after receiving defective articles or failing to receive articles is characterized and an overview of relevant related research into reputation models is provided. Then a game-theoretical analysis of the individual motivations of supplier and customer is introduced. Afterwards, the customer complaint handling is modified for automation purposes by introducing a reputation mechanism which would reduce the number of manual inter-actions to a minimum. Subsequently, a brief description of its technical imple-mentation by the use of EDI standard messages is given.

5.2.1   Reputation and EDI-based Process Automation

The need for efficient communication arises whenever independent business partners have to coordinate their interdependent activities (Malone et al. 1994). The implementation and use of EDI meets these economic demands and has therefore attracted academic attention for decades. The benefits of EDI, such as avoidance of redundant data entry, reduced error rate of data en-try, reduction of non-value time, improved supply chain management and re-duced transaction costs, have been identified as the most important advan-tages of EDI (Emmelhainz 1993; Wigand 1994).

5.2.1.1 EDI Research Fields

Based on these unquestioned benefits of EDI, several articles have analyzed the effects of the adoption, diffusion, impact, and integration of EDI on both the micro- and macroeconomic levels. The adoption of EDI can be analyzed on the level of small and medium-sized enterprises (Chau et al. 2001; Iacovou et al. 1995; Ketler et al. 1997), as well as industry wide, e.g., in the retail sector (Jimenez-Martinez et al. 1998; Vijayasarathy et al. 1997), the pharmaceutical industry (Howells et al. 1995), or the automotive industry (Mackay et al. 1996). The diffusion of EDI driven by powerful EDI champions is focused on in (Webster 1995). The impact of EDI associated with the level of integration is analyzed as a de-facto benefit outcome (Fearon et al. 1999) or at least as the perceived value (Williams et al. 1998) using a multidimensional approach. The technological integration of EDI includes the external transmission layer such as Internet-EDI (Segev et al. 1997) or WebEDI (Beck et al. 2003d) as a solu-tion aimed at reducing the necessity of special EDI technological knowledge or to lower the EDI entry barrier (Muller 1998). From an in-house point of view, the internal technological implementation is focused on the degree of integra-tion, i.e. the application-to-application integration (Swatman et al. 1991).

Different reasons have been analyzed as being responsible for the diffusion of EDI. When (often larger) partners exercise power or due to competitive pres-sure, business partners can be forced to adopt EDI (Barua et al. 1997). Be-sides power, trust can also be the reason for EDI adoption in long-term business relations between business partners (Hart et al. 1997; Hart et al. 1998). EDI is therefore more than just electronic communication: it is also a coordination arrangement based on trust and control for ex-ante designed collective behavior rules (Brousseau 1994). Therefore, trust or reputation can be both the necessary prerequisite for establishing EDI with other business partners and the outcome of a successful EDI-based business partnership. On the other hand, opportunistic behavior is negative in terms of trust.

The research approach presented here is to use the trust perspective of EDI relations to remodel the traditional processes for dealing with defects or customer complaints by developing a reputation model for established EDI-based business relations. This innovative use of EDI may help to reduce handling costs and increase efficiency in supply chains at the same time.

5.2.1.2 Automation-oriented Business Process Reengineering

As mentioned earlier, apart from the electronic exchange of order or invoice messages there are manifold businesses processes which are not yet fully implemented at industry level or discussed in the literature. Most of them are related to trust or reputation factors, i.e. are the data submitted up-to-date, is the sender or receiver reliable and solvent, or is a partner's claim justified? Especially when it comes to irregularities in the value chain not covered by standardized processes, costly human interaction is necessary to fix any problems that arise. A common type in every day product delivery is the handling of customer complaints about articles that are broken or missing from an order. This general process is described briefly: After submitting an order and receiving a delivery note from the supplier, the incoming orders have to be checked physically by the stock receipt department. In the case of broken or partially missing articles, the supplier has to be contacted and/or the broken parts have to be sent back. Afterwards, the supplier has to send replacements for the missing articles and the customer has to track the claim until all parts are received. If the defective items are regular in-stock articles, the redelivery may be delayed until the next routine order. In this case, a credit note has to be sent to the customer.

Especially where missing or broken low-value products such as raw materials and supplies are concerned, the customer complaints management process itself might be more expensive than the replacement value of the product. The customer has to decide whether to reclaim or not. If she does not, she has to pay for the incomplete delivery and the supplier cannot adjust her distribution because her quality management never receives the information that products have reached customers in an unsatisfactory condition. In the worst case, these unsatisfactory circumstances can lead to the loss of customers while the supplier is unaware of the underlying reason. A possible solution might be a system of reputation, trust and EDI-based information exchange where customers do not have to prove that parts are damaged or missing. Instead, the supplier believes her based on the reputation and trust the customer has acquired in past transactions. In the following section, a brief overview of the concepts of reputation and trust is provided.

5.2.1.3 Reputation and Trust

In the business world, reputation reflects an aggregate ratio incorporating multiple factors: quality of merchandise, reliability of financial transactions, and/or level of customer service. It is often observed that reputation and trust acquire fundamental importance in long-term business-to-business (B2B) relations. According to (Mui et al. 2002b), reputation is a "perception that an agent creates through past actions about its intentions and norms" and trust is the "subjective expectation an agent has about another's future behavior based on the history of their encounters". It can be shown that reputation reduces the complexity of the decision process by enabling a better assessment of the likelihood of failed orders and a reduction in the number of quality tests needed for a product (Marsh 1992).

It is important to distinguish between the individual and the social dimensions of reputation (Sabater et al. 2002). This paper focuses on the individual dimension of reputation which arises in direct interactions between two business partners. Experience of transactions with a partner is directly reflected in an assigned reputation value. The social dimension of reputation relies on intermediates to propagate common reputation assessments. Due to the specific setting of bilateral supplier-customer-relationships, the social aspect of reputation can be neglected because there are only two partners involved in the complaints handling process addressed here.

Models of reputation and trust have been developed, especially in agent-based computational economics. A broad overview of approaches to the use of reputation in multi-agent systems is provided by (Mui et al. 2002a). Sabater and Sierra (Sabater et al. 2001) introduce a reputation model which takes the individual and social dimension of reputation into account for a multi-agent society. Carter, Bitting, and Ghorbani (Carter et al. 2002) propose a formalization of reputation for multi-agent systems, applying the sociological concept of role fulfillment to establishing a positive reputation and examining the link between reputation and trust. The role of trust in supply relationships and the underlying implications are addressed by Lane and Bachman in an empirical study of business relationships in Germany and Britain (Lane et al. 1996). As they point out, trust relations are highly dependent on stable social, institutional and legal structures. Moorman et al. investigate the specific relationship between the providers and users of market research reports and provide a good introduction to the role of trust in relationships (Moorman et al. 1992).

Das and Teng (Das et al. 1998) argue that trust and control are the two pivotal sources of confidence in the cooperative behavior of business partners in strategic alliances. Both sources of confidence are highly interdependent. A large amount of control reflects a low amount of trust and vice versa. Without any control, the trusting party takes on the whole risk of the trustee's behaving opportunistically. As they point out, trust or control are two completely different kinds of approach to business relationships.

In the following model, extensive control in the customer complaint-handling process should be replaceable by trust in order to reduce costs for suppliers and customers. A supplier establishes reputation accounts for her customers and tracks their past behavior to inhibit opportunistic behavior. Customers are assigned individual reputation values by tracking past behavior in complaints issues. This reputation value can then be used by the supplier to decide whether to trust the customer and accept the complaint without checking the correctness of the customer's claim or to initiate a detailed investigation.

5.2.1.4 Reputation and Transaction Costs

Increasing the level of control by establishing contracts or mechanisms to prevent opportunistic behavior can result in higher transaction costs so that—in the worst case—the handling of an order might be more cost intensive than the expected benefit. In the context of reputation and trust, ex-post transaction costs are of particular importance (Williamson 1975; Williamson 1985). "Ex-post transaction costs" refers to costs that emerge after the order has been shipped and before the entire transaction is completed. Consequently, the ex-post transaction costs will increase if the trust level decreases or in other words, the monitoring and enforcement costs to prevent ex-post bargaining will be higher if the incentive to opportunistic behavior increases (Dahlstrom et al. 1999). For suppliers, such costly uncertainties are based on unanticipated changes in the behavior of business partners (Noordewier et al. 1990). The greater the level of uncertainty, the more difficult it is to formulate, negotiate, and enforce a contract to reduce the risk of being a victim of opportunistic behavior. In long-term relations, expensive tracking and monitoring instruments may be replaced by mutual trust. However, trust and reputation have to be managed in an effectively automated way when the number of business partners increases.

5.2.2   Customer Complaints Handling, Reputation Mechanism, and Simulation Model

5.2.2.1 Customer Complaints Alternatives and Implications

As mentioned earlier, many business processes are not yet fully automated. Some of them are related to trust or reputation factors, i.e. are the data submitted up-to-date, is the sender or receiver reliable and solvent or is a partner's complaint justified? Especially when it comes to irregularities in the supply chain not covered by standardized processes, costly human interaction is necessary to handle problems that arise. A common process in every day product delivery is dealing with customer complaint about items that are broken or missing from an order.

In order to discuss the customer complaint process on the customer and supplier side in more detail, the alternatives and relevant business cases are depicted in the following. Drawing on the "exit, voice, and loyalty" model provided by Hirschman (Hirschman 1970), and the customers' "problem impact tree" framework of Rust, Subramanian, and Wells (Rust et al. 1992) the problem tree with "voice" a complaint or "exit" without making a complaint is illustrated. According to Hirschman, customers have two potential feedback options: to voice complaints and thereby express their dissatisfaction directly to the supplier or to stop buying and exit the relationship. Both options may have different but always unfavorable impacts on suppliers, who have to respond with appropriate defensive strategies to overcome those problems. Therefore, all possible customer complaints scenarios are first described briefly: After submitting an order and receiving a delivery note from the supplier, the incoming orders have to be checked by the stock receipt department of the customer.

In the case of a faultless shipment, one might expect that customers have no reason to complain (upper branch of Figure 22). This is indeed true in nearly all cases: Customers receiving correct deliveries will be satisfied, continue with the supplier and will not make any complaints. The situation is slightly different if complaints are not too costly and the supplier does not normally ask for defective items to be returned in order to check the correctness of the complaint. If customers are not afraid of any such controls, then they might be tempted to cheat and complain about faultless shipments. Avoiding such an incentive is a pivotal element when designing an automated customer complaint solution.

Figure 22: Customer Complaint and Alternatives

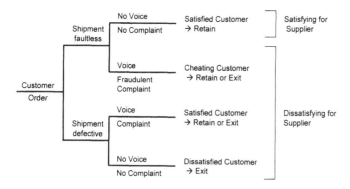

In the case of defective or partially missing items in the shipment (lower branch of Figure 22), the supplier has to be contacted and/or the broken parts have to be sent back. Afterwards, the supplier has to replace the defective parts and the customer has to track the complaint until all parts have been received. If the supplier handles the complaint satisfactorily, the customer will continue and buy again. If this is not the case and the customer is dissatisfied with the process management, then the exit strategy might be chosen. In contrast to the latter case, the supplier has no opportunity to contact the dissatisfied customer if a defective shipment is delivered and the customer decides not to complain. It is very likely that such a customer will discontinue the business relationship temporarily or permanently.

As Figure 22 reveals, cost-intensive additional work and therefore dissatisfying scenarios can emerge for suppliers, even when the shipment was faultless. A possible solution to the dissatisfying results for customers and suppliers might be offered by a combined reputation and EDI-based new solution where customers do not have to prove that parts of a shipment are damaged or missing. Instead, the supplier simply believes the customer based on the reputation and trust the customer has acquired in past transactions. How this might work is illustrated in the following section.

5.2.2.2 A Simplified Complaints Handling Process Model

In this section, a simplified customer complaint process which would reduce handling costs for suppliers and customers is described. It will be shown that, from a game-theoretical point of view, the simplified customer complaint-handling process dominates the conventional process if customers are always truthful. If customers cannot be assumed to be truthful, a reputation mechanism is introduced to inhibit cheating behavior by customers.

The model is based on the following assumptions:

- Neither supplier nor customer knows the exact value of the ratio of defective items d. The exact quality of the products is not known (e.g., due to unknown conditions during the shipment).

- There is a long-term recurring relationship between supplier and customer. Products are frequently exchanged between them.

- The value of a single order is relatively low, as can be observed for raw materials or office supplies.

- The customer complaints-handling costs of the *simplified process* can be ignored. In the simplified process, the customer only has to send a notification to the supplier; the supplier does not have to check if the products are indeed defective.

- Legal issues are not addressed.

A game-theoretical approach will be used to analyze the trade situation for the conventional and the simplified complaints handling process. In a conventional complaints handling process, the customer checks the shipment and if there are defects, the defective parts of the shipment are sent back to the supplier. The supplier has to check whether the complaint is justified or not. Both partners incur expenses due to the manual processing and shipment of products. Table 21 depicts the cost matrix in a game with a conventional customer complaint process.

Table 21: Conventional Customer Complaint Process Cost Matrix

		Customer Complains?	
		Yes	No
Shipment Defect?	Yes (*d*)	Customer: complaint costs (c_C^C) Supplier: proportion of shipment defective (v)+ complaint costs (c_S^C)	Customer: {0; proportion of shipment defective (v)} Supplier: 0
	No (1-*d*)	Customer: complaint costs (c_C^C) Supplier: complaint costs (c_S^C)	Customer: 0 Supplier: 0

If the shipment is indeed defective and the customer decides to reclaim, both customer and supplier have to pay for the cost-intensive manual handling of the customer complaints c_C^C and c_S^C respectively. Additionally, the supplier will not be paid for his defective products and the value *v* (ranging from 0 to the total value of the shipment if all parts are defect) of these parts is lost for him. When the customer decides not to reclaim the defective products, his loss equals the value of the defective shipped products *v*. If the shipped products have only minor defects, the consumer may be able to use the products to some extent, thereby reducing his loss to a fraction of *v*, indicating the shipment's remaining utility. Nonetheless, compared to flawless products, the consumer encounters loss costs ranging from 0 for minor defects to the value of the shipment *v* for major defects.

If the shipment is not defective and the customer decides to issue a complaint, both partners will have to pay complaint costs c_C^C and c_S^C. After the order is sent back, the supplier checks the products and finds them non-defective, so she or he may re-ship them or sell them to another customer, so there are no further costs despite the complaint processing costs. In regular cases when the shipment is not defective and the customer does not decide to reclaim, the transaction is completed as originally intended.

Now a simplified customer complaint-handling process is implemented, significantly reducing complaint costs for both partners. In cases where the customer decides to complain about a shipment, the supplier trusts her customer, assuming the products are indeed defective without testing. The customer subtracts the invoice accordingly or a new shipment is immediately scheduled and the complaint is not audited any further by the supplier. This new setting is described in Table 22.

Table 22: Simplified Customer Complaint Process Cost Matrix

		Customer Complains?	
		Yes	**No**
Shipment Defect?	Yes (d)	Customer: 0 Supplier: proportion of shipment defective (v)	Customer: {0;proportion of shipment defective (v)} Supplier: 0
	No (1-d)	Customer: - proportion of shipment defective (-v) Supplier: proportion of shipment defective (v)	Customer: 0 Supplier: 0

If the shipment is not defective and the customer decides not to claim, the situation is unchanged. In cases where the products are defective, the situation is unchanged despite the lack of complaint costs. The critical case is a cheating customer who pretends to complain about a shipment that is not defective at all. In this case, the customer does not have to pay for the products although she has received faultless products. The customer immediately earns the value of the products ("negative loss costs (-v)"). On the other hand, the supplier loses the value of the products shipped.

Comparing both situations reveals that for defective product shipments, the second scenario with a simplified customer complaint process is advantageous in all situations. If supplier-side complaint costs are less than the value of the shipments, only the lower left quadrant of the cost-matrix is disadvantageous. This outcome, which implies a cheating customer, must therefore be avoided.

Despite the savings made by skipping claim checks, it can be rational for the supplier to ask the consumer to return the defective goods in order to be able to determine the source of the defects and improve quality by taking appropriate counter measures. Even if consumers always act truthfully or a reputation mechanism is applied, a random sample of shipments claimed to be defective should be returned for the supplier to analyze the source of defects.

The costs of shipping and handling complaints in a specific market are also important for the applicability of the simplified customer complaints process. In the case of low or negligible shipping and complaint handling costs, it might be rational always to return defective shipments. It depends on the relationship of total complaint costs to the individual value of a shipment whether the simplified complaint process is applicable or not. If total complaint costs are high in relation to the shipment's value, the simplified complaint process can realize substantial cost savings.

5.2.3   A Reputation Mechanism to inhibit Opportunistic Behavior

In the case of accurate shipments, there is a significant difference between the conventional and simplified scenario. If the customer decides to complain about a faultless shipment, then she will not have to pay for the faultless products and immediately gains their value. On the other hand, the supplier loses the equivalent value because she trusts her customer and does not perform a quality check on the products complained about. If there is no additional monitoring or control structure, the customer will always claim the delivered shipments are defective, independent of the actual status of the shipment (whether it is indeed defective or not). It is the best strategy for the customer to complain always. The supplier therefore always loses the equivalent value of the shipment if no mechanism to counter cheating behavior is applied.

In an ideal world, a truthful customer would be the optimum to reduce transaction costs. Both partners could improve their respective position in all cases, because only the upper left and lower right sections in Table 22 would be relevant. Assuming a customer who always tells the truth reveals that the conventional complaint-handling mechanism is inferior to the simplified automated complaint handling. Both parties benefit from the reduction of transaction costs when processing complaints. Nevertheless, the customer might be tempted always to complain that products are defective even if this is not justified. The pivotal question is how to ensure that the customer has no interest in cheating the supplier by applying an inexpensive mechanism at the same time.

At this point, an automated complaint-handling mechanism might be suitable. Reputation in this context is based on business transactions with a certain customer in the past. The more orders successfully processed in the past, the higher the reputation account. By contrast, the customer withdraws from her reputation account on the supplier side if transactions have failed in the past. For example, in the simplest case the supplier could estimate a rate d of defective items among his/her products r and adjust the customer's reputation account if her complaints rate differs significantly from the estimated quality, e.g., by applying a χ^2 test.

The supplier's plausible threat is to switch back to the conventional customer complaints handling mechanism, inducing complaints processing costs on future transactions. This threat only works for infinitely repeated games as assumed for this model. Nevertheless, this assumption seems to be appropriate for the setting, since B2B-relationships can often be characterized as long-term, frequently recurring relations.

The supplier can implement several strategies to ensure that the customer is truthful. The following strategies can be applied if the supplier knows the defection rate d with a high degree of accuracy:

- The supplier can randomly select shipments claimed to be defective and request the customer to return the products for an intensive test. If the products are faultless, the customer cannot be trusted and she is removed from the simplified customer complaints handling process. The process is immediately switched back to the traditional handling process. This trigger-strategy is misleading if the customer accidentally complains about products that are not defective.

- The supplier can switch back to the conventional complaints handling process if the ratio of products complained about significantly exceeds the defectiveness ratio d. This mechanism only works if the supplier knows the defectiveness ratio d with a high degree of accuracy.

- Each customer receives a reputation account for a given period, calculated as the product of the mean ordered value and the quality parameter d. If a customer claims a shipment, the shipment's value is subtracted from this account and if the account is exhausted, the customer has to justify her behavior. This mechanism also relies strongly on the accuracy of the parameter d.

The threshold for identifying cheating behavior on the part of a customer should be chosen according to the accuracy with which d is known. If d is not exactly known and is subject to change, this threshold should be increased and vice versa.

If the supplier herself does not know the defectiveness ratio d, she can improve the reputation mechanism by taking the responses of all other customers for each product into account. Each customer has individual reputation accounts for each product. If a customer claims a shipment, the value of this shipment is subtracted from her product reputation account. Afterwards, the reputation accounts of all customers receive a bonus. This bonus for product r and customer i is calculated as an adjusted ratio of the mean quantity ordered by the customer. This value can be regularly recalculated for all orders in a given period (e.g., monthly). The following equation calculates the reputation bonus for each customer i and product r.

$$bonus_r^i = \frac{q_r^i}{\sum_{j=1}^{n} q_r^j} * p_r q_r^d$$

Equation 2: reputation bonus

p_r: price of product r

q_r^i: aggregated quantity of product r ordered by customer i in a given period

q_r^j: aggregated quantity of product r ordered by customer j in a given period

n: number of customers with reputation accounts

q_r^d: quantity of defective product r that is claimed

If all customers are acting truthfully, the individual reputation accounts for every product will be zero on average. A simple example should illustrate the mechanism: a defectiveness ratio of 10%, a price of 1 for a given product r and three customers are assumed. The first customer regularly orders 1000 units, customer 2 orders 50 units and customer 3 orders 200 units. Each customer truthfully claims 10% of the shipments. When the first customer claims in total 100 units, her reputation account is immediately reduced by 100, equivalent to the total value of the complaint. Afterwards, all customers' reputation accounts are given a bonus (including the customer initiating the claim), resulting in 80 bonus points for customer 1, 4 bonus points for customer 2 and 16 bonus points for customer 3. This process is also applied for the complains of the other customers, leading to neutral reputation accounts at the end of the selected period.

If one of the customers decides to cheat and complains about a higher ratio, e.g., 15%, then her reputation account will be negative while the accounts of the other customers will be positive. If the first customer complains about 15% of her shipments and the other customers complain about 10%, their respective reputation accounts for the illustrative example will be -10, +2 and +7.2. Customers with a higher complaint ratio than other customers can be identified by their negative reputation accounts. The first customer to cheat will put herself into an inferior position compared to truthful customers.

This system can only be cheated on if all customers together increase their complaints ratio. Furthermore, it does not work with a small number of customers. If there were only one customer, then this reputation account would always be neutral.

From a macroeconomic and an individual perspective, both partners can reduce their costs when the simplified mechanism is applied and supported by reputation accounts to foster truthful behavior on the part of customers. The implementation of the reputation model within the existing EDI infrastructure is described in the following section. The communication messages necessary to cover all information flows for the reputation model already exist within the UN/EDIFACT standard.

5.2.4   Developing an Automated Customer Complaints Processing System

Based on the already discussed reputation accounts, an automated customer complaint handling system is shown in Figure 23, based on and exemplified using existing UN/EDIFACT message types.

The process starts with an initiating order submitted (ORDER) by the customer to the supplier. The supplier sends in parallel to the physical shipping of the ordered products a dispatch advice (DESADV) including detailed information about date of delivery, product prices and further information, similar to an invoice. After receiving the ordered products, they are checked at the point of stock receipt. If there is any reason to claim for defective or missing products, the customer does not return the relevant items but sends an optional commercial dispute message (COMDIS) to inform the supplier or a revised invoice document (INVOIC) directly back to the supplier listing the de facto order items the customer is willing to pay for. The information system of the supplier now has to decide whether this revised invoice is justified or not. The proposed reputation mechanism decides whether the consumer's reputation account suggests defective or truthful behavior on the part of the consumer. If defective behavior is presumed, the consumer is asked to return the shipment that is being claimed for.

Figure 23: Automated EDI-based Customer Complaints Handling System

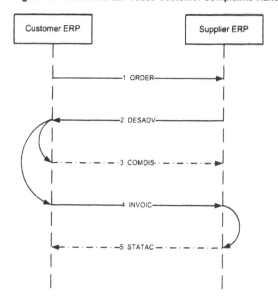

If the supplier agrees and assumes truthful behavior, the customer sends a pay order based on the invoice she has generated. The supplier can optionally send an account statement (STATAC) providing information about as yet unpaid invoices.

5.2.5   Trust versus Control in long term Relations

The combination of traditional information systems standards such as EDI together with game-theory inspired reputation accounts establishes new solutions to automate more business transactions where formerly human decision makers were necessary. The author believes that an economic view of existing information systems technologies may help to reveal still unrealized potentials for more computer-mediated application areas. Apart from the reduction in manual handling and shipping costs, the process quality may be increased for customers and suppliers, resulting in higher customer loyalty.

Mechanisms based on trust and reputation can be used to foster otherwise less favorable situations and create situations where all participants benefit. Information systems such as EDI can be used in business processes that could not previously be applied successfully because of the threat of opportunistic behavior. The full potential of EDI automation may only be realized if mechanisms that allow one to lower the extent of manual control and to increase trust among business partners at the same time can be applied. By deploying a reputation mechanism, not every single shipment claimed has to be checked. Even when a reputation mechanism as proposed is deployed, a random proportion of defective shipments should be checked to improve quality by determining the source of defects.

Apart from opportunistic behavior on the customer side, another behavior is also plausible in a long-term business relation, namely too much trust on the customer side: customers receiving broken items of low value could decide in favor of discarding these items from a shipment without notifying or charging the vendor because of their otherwise excellent business relationship. The vendor will never notice that her products were not delivered in perfect condition and lose the chance to improve his production or delivery process. If customers behave like that, the supplier will not be harmed by cheating customers but will also not have the opportunity to improve production or logistics because she never receives any feedback from her customer.

The model as described here is focussed on the individual dimension of reputation in direct interactions between two business partners and has not yet implemented the social dimensions of reputation, which relies on intermediates to propagate common reputation assessments. Since it seems obvious that the social dimension has some influence on the resulting reputations, the social dimensions will be taken into account in future research. In order to make the model more flexible, e.g., in the case of new customers and therefore new reputation accounts, the next step will be to integrate these changes into the model.

Although the presented model needs some fine-tuning before it is adopted in real world scenarios, the linkage with existing UN/EDIFACT message types reveals its immediate potential. The model aims to increase the number of possible electronically processable business transactions. Starting from the current "networked economy" with a certain degree of electronic data interchange and automation already in use, the proposed solution might contribute to the vision of a perfect "network economy" in the future.

The WebConverter and the reputation accounts are two possible solutions which primarily increase the indirect benefits related to the adoption of communication standards. At the same time, due to increased use, the communication related direct benefits of interchanging data with business partners increase as well. Since both network effects are related to each other by the installed base of standard users it is difficult to predict which combination might be the initial reason for adopting a communication standard. Even more, the changing number of network participants using the same standard leads to different magnitudes of potentially achievable network benefits over time. Since the dynamic change and magnitude of both network effects (characterized as the network effect helix) is important in enabling us to understand the adoption decision of potential adopters, the network-size-related external effects are analyzed in more detail in chapter 1 by applying an agent-based computational simulation analysis.

6 Simulation of the Diffusion of Network Effect Goods

The diffusion of communication standards such as traditional EDI standards, but also newer ones such as InternetEDI, WebEDI, or even XML-based data communication standards is lagging behind the expected degree of wide-spread use although the benefits accompanying with these standards were never in doubt. It is not only SMEs who have not completely adopted these standards, but also even large enterprises with massive communication traffic are often reluctant to adopt, and therefore do not use all possible electronic data communication standards. EDI standards and communication standards in general seem to be special and different from other products or goods that can be used without the necessity of being a product that is widely adopted among other market participants. Therefore, the diffusion of such network effect standards is difficult to predict and often remains below the expected degree of diffusion. Standards which are not able to overcome the early phase of diffusion (from the start-up until reaching critical mass or threshold) will never become accepted market standards. Apart from the diffusion of open, unsponsored EDI standards among firms this phenomenon is also observable for proprietary, sponsored standards in the telecommunication markets, such as for WAP, i-mode, or UMTS.

While the anticipation of the possible diffusion paths of communication standards in unsponsored networks is of importance primarily for adopters (or potential adopters) of a new standard to enable them to decide whether to standardize or not, the anticipation of consumer behavior is also of importance for providers. If, e.g., a sponsored standard is competing with an unsponsored one, then a provider has a choice of certain market parameters for her penetration strategy. Apart from subsidized prices or side payments, a provider can also stress certain components of a standard during the diffusion stage to meet the demands of potential adopters in accordance with the results of the market simulation.

From an economic perspective, a focus on the user of a standard rather than concentration on the supplier is more interesting in terms of understanding the development of a user network characterized by adopter-side economies of scope. The findings of the microeconomic bottom-up view of the adoption behavior of single market participants reveal market strategies for suppliers, while an inverse macroeconomic top-down view cannot.

As described earlier, the question of how to describe or even solve the start-up problem for communication and compatibility standards in network effect markets remains unanswered. Due to the complex interplay between adopters of standards and the network benefits which change constantly during the diffusion process, the detailed analysis of all network externalities linked with the adoption is necessary to describe all possible paths of diffusion.

Earlier research work on the diffusion of standards in network effect markets has focused on the allocation implications and market structure after overcoming the start-up problem, i.e. the market concentration tendency of sponsored standards towards a monopolistic market. But whether, however, the critical early diffusion phase up to the point of reaching critical mass can be overcome and described methodically, remains open so far. Due to the network effects that arise, the individual benefit of a new communication standard for prospective adopters is difficult to determine, resulting in a tendency to under-supply with standards (excess inertia). Particularly for the important, but still not carefully enough analyzed, phase between the roll-out, start-up and reaching of the critical mass or threshold, there are still no suitable methods of explaining the individual adoption decision and the overall diffusion at the same time.

6.1 Application of Network Effect Theory to Developing a Network of Mobile Service Users

In order to be able to analyze the dynamically changing effects with each new adopter and its degree of integration within the developing network over time, a simulation-based approach was chosen. Doing this allows potential adopters to determine the net present value of communication standards in a developing network by consideration of direct and indirect network effects for different environmental conditions. This agent-based computational economics approach to agents' standardization decisions extends the empirical view of communication standards diffusion and allows one to test and to extend network effect theory and related aspects such as learning behavior among simulated market participants in a controlled environment. In general, a simulation-based approach is chosen since it offers several advantages:

- Agent-based simulation models make it possible to analyze learning behavior, asymmetric information distribution, and heterogeneous preferences among virtual market participants. Very often such explicit information about the adoption decision-making process is not available from surveys on human-based organizational adoption decisions. Furthermore, decision makers often do not know that network effects are the real source of the benefits of their adoption and therefore underestimate or simply do not know the external network effects occurring in interorganizational systems.

- Agent-based simulation models provide the possibility of fast motion analysis of communication standards diffusion under certain premises in order to derive insights into current developments. Otherwise, longitudinal studies would be necessary in order to be able to analyze communication standards diffusion paths from the past, which might be inadequate for the diffusion analysis of competing standards today. Consequently, simulations attempt to capture potential macroeconomic paths of diffusion over the life cycle of a standard based on iterative microeconomic adoption decisions on the individual level.

- Agent-based simulation models can be used to analyze environmental changes and their impact on the diffusion result by adjusting the parameters used. Heuristic elements such as estimators about the standardization decision of other agents in a non-deterministic system allow an analysis under uncertainty. Experimenting with different parameter settings can reveal potential changes in agents' diffusion behavior, which enables providers of communication standards to test their market strategies.

The simulations are based on ex ante observable qualitative criteria of the available communication standards available in sponsored and unsponsored markets. Anticipating the quality of a standard is already difficult enough since the quality of a network is related to network externalities characterized by the number of existing adopters (Bental et al. 1995). Depending on individual preferences, adopters can decide when the optimal adoption time has come for them. Organizations providing communication standards and service providers for such standards can redesign the standard to increase their market expectations.

Providers can use the simulation results to improve their understanding of the utility components, as well as the variation of these components over the life cycle of a standard in order to develop market-oriented standards and diffusion strategies. Communication or compatibility standards as a source of network effect benefits guarantee the compatibility among adopters which enables them to gain positive network effects (Köster 1998) and therefore require special attention in the diffusion analysis. Since these standards offer no standalone benefit in unsponsored markets (Borowicz et al. 2001; Weiber 1992), the question of how to overcome the start-up problem arises. A first analysis of the network effect helix simulation reveals the changing importance and strength of the two network effect types during the diffusion process (Beck et al. 2003c).

Communication standards in pure network effect markets are subject to the chicken and egg problem. As long as no users of a standard have entered the market, other users are hardly likely to adopt and vice versa. However, after a communication standard is established and has revealed its true value, this standard has an advantage and will potentially be adopted by further market participants. Often in this context one refers to the penguin effect (Farrell et al. 1986, p. 943) or herd behavior (Choi 1997). Hungry penguins sitting on an ice floe wait until one jumps first in order not to run the risk of being eaten by sharks or sea lions. After the first one has jumped and the water seems to be safe, then the others will follow. This is equivalent to the risk of adopting a communication standard that is only useful if other market participants likewise jump (or adopt). However, this does not explain why the first penguin jumps if it is assumed that all penguins feel equally hungry and that they have equivalent expectation of the existence of predators in the water.

The start-up problem is also more like the chicken and egg paradox. The start-up would not be difficult, if there were already an installed base of users in the network; as soon as the critical mass of network participants is established, the uncertainty about the success of a standard at the time of the adoption decision has vanished. That is the reason why new standards try to benefit from the installed base of adopters of an earlier standard network. Thus, overcoming the start-up problem under imperfect information is closely related to reaching the critical mass of network participants. Although intuitively comprehensible, substantial explanation difficulties and criticism connected with the concept of critical mass exist (Kubicek et al. 1996). Apart from the difficulty of proving empirically that there is market failure in network effect markets when the critical mass is not reached (Liebowitz et al. 1999), the generally assumed market tendency towards a monopoly is over-estimated (Köster 1998; Weitzel 2004). Unrealistic assumptions like continuously increasing homogeneous network effects (criticized by (Liebowitz et al. 1995b)), as well as the insufficient consideration of the structural characteristics of networks (network topologies, as described by (Weitzel et al. 2003b)) are further research areas which should be considered in the context of the analysis of the diffusion of communication standards. In sociological approaches, network topologies found early consideration, e.g., in form of opinion leaders and personal network densities (Coleman et al. 1957). Network topologies such as social networks or "small world networks" define the way information flows, e.g., in co-authors' networks or even terrorist networks (Ebel et al. 2003). The influence of a network topology (Granovetter 1973) and its impact on applicable price strategies for software providers is analyzed by Westarp (Westarp 2003), while the impact of networks on the diffusion of standards in general is discussed by Weitzel (Weitzel 2004).

In the ACE-based network effect helix model it is assumed (by analogy with transaction cost theory) that agents have imperfect information (agents have to estimate the network benefit of other network participants and the quality of a communication standard) and that agents have to maximize their individual utility function under uncertainty. The efficiency criterion for the adoption of a communication standard is the expected benefit surplus in comparison to the process or standard previously used. The simulation however only reveals the benefits of the direct and indirect network effects of the chosen standard, assuming that the surplus benefit of an adopted standard is at least zero in comparison to an older one. This is a realistic assumption, because swapping from an old but superior standard to a new but inferior standard would not make sense at all. In contrast to transaction costs theory, where contracts are often regarded as fixed, contracts in the network effect helix model can be renegotiated anew every period. Thus no artificial lock-in by contract is possible in the model.

The simulation of micro-behavior-based adoption decisions on the diffusion, together with macroeconomic effects such as the bandwagon or path dependence are increasingly being analyzed by using ACE approaches (Tesfatsion

2002). For an overview of the applicability of ACE to analyzing path dependence by using different agent decision rules see Vriend (Vriend 2000).

The objective in this chapter is now to analyze the start-up of standards from a microeconomic perspective in order to be able to forecast possible diffusion scenarios. The initial point of research is the competition between two incompatible communication standards, one already established on the market (installed base) and a new one. Using the decentral standardization model (Weitzel 2004) extensions are made to analyze direct and indirect network effects and their importance for the start of the diffusion of standard. The following questions are particularly considered:

- What quality attributes of a standard are particularly relevant during the market rollout and do they change during the ongoing diffusion process?

- What network parameters are necessary in order to explain and predict the diffusion of standards?

- How do different preferences and heterogeneous market participants affect the early phase of standards diffusion?

In the following, the network effect helix approach is applied to two different markets for communication standards in order to analyze the diffusion of mobile communication standards (WAP versus i-mode) and the diffusion of electronic data interchange standards among SMEs. The two different markets were chosen in order to test the simulation model for the generalizability of its results. For both simulation scenarios, real world data is used to customize the simulation parameters according to the particular network market. Communication standards service providers can use the results of the simulations in order to develop market strategies that work in different market environments. The limitations of simulation-based approaches are discussed at the end of chapter 6 in section 6.2.6.

Wireless communication standards and technologies hold great promise for extending e-business and e-commerce applications to the dimension of mobile commerce. However, despite potential benefits such as ubiquitous Internet access and flexible information system infrastructures there is a substantial lack of strategies to develop large mobile communication networks of individually adopting users. Most research so far has focused on technical factors, neglecting the importance of business models and strategies for attracting a critical mass of users to adopt the same communication standard.

The critical challenge is how to attract the first users to a technology that promises to be useful only if others are using it as well. So the strategic question is: how does one build up an installed base of users to "tip the dominoes", i.e. to create an installed base generating sufficient network effects to initiate a bandwagon effect. Without an installed base of existing users, nobody else is willing to adopt a new standard: a typical chicken and egg problem arises. Hence, a major challenge for mobile service providers seems to be the development and evaluation of business strategies aimed at establishing a variety of mobile services based on a widely diffused mobile communication standard. Therefore, based on the network effect helix approach, a decision support model and toolset is developed addressing the main research question: what are the adoption drivers of communication standards and how can mobile service providers influence these drivers to develop an installed base of mobile service users?

According to the literature on network effects (see chapter 1) and the diffusion of innovation theories (see chapter 2), a conceptual model of mobile data communication standard diffusion is developed. In section 6.1.4, the findings are incorporated into a simulation model of the battle between i-mode and WAP services, focusing on the interplay between direct and indirect network effects as the main utility drivers. Using the proposed model supports the decision of mobile service providers in terms of their strategy of communication pricing versus content services.

6.1.1   Theoretical Foundation: Standards and Network Effects

Network analysis is often based on the theory of positive network effects, which describes a positive correlation between the number of users of a network good and its utility (Katz et al. 1985). A common finding is the existence of *network effects*, i.e. the increasing value of a network as the number of its participants increases (demand side economies of scale) leading in many cases to unfavorable outcomes (Pareto-inferior results of diffusion processes such as, e.g., insufficiently developed ICT infrastructures) or unpredictable multiple equilibriums (Hildebrand 1976). Network effects describe "the change in the benefit, or surplus, that an agent derives from a good when the number of other agents consuming the same kind of good changes" (Liebowitz et al. 1995b; Thum 1995). Katz and Shapiro (Katz et al. 1985, p. 424) first differentiated between *direct network* effects in terms of direct "physical effects" of being able to exchange information and *indirect network effects*, arising from interdependencies in the consumption of complementary goods (Chou et al. 1990; Church et al. 1992; Teece 1987). Since network effects are found especially where *compatibility* is important, in terms of the definition above, the term network often describes the "network of users" of certain technologies or standards such as the network of MS Word or SAP R/3 users (Besen et al. 1994, p. 117) or subscribers to a mobile services network (Beck et al. 2003a; Beck et al. 2003c).

The pattern of argument in network effect theory is based on asymmetries between micro and macro effects: the discrepancy between private and collective gains in networks under increasing returns may possibly lead to Pareto-inferior results. With incomplete information about other agents' preferences, *excess inertia* ("start-up problem") can occur, as no agent is willing to bear the disproportionate risk of being the first adopter of a technology and then becoming stranded in a small network if all others eventually decide in favor of another technology. This already discussed *start-up problem* prevents any adoption of the particular technology at all, even if it is preferred by everyone. In the context of cellular services, many vendors observed that user clusters such as students postponed their decisions to subscribe to a particular network service until a threshold number of friends had adopted. The reason is that communication within a provider network is less expensive than using other networks. Everyone who has experienced roaming fees knows this painful difference. The wait-and-see strategy of postponing the adoption decision is known as the *penguin effect* in network effect theory.

While the traditional network effect models contributed greatly to the understanding of a wide variety of problems associated with the diffusion of standards (the evolution of networks), more research is still needed when trying to develop solutions to the aforementioned problems (Liebowitz et al. 1994b). The specific interaction of potential standard adopters within their personal socio-economical environment in particular is often neglected. As a result, important phenomena of modern network effect markets such as the coexistence of different products despite strong network effects or the fact that strong players in communication networks force other participants to use a certain solution cannot be sufficiently explained by the existing approaches (Liebowitz et al. 1994b; Weitzel et al. 2000b). In addition, most contributions lack direct applicability to real life problems and therefore cannot be used to explain decisions in networks.

A thorough review of the literature shows that the distinction between direct and indirect effects is commonplace in the introduction to most articles on network effects. Nevertheless, apart from theoretical and empirical evidence (Weitzel 2004) of their different economic implications, the distinction is not carried through to the models and analysis (Weitzel et al. 2000b). Therefore, it appears promising to apply network effect theory to the telecommunications application domain and at the same time extend the traditional view of network effects by differentiating between direct and indirect effects as diffusion drivers of communication standards in a single diffusion model. To overcome these deficiencies of the traditional theory we need a model that incorporates

- ...the dynamic interplay between direct and indirect network effects (*direct and indirect network effects*),

- ...the individual standardization costs and benefits (*user view*),

- ...the influence of network clusters (neighbors) on the adoption decision and duration of diffusion (*network topology*).

Accordingly, in section 6.1.2 basic findings from network effect theory are extended and incorporated into the network effect helix model.

6.1.2   Concept of a Network Effect Helix

The problem of developing a network of users a communication standard has long attracted academic and public attention (Funk 1998). Nevertheless, as has been shown, there is still a substantial lack of both a sound theory of networks as well as a lack of adequate models and tools to support providers trying to establish a new communication network. From a theoretical perspective, the externality property associated with network effects still creats a quite complex coordination problem that has not been solved so far. For the diffusion of i-mode, earlier research already assumed a self-reinforcing dynamic between voice calls and data services (Barnes et al. 2003).

Network effects can result from both horizontal and vertical compatibility requirements. In the case of cellular networks, communication requires horizontal compatibility (direct network effects), while accessing content offered by the MSP (e.g., stock quotes) necessitates vertical compatibility (indirect network effects) (Katz et al. 1985). The aim here is to develop a decision support model and network toolset to incorporate the effects that have so far been considered as individual factors into a model of compound network strategy. Depending on the varying magnitudes and importance of direct and indirect network effects in different stages of diffusion over a network life cycle, the providers' pricing and market penetration strategies have to be adapted. Applying the model to real world data taken from a mobile service network in section 6.1.3 will show that for establishing a threshold number of standard users (installed base) promoting direct network effects is pivotal, while for expanding the network beyond that point of diffusion, indirect effects might become important. As the network grows, the potentially achievable direct and indirect network benefits also grow and influence each other positively, while propelling the diffusion like amino acids doublets in an upward spinning spiral. A similar fundamental dynamic can be found in the development of EDI networks and is called the network effect helix.

6.1.3   The Standard Battle: i-mode vs. WAP

The huge success and the rapid diffusion of cellular phones, together with the ability to use the devices as mobile Internet gateways, led to promising forecasts for mobile network markets. In spite of the large number of cellular phones and the heavy usage in the areas of voice telephony and Short Messaging Service (SMS)—at least in Europe and Asia—the use of cellular phones as true alternative to PC-based Internet access is still in its infancy (Siau et al. 2001). Two mobile communication standards are competing in this area in Germany, France, The Netherlands, Australia, and Japan: i-mode and WAP. While WAP offers only relatively restricted use of Internet applications, i-mode is based on cHTML (a proprietary subset of HTML) and therefore offers the regular Internet-like browsing experience. Furthermore, i-mode comes with a billing business model, which allows the consolidation of charges for the use of third-party content providers' services into a single telephone service invoice. Therefore, the micro-payment problem is solved, e.g., charging for downloading stock market or weather forecast information on demand. Choice of mature technology (cHTML-based) coupled with a liable business model (in the case of i-mode) can be seen as an improvement or innovation compared to WAP (Barnes et al. 2003). The two network effect sources for the competing standards are illustrated in Table 23.

Table 23: Network effect benefits of WAP (SMS) i-mode (i-mail)

	Direct network effects	Indirect network effects
WAP	SMS (up to 160 characters) (not an original WAP feature)	WML-based Websites, number of content providers unknown
i-mode	i-mail (with rich media content, up to 1000 characters)	cHTML-based, ca. 150 official and 7,000 independent content providers in Germany (official, certified vendors gain benefits from the integrated payment model via telephone invoice)

Indirect network effects in this case result from the existence of complementary products, content and/or services for the installed base of users of a special technology (Farrell et al. 1986). An example is the availability of WAP content services, depending on the number of WAP-capable cellular phones. After the specification of cHTML in XML, i-mode will also operate with WAP 2.0. Offering i-mode today as a mobile services provider probably means gaining a competitive advantage by installing an early market entrance for 3rd-generation mobile communication standards in the future. i-mode mobile Internet content includes a large variety of different resources, such as route planners, city guides, on-line brokerage, newspapers, weather information, and adult entertainment.

Direct network effects accrue from multilateral exchange of text-oriented data in form of SMS and i-mail among adopters. Unlike i-mode, WAP does not come with a special WAP mail service. A comparable standard here is SMS. Generally, SMS allows cellular phone users to send and receive short messages of up to 160 characters. Unlike i-mail, SMS is displayed in a monochrome alphanumeric mode without the possibility of attachments. The introduction of Multimedia Messaging Service (MMS) can be seen as technological progress providing potentially higher direct network effect benefits due to superior technological features. The current widespread use of SMS in Europe and Asia is driven by the relatively inexpensive pricing due to its low transferred data volume. Lower costs for exchanging SMS messages are accompanied by lower network benefits in comparison with i-mail. With up to 1000 possible characters, i-mail provides six times more characters per mail than SMS.

6.1.4   A Simulation Model for Mobile Service Markets

To internalize the interdependencies described in the previous sections into a decision support process for the development of strategic pricing models, the simulation model presented in this section considers the features and aspects of the different technologies responsible for two sources of network effects as described in chapters 2 and 3. Strategic pricing in order to gain monopoly benefits (Economides et al. 1995b; Katz et al. 1986b) is not incorporated yet. The simulation model combines both direct and indirect network effects for adopters. The resulting utility strongly depends on the network topology and communication preferences of each user (Wendt et al. 2000).

A network of n independent agents already using WAP-enabled cellular phones as installed base is assumed. Due to the broad distribution of WAP enabled mobile phones, nearly all users can be seen as potential WAP customers. Each agent i has to decide in each period (i.e. one month as the minimal i-mode subscription period in Germany) to continue to use only WAP or to shift to a new standard such as i-mode, i.e. adopting an i-mode cellular phone (i-mode capable devices also support WAP but not vice versa). As a result, agents are able to decide anew for or against i-mode in each period. Depending on their bounded and dynamically adapted information set deriving—among other things—from past technology adoption decisions made by the direct neighbors of i, agents can adopt i-mode in one period and drop it in the next. Furthermore, the agents use mobile data services such as SMS or i-mail to communicate directly with their nb_i neighbors. To visualize the communication relationship, agents and their relationships can be described as nodes and edges in a graph. To create a close network topology, the participating agents are randomly located in a unit square. Afterwards, agent i activates a vectored communication to the nearest neighbors nb_i in Euclidian distance. Such a graphic illustration represents the social network of agents and does not determine the geographical location.

The decision calculus of each agent is to evaluate the monthly benefit surplus when using i-mode and i-mail in comparison with WAP and SMS. This benefit surplus accrues from the additional possibilities and features offered by i-mode, given that relatives, friends, business partners, etc. (the "neighbors" of the agent) also adopt i-mode. The following cost and benefit aspects illustrate the adoption scenario for potential i-mode users in Germany:

Set-up costs: Compared with the widespread penetration of WAP-capable cellular phones as quasi standard, adopters of i-mode have to invest in new mobile devices. In 2003, the lowest subsidized retail price for an i-mode cellular phone (which also enables WAP) was € 1.- , including a 24-month contract. Besides these negligible set-up costs, an adopter had to pay € 5.- per month as additional fee for i-mode services in 2003. Adopters of WAP-services have no further monthly basic fees to pay. These monthly fixed costs K are equal for all users. The aforementioned scenario is based on the mobile telecommunication market in Germany. Interested readers are invited to customize other market constellations and scenarios using the simulation applet available on the Internet.

The simulation model does not consider any additional stand-alone benefits of an i-mode cellular phone, compared to non-i-mode-capable cellular phones. The integration of conceivable stand-alone benefits into the simulation model would accelerate the speed of adoption.

Direct network effects: Because she can use i-mail, the i-mode adopter i gains more benefits from the new mobile standard through communicating with i-mail capable neighbor j in comparison with the use of SMS. The additional direct benefit u_{ij}^{D}, using i-mail per period per communication with neighbor j (communication partners), is calculated as the difference of $u_{ij}^{D,i-mail}$ less $u_{ij}^{D,SMS}$:

$$u_{ij}^{D} = u_{ij}^{D,i-mail} - u_{ij}^{D,SMS}$$

Equation 3: additional direct network benefit

Analogous to the benefits, the additional direct costs c_{ij}^{D} can be described as the additional costs of the communication relations between i and its neighbors j:

$$c_{ij}^D = c_{ij}^{D,i-mail} - c_{ij}^{D,SMS}$$

Equation 4: additional costs of the new communication standard

The resulting additional net benefit coefficient nu_{ij}^D is:

$$nu_{ij}^D = u_{ij}^D - c_{ij}^D = u_{ij}^{D,i-mail} - c_{ij}^{D,i-mail} - \left(u_{ij}^{D,SMS} - c_{ij}^{D,SMS} \right)$$

Equation 5: overall additional net benefit coefficient

subject to: $nu_{ij}^D \geq 0$

Indirect network effects: The model describes a unique monotonously increasing correlation between the diffusion of a new technology in an existing network and the i-mode services and content offered. Since no installed base of i-mode users is available at the very beginning, third-party i-mode content providers are not necessarily willing to bear the risk of investing in i-mode content. By contrast, without i-mode content, potential users will not decide to adopt and a typical chicken and egg problem occurs. With close interdependencies between providers and users (and among users), the network related benefit of i-mode will arise only after a certain number of users have adopted. After this vicious circle is eventually broken, the steadily increasing number of adopters and users of i-mode services and content will motivate additional content and service providers to augment their supply, which will again lead to further network effect benefits. As the network grows, the ratio of achievable direct and indirect network benefits grows and varies with positive feedback to each other. A self-perpetuating *network effect helix* occurs. Due to the compatibility of i-mode cellular phones with WAP-content sites, the indirect network benefit is ≥ 0 for i-mode adopters in each period. The resulting indirect network effect benefits per period linked to use of the communication standard are therefore a function of all standard adopters $B_{q,t}$ of the same standard q:

For WAP adopters:

$$U_{WAP,j,t}^N = U_{WAP,i}^N \left(B_{WAP,t} \right) \text{ with costs}$$

Equation 6: resulting indirect network utility for all WAP adopters

$$C_{WAP,i,t}^N = C_{WAP,i}^N \left(B_{WAP,t} \right)$$

Equation 7: resulting costs for all WAP adopters

For i-mode adopters:

$$U^N_{i-mode,i,t} = U^N_{i-mode,i}\left(B_{i-mode,t}\right) \text{ with costs}$$

Equation 8: resulting indirect network utility for all I-mode adopters

$$C^N_{i-mode,i,t} = C^N_{i-mode,i}\left(B_{i-mode,t}\right)$$

Equation 9: resulting costs for all i-mode adopters

The simulation model uses the absolute number of i-mode users instead of the proportion of users in relation to an imaginary N of population, because both the de facto number of total i-mode adopters today as well as the (growing) number of users in the future is hard or nearly impossible to predict. In fact, a provider in network markets not only wants to cannibalize users from other MSPs but also wants to attract completely new users who are buying a cellular phone for the first time. Furthermore, the interpretation of the functions used (or in more detail: the coefficients used in equations 10 to 13) would be quite difficult. The computer-based simulation model uses a linear proportional function. Although a sigmoid form of the function curve seems to reflect the potential diffusion path better, analogous to an initial slow diffusion start, followed by a rapid growth and finally a saturation-like slower adoption, a linear function was chosen, since this already reveals the dynamics between direct and indirect network effects. Furthermore, using a sigmoid function would require a more complex parameterization, making the traceability of the results more difficult.

$$U^N_{WAP,i,t} = u^N_{WAP,i,} \cdot B_{WAP,t}$$

Equation 10: total indirect benefits of WAP subject to installed base

$$C^N_{WAP,i,t} = c^N_{WAP,i} \cdot B_{WAP,t}$$

Equation 11: total costs of WAP subject to installed base

$$U^N_{i-mode,i,t} = u^N_{i-mode,i} \cdot B_{WAP,t}$$

Equation 12: total indirect benefits of i-mode subject to installed base

$$C^N_{i-mode,i} = c^N_{i-mode,i} \cdot B_{WAP,t}$$

Equation 13: total costs of i-mode subject to installed base

subject to:

$$u_{WAP,i}^{N} \; ; c_{WAP,i}^{N} \; ; u_{i-mode,i}^{N} \; ; \; c_{i-mode,i}^{N} \geq 0$$

Using Equations 10 to 13, the following indirect network effects net benefit co-efficients $nu_{WAP,i}^{N}$ (Equation 14) and $nu_{i-mode,i}^{N}$ (Equation 15) can be derived:

$$nu_{WAP,i}^{N} = u_{WAP,i}^{N} - c_{WAP,i}^{N}$$

Equation 14: indirect net benefit coefficient WAP

$$nu_{i-mode,i}^{N} = u_{i-mode,i}^{N} - c_{i-mode,i}^{N}$$

Equation 15: indirect net benefit coefficient i-mode

In the case of indirect network effects, the term "net benefit" refers to the total i-mode content benefit while in the case of direct network effects, benefits are defined as the difference in the net benefit coefficient nu_{ij}^{D} (see equation 5) between i-mail and SMS. Because an i-mode user is still able to use SMS and WAP services, a further parameter has to be integrated to describe the substitution relation of i-mode services in comparison to WAP services. A substitution rate of $sub=1$ means, e.g., that there is no WAP service an i-mode adopting agent will use any more. A substitution rate of 0.8 would be equivalent to an adopter using 80% i-mode and 20% WAP. Consequently, a substitution rate of 0 is equivalent to a WAP user not using i-mode at all. The overall individual net benefit deriving from indirect network effects is defined as $U_{i,t}^{INE}$.

$$U_{i,t}^{INE} = \begin{cases} \left(nu_{i-mode,i}^{N} \right) \cdot B_{i-mode,t} - sub_{i} \cdot \left(nu_{WAP,i}^{N} \right) \cdot B_{WAP,t} & if \; U_{i,t}^{INE} > 0 \\ 0 & if \; U_{i,t}^{INE} \leq 0 \end{cases}$$

Equation 16: overall individual net benefit from indirect network effects

The value of indirect network effects is defined as greater than zero because an i-mode device offers the possibility of using WAP services even when the substitution rate sub is equal to one, since an adopter could still use WAP services.

Decision Calculus: The overall i-mode adoption benefit is defined as:

$$U_{i-mode,i,t} = -K + \sum_{j \in NB_i} \left(nu_{ij}^D \cdot x_j \right) + U_{i,t}^{INE}$$

Equation 17: decision calculus for i-mode adoption

subject to:

$x_j \in \{0;1\}$ (indicator for the i-mode adoption by agents' j)

$0 < sub_i \leq 1$ (agents' substitution behavior using i-mode instead of WAP)

$n = B_{i-mode,t} + B_{WAP,t}$

The adoption decision is based on uncertain and imperfect information about the adoption decision of other users, so adopter i has to estimate the adoption decisions of neighbor j heuristically. Drawing on the decentralized standardization model (Weitzel 2004), the probability p_{ij} describes agent i's estimation that agent j will adopt a new standard. If the estimated benefit of adoption is $E[U_{it}] > 0$, then agent i will adopt. If agent i is certain about the adoption behavior of her communication partners, p_{ij} corresponds to 0 (no adoption) or 1 (adoption). Every additional communication edge ij between agent i and her neighbor j (with costs c_{ij}) contributes to the amortization of the adoption costs of the initially adopting agent i. The decentralized standardization model furthermore assumes that the initial standard adoption costs K and the variable communication costs c_{ji} are the only costs known to agent i regarding j's adoption situation. Therefore agent i can assume that the edge ji is representative of all of j's edges.

Combining all assumed data, agent i can then develop the following probability estimate p_{ij} for the probability of technology adoption on the part of agent j, where c_{ji} is equivalent to nu_{ij}^D and K equivalent to 5:

$$p_{ij} = \frac{c_{ji} \cdot (n-1) - K}{c_{ji} \cdot (n-1)}$$

Equation 18: general individual standard adoption probability

Further structural adaptations of the decentralized standardization model are necessary for the simulation model. In the case of mobile telecommunication, a low density of related agents (similar to few communication edges) is assumed to perform the computer based simulation. This is equivalent to only a few individually relevant i-mail communication partners in contrast to all i-mode adopters. The general standardization model assumes communication edges between all adopters. This seems to be unrealistic for the observed cellular phone case. As mentioned before, network topology has to be taken into account and leads to different results (lower network effect utility compared to MetCalfe's law) as previously shown by (Weitzel 2004) and (Wendt et al. 2000). In general, the fact that a new adopter could benefit—at least theoretically—from having the potential to call all adopters is not as important as the number of relatives, friends, and business partners also adopting the same standard. As argued in the next chapter, the simulated network structure has a low density and represents close topology. The term $n-1$ is therefore replaced by nb_j which describes the number of communication partners of agent j. Further, the heuristic estimation used has to consider the indirect network effects of the technology adoption decision of neighbors. Therefore, the numerator in this model is extended to the expected indirect network effect net benefit of the neighbors ($E\left[U_{jt}^{INE}\right]$).

$$p_{ijt} = \frac{nu_{ji}^D \cdot nb_j - K + E\left[U_{jt}^{INE}\right]}{nu_{ji}^D \cdot nb_j}$$

Equation 19: adapted individual standard adoption probability

If neighbor j uses i-mode in the previous period, p_{ijt} is equivalent to 1. Agent i believes that it is absolutely implausible for neighbor j to switch the current chosen new standard immediately in the next period. A simplification of the model is the supposed assumption that agent i has complete information about the direct and indirect net benefits components of its neighbors j.

In contrast to direct network effects, the impact of indirect network effects depends on the total number of adopters. To forecast the adoption rate, concepts from diffusion theory such as relational and structural interaction patterns (neighborhood concept) to explain the diffusion of innovations have been incorporated in this model. This simulation model refers to a restrictive estimation for adopting i-mode ($B_{i\text{-}mode,t}$), based on the installed base of i-mode users in the previous period:

$$E\left[B_{i-mode,t}\right] = B_{i-mode,t-1} + 1$$

Equation 20: estimated adoption of i-mode in period *t+1*

$$E\left[U_{i,t}^{INE}\right] = sub \cdot \left(\left(u_{i-mode,i}^{N} - c_{i-mode,i}^{N}\right) \cdot B_{i-mode,t-1} - \left(u_{WAP,i}^{N} - c_{WAP,i}^{N}\right) \cdot \left(n - B_{i-mode,t-1}\right)\right)$$

Equation 21: anticipated utility of indirect network effects in period *t*

The calculus of decision of a risk-neutral agent i in period t depends on the estimated total benefit $E\left[U_{i-mode,i,t}\right]$. If the benefit is >0, then agent i will adopt an i-mode-capable cellular phone. Each agent can decide once per month (i.e. per period). The calculus of adoption is:

$$E\left[U_{i-mode,i,t}\right] = -K + \sum_{j \in NB_i}\left(nu_{ij}^{D} \cdot p_{ijt}\right) + E\left[U_{i,t}^{INE}\right]$$

Equation 22: overall calculus of adoption for i-mode

Provider strategies: MSPs are able to determine different parameters which drive or inhibit the diffusion of i-mode in the network. They can influence cost and utility parameters by setting prices or mobile services features to distinguish them from WAP to raise the net benefits from direct and indirect network effects. Consequently, MSPs often provide content or services implemented as a virtual base to generate indirect network effects to attract adopters even without an established installed base of users.

Table 24: Analyzed strategy set for mobile service providers to lock-in users

	Benefit drivers		
	Stand alone	Direct network effects	Indirect network effects
Technology	Implementing any stand-alone functionality in the i-mode browser (or in the device by product bundling)	Increasing marginal utility of switching to i-mode (u_{ij}^{D}), e.g., increasing message capacity for images or movies	Increasing marginal utility of switching to i-mode ($u_{i-mode,i}^{N}$), e.g., providing unique browsing functionalities
Pricing	Decreasing basic fee	Decreasing costs for inter-customer communication (c_{ij}^{D})	Decreasing prices for using content and services ($c_{i-mode,i}^{N}$)
Subsidizing		Subsidizing messages (e.g., offering a number of free messages per month)	Subsidizing content and service providers to establish a virtual base (*VB*)

One possible strategy for generating such a virtual base is to subsidize content and service providers in early periods of market penetration. Due to the close relation between provision of content and services on the one hand and the number of i-mode users on the other hand, eligible adopters will use the virtual base as estimator for prospective indirect network effects. A dominant MSP strategy is therefore to signal the hopefully increasing indirect network effect benefits in the future by implementing a virtual base *VB* previous to the market launch. A *VB* = 100 means that an MSP subsidizes content providers as a virtual base, corresponding to a real existing adopters' network of 100 users, i.e. the amount of the subsidy corresponds to the revenue which the content provider would get from 100 users. Having such a subsidized number of content providers in place, a potential adopter can take *VB* into her adoption decision.

Implementation: The model is implemented in Java 1.4. The parameters used in the simulations are chosen in a conservative way with regard to the application case discussed. 1,000 agents are defined as the network population n. This is a relatively small population compared to the large number of cellular phone users, but a necessary limitation for better performance of the model. The substitution rate is $sub_i = 1.0$ $\forall i$, as defined above. The density of the network topology is assumed to be $nb_i = 5$ $\forall i$ (that means that agent *i* has 5 direct neighbors, i.e. communication partners). As mentioned before, the monthly fixed fee is set to € 5.- for all actors. The net benefit expectations for direct and indirect network effects are assumed to be normally distributed. The expectation varies in the ranges provided by to equations 21 and 22, while the variation coefficient is a constant 0.2 for all parameters.

The expectation varies for direct network benefits in the ranges between $\mu(nu_{ij}^D) = [0.5; \ 2.0]$ and for indirect network benefits (for i-mode and WAP) $\mu(nu_{i-mode,i}^N) = [0.004; 0.35]$ $\mu(nu_{WAP,i}^N) = [0.003; 0.35]$, respectively, while the variation coefficient is a constant 0.2 for all parameters.

During the simulation runs, the parameter values are varied in incremental steps of 0.1 (nu^D) and 0.02 (nu^N) allowing a (ceteris paribus) sensitivity analysis. The virtual base *VB* was varied from 0 to 200 during the different simulation runs and existed only in the first period (i.e. content providers were only subsidized in the first period). Each simulation run represents one mobile communication network. Having generated the close network topology, the agents' behavior as modeled above is simulated over multiple periods until a stationary state is reached (i.e. no more adoption or switching activities). The total number of simulation runs conducted was 19,607.

6.1.5 Mobile Network Simulation Analysis

The results presented in this section are structured as follows: the first step is to analyze what circumstances (combinations of different levels of net benefits from direct and indirect network effects) lead to the adoption or not i-mode. In the latter case, we analyze whether if a virtual base can "heal" this start-up problem from the MSP's perspective. The second part will focus on a single simulation run to analyze and to visualize the impact of the network effect helix. The last section investigates the duration of the adoption process and the VB's influence on it.

Direct and indirect network effects and the emergence of i-mode networks: The first simulation results presented in Figure 24 depict the number of i-mode adopters at stationary state (stable equilibrium in the period after the last adoption activities). During the simulation, the expectations concerning the normally distributed direct and indirect additional benefits nu_{ij}^D, $nu_{WAP,i}^N$, $nu_{i-mode,i}^N$ were varied while $nu_{i-mode,i}^N$ had to be greater than $nu_{WAP,i}^N$. Further, the simulations were conducted for different levels of VB.

In the following, variations of all possible set screws of the MSP (costs and benefits resulting from technical features influencing direct or indirect network effects, as well as subsidizing content providers) are captured by the simulations. The results directly depend on the expectations of net benefit nu_{ij}^D and $\Delta nu_i^N = nu_{i-mode,i}^N - nu_{WAP,i}^N$ which represent the two independent dimensions in figure 1. Note that the transformation to Δnu_i^N is only possible if sub_i equals 1 for every agent i.

In Figure 24, each data spot represents the result of a single simulation run. In a basic simulation with a virtual base $VB = 0$, two main sections and a small interfacial area can be identified. In the lower section, nobody adopts i-mode. The results are only slightly influenced by indirect network effects. on the other hand, if the direct network effect parameter $E[nu_{ij}^D]$ is greater than 1.6, the network will be completely equipped with i-mode capable cellular phones. The most interesting region is the interfacial area around $E\left[nu_{ij}^{D}\right]=\left[1.5\right]$. Here, the typical dilemma known from standardization research appears, i.e. the start-up problem (penguin effect (Farrell et al. 1986)) or tippy networks (Shapiro et al. 1998). In this area, the frequency of mixed solutions (i.e. an only partial market penetration by i-mode where only some agents adopt i-mode) is highest. These mixed solutions have a maximum of 226 i-mode users in the stationary state; more adopters will lead to tipping of the whole user base to the i-mode network.

Figure 24: Number of i-mode users in the stationary state, depending on the net benefit parameters

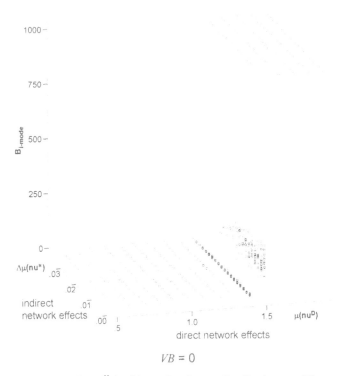

$$VB = 0$$

The influence of Δnu_i^N in this region forces the tippiness of the network (Arthur 1989; Besen et al. 1994; Shapiro et al. 1998), which means that an increase of Δnu_i^N does not increase the number of i-mode adopters ($B_{i\text{-mode}}$) in mixed networks, but rather enforces the shift towards an i-mode monopoly. Due to the low variance of marginal benefits (mostly representing the homogenous interests of network participants), only a few mixed networks occur. For a sensitivity analysis, the variation coefficient was raised from 0.2 to 0.4, covering the larger heterogeneity of individual utility parameters which i-mode users might perceive in reality. As a result, the percentage of oligopoly solutions (mixed networks, see (Weitzel 2004, pp. 127-150) increases by factor 1.12, i.e. the simulation results react quite insensitively to varying the variance parameters.

If the MSP supports a virtual base, further diffusion activities are possible as displayed in the middle and right part of Figure 25. By implementing a virtual base of VB to 200, the network switches completely to i-mode, even if the benefit from direct network effects is marginal ($E[nu_{ij}^{D}] \rightarrow 0.0$) while the indirect network effects are sizeable. In contrast to a market rollout of i-mode without an installed VB, where direct network effects are responsible for the market penetration, a pivotal element for the successful diffusion of i-mode with VB are the indirect network effect benefits of WAP ($nu_{WAP,i}^{N}$) as shown in Figure 26 with $nu_{WAP,i}^{N}$, $nu_{i\text{-}mode,i}^{N}$ and nu_{ij}^{D} as decision variables of potential i-mode adopters.

Figure 25: Number of i-mode users in the stationary state, depending on the net benefit parameters for different sizes of virtual bases VB

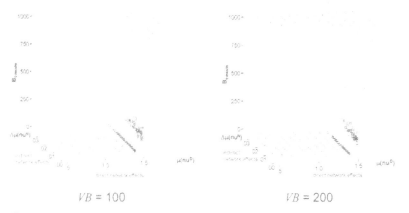

In Figure 26, the scatter plots provide all parameter constellations of $nu_{WAP,i}^{N}$, $nu_{i\text{-}mode,i}^{N}$ and nu_{ij}^{D} which lead to a complete adoption of i-mode under a certain parameterization for different VB.

Consequently, the overlapping areas in Figure 25 for $\Delta nu_i^N = [0.02, 0.03]$ are caused by different levels of $nu_{WAP,i}^N$: the higher the indirect network effects benefit resulting from the use of WAP, the less likely it is that users of WAP will adopt i-mode, although their benefit would also increase with i-mode.

Figure 26: Parameter constellations, leading to a network-wide adoption of i-mode

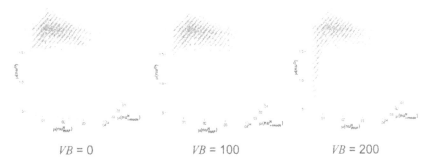

$$VB = 0 \qquad\qquad VB = 100 \qquad\qquad VB = 200$$

By combining the direct (bidirectional data communication) and indirect (service and content, provided upfront as VB) network effect benefits in one diagram (Figure 27), an MSP can choose which set screws have to be adjusted to reach a certain level of i-mode diffusion. Each frequency level can be seen as the combinations of nu_{ij}^D and VB (isoquants) which may substitute each other on the same isoquant (as a range for MSPs to choose their strategy, aiming at a certain level of market penetration) to switch a WAP network into an i-mode network.

Figure 27: Relative frequency of i-mode networks for different VB and direct network effects

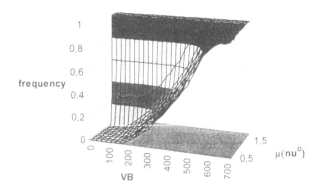

The analysis allows a clear insight into the interdependent impact of the different set screws on i-mode market penetration. Without subsidizing any content providers, the direct effects are the only force available to launch the diffusion process, while indirect network effects help to ensure market penetration. By using the subsidizing strategy ($VB > 0$) the MSP will increase the importance of indirect network effects which can partly substitute the impact of direct network effects. The substitution rate between the impact of direct and indirect network effects in the stationary state is moderated by the level of the initial virtual base.

User view of adoption process and network effect helix: In the following, we focus on particular simulation runs to investigate the role and interplay of direct and indirect effects on an agent's adoption behavior from a potential user view over time.

Figure 28 provides two exemplary diffusion paths over time, which lead to different results based on almost identical parameterizations.

In the left scenario, the network switches completely to i-mode, while in the right scenario (where Δnu_i^N is slightly lower), an oligopolistic equilibrium appears, although the diffusion process is almost identical for the first 20 periods. The differences are caused by some marginal deviations in the local adoption behavior. They are consistent with (Arthur 1989) who discovers micro-behavior leading to unpredictable system behavior in the presence of network effects.

Figure 28: Diffusion process of i-mode vs. WAP ($VB = 0$ in both cases)

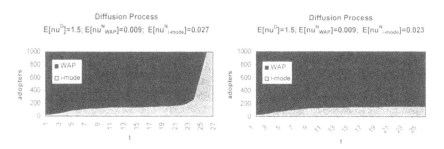

The diagrams in Figure 29 illustrate the average expected user benefit (neglecting setup costs), based on direct and indirect network effects ($E[U_i^{INE}]$), visualizing the network effect helix character.

Figure 29: Diffusion process and progression of net benefit, based on direct an indirect network effects for an exemplary parameterization with _VB_ = 0 (left) and _VB_ = 100 (right)

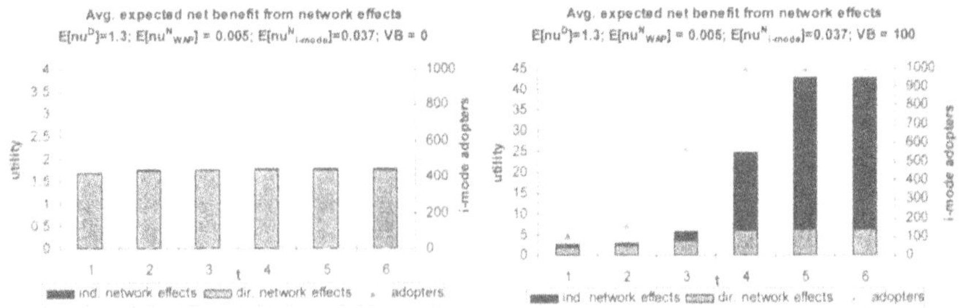

The left diagram depicts a scenario with _VB_=0, while in the right scenario the diffusion process is driven by a virtual base of 100. In the first case, the diffusion process is only driven by the expected direct network benefits, which are not strong enough to establish i-mode network-wide, but only among 16 i-mode adopters. In the second case, the virtual base is responsible for immediately accessible indirect network effects, high enough to trigger a network-wide diffusion process. In the second period, the estimated indirect network effects decrease because some agents assume that content providers will leave the market after they end the subsidies in the second period. This contradictory effect can be overcompensated by increasing direct effects, which again push the indirect network effects $E\left[U_i^{INE}\right]$ in the following periods. Nevertheless, the stationary state is reached after five periods. Different network effects may have different impacts (in strength and direction) on the diffusion behavior, which should be reconsidered and structurally analyzed by MSPs when developing pricing strategies.

Network topology and diffusion duration: After determining the strategic importance of direct and indirect network effects during the market introduction of new mobile communication standards, the question of how the network topology influences the duration of such a market rollout t_{stat} now has to be answered. Assuming the periods to be months, the diffusion process needs quite a long time in only a few cases (see Figure 30), depending on the variation of coefficient and disregarding existing diffusion time lags in reality.

For $E\left[nu_{ij}^D\right] \approx 1.5$ the simulations need the most processing time, up to 28 periods. Interestingly, even in these cases the duration can only be reduced marginally by increasing the virtual base *VB*, as shown in the right diagram of Figure 30 for *VB*=200.

Figure 30: Diffusion process and progression of net benefit, based on direct and indirect network effects for an exemplary parameterization with VB = 0 (left) and VB = 200 (right)

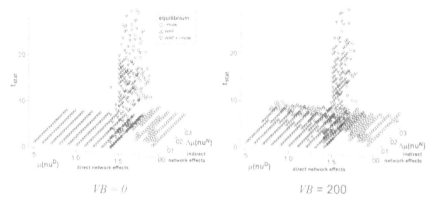

The direct network effect benefits nu_{ij}^D show the most important impact on the diffusion duration t_{stat}. The virtual base *VB* only influences the velocity of the diffusion process in the area around nu_{ij}^D =1.5, while the indirect network effects Δnu_i^N have no significant impact on the duration of the diffusion process. In order to provide a complete view, Figure 31 finally presents the average t_{stat} for all combinations of nu_{ij}^D and VB.

Figure 31: Average t$_{stat}$ for different combinations of VB and direct network effects

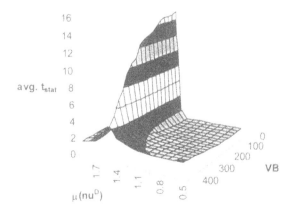

In this section, the simulation approach was able to reveal the relations between (a) direct and indirect network effects on the path of diffusion, (b) the user view and its influence on the diffusion process, and (c) the network topology and its impact on the diffusion duration. In the following, the implications and possible MSP strategies based on these results will be discussed.

6.1.6   Implications for the Diffusion of i-mode

Using the standards battle between WAP and i-mode for establishing a network of mobile service users, the significant influence of direct network effects (communication) is often neglected in early diffusion stages and their dynamic interplay with indirect effects (content provisioning) is not analyzed systematically. If a new standard, like i-mode, has not reached the critical mass of adopters in the early phase of market introduction, then the probability increases that the standard cannot be established on the market at all. Based on the network effect helix model, the simulation model shows that to reach this critical mass, the MSP has to consider the changing ratio and magnitude of direct and indirect network effects. In addition to the conventional wisdom of applying low price strategies for successful market rollouts, equivalent to low communication prices at the beginning until an installed base of users is established, MSPs have to orchestrate the next wave of network growth by focusing on content-based services. This probably fundamental network phenomenon of direct and indirect network effects amplifying the number of adopters and stabilizing the ongoing diffusion process is called *the network effect helix*. By applying the model, MSPs can analyze various diffusion scenarios in order to identify interesting and promising market and price strategies for their planned content and mail services.

When trying to win and exploit new markets, MSP strategies have often focused on strategically promoting content as the main diffusion driver while ignoring the importance of direct network effects (e.g., derived from SMS or i-mail exchange). In fact, as the simulation results have revealed, establishing a subsidized base of service and content providers—even without a single adopter of i-mode in the market—is important for a successful market rollout. On the other hand, the virtual base as strategic instrument loses its strategic importance after the market introduction. At this point, the users' assessment of future direct and indirect network effect benefits predominates. While indirect network effects certainly are of great importance for the ongoing diffusion process, the possibility of direct bidirectional communication (direct network effect) is at least as important as an initial subsidized base of service providers. In the case of the i-mode launch in Germany, the MSP offered around 70 service and content providers as *VB*. Due to the unsatisfying adoption rate of i-mode in the early phase, the MSP reduced the price for i-mail (as source of direct network effects) significantly. Afterwards, the initially slow diffusion process accelerated in 2004 quadrupling the number of i-mode subscribers in Germany from 191,000 to 855,000. The changed market strategy was apparently highly effective in penetrating the mobile market.

Despite the fact that it was only a coincidence that the MSP acted according to these research results, it validates (to a certain degree) the explanatory power of the simulation model. Further important factors such as market heterogeneity, users' risk preferences, or type of diffusion function will be incorporated in the model as part of future research.

The model may also provide valuable insights for analyzing the stability of lock-in effects, i.e. how many parameters (such as costs) can be altered by the MSP until the network switches back to WAP or to a new standard. This is especially interesting, since the MSP providing i-mode in Germany has announced that they will use the i-mode platform as the basis of future 3rd-generation services and content. At the same time, an MSP competitor announced the introduction of i-mode in 2006 in Germany to serve its UMTS customers. The use of an installed i-mode network as a pre-installed network of potential UMTS adopters is of strategic importance for MSPs to enable them to carry out inter-temporal pricing strategies.

The main contribution of this research is thus to provide strategic decision support or building blocks towards a better and systematic understanding of the dynamics of value drivers in networks. The model and the simulation software can support the development and evaluation of mobile service networks and thus contributes to establishing a networked infrastructure in a variety of domains, as the adaptation of the model on the EDI market in the following section demonstrates.

6.2 Application of Network Effect Theory to Developing an EDI Network

The diffusion of standards such as electronic data interchange (EDI) among small and medium sized enterprises (SMEs) seems to be one of the most challenging tasks in the history of information technology adoption (Chen et al. 1998; Ketler et al. 1997). While traditional EDI among large enterprises has been discussed for decades in the context of efficiency potentials and costs savings from standardization, it has been almost impossible to incorporate SMEs into electronic supply chain networks (Iacovou et al. 1995). The main reasons discussed in literature are the high setup and maintenance costs for EDI, as well as the frequent lack of IT know-how among SMEs (Beck et al. 2003d), as an overview of EDI adoption studies among SMEs suggested (Chau et al. 2001). Another important reason is that EDI-standards were traditionally designed to serve high data traffic among large enterprises, focused on the reduction of external communication costs in data transfer. Therefore the EDI adoption decision for large enterprises, which focuses on compatibility, is less difficult as long as their large business partners also use the same EDI standards (Bendoly et al. 2003).

In this section, it is argued that focusing on all benefits accompanying EDI rather than focusing on pecuniarily measurable costs can improve the understanding of EDI and its overall impact on adopters. By the systematic application of network effect theory to the analysis of EDI diffusion, the sources of benefit which are responsible for the adoption decision can be revealed. More precisely, the dynamic interplay between direct and indirect network effects is described, associated with the adoption and use of EDI in a single diffusion model. In doing so, it can be shown that the absence of stand-alone benefits in the context of communication standards must be compensated for start the diffusion process in order to exceed the necessary critical mass of network participants. It is demonstrated that both forms of network effects contribute dynamically to the overall value of a network during the diffusion process. Thus, the goal of this contribution is to elaborate on the dynamic interplay of direct and indirect network effects during the diffusion of communication standards, as exemplified by the diffusion of EDI.

Dealing with the diffusion of EDI as an example is not merely a retrospective way of discussing important standards of the past in the presence of XML-related standards. To define it precisely, EDI is "the interorganizational, computer-to-computer exchange of business documentation in a standard and machine-processable format" (Emmelhainz 1993). This definition includes all kinds of EDI varieties such as traditional EDI, EDI-over-the-Internet, or XML-based EDI. Therefore, even new forms of e-business "languages" or standards are confronted with the same old diffusion problem that can be observed for EDI.

In the following, it will be shown how direct and indirect network effects can cause critical mass and inertia phenomena, while at the same time providing the main value source for the standardization decision. In the context of EDI communication, direct network effects are based on the direct interchange of data among business partners in an industry, while indirect network effects result from the internal use of article and price master data available from industry-specific data pools.

The results will help one to develop improved strategies which are capable of incorporating SMEs in electronic communication networks as well. The critical discourse on network effect theory allows us to derive an EDI diffusion model, which is applied as a simulation model based on empirical data from a survey among small retailers and large industrial suppliers in the German office supply industry.

6.2.1   Network Behavior under Network Effects: the Start-up Problem

The basic pattern of argument in network effect theory is that the discrepancy between private and collective gains in networks with increasing returns may possibly lead to Pareto-inferior results. With incomplete information about other agents' preferences, *excess inertia* ("start-up problem") can occur, as no agent is willing to bear the disproportionate risk of being stranded with his adopted standard in a too small network if other market participants eventually decide in favor of another standard. Such inferior standards cannot establish a network of users since a *critical mass* cannot be reached. If potential adopters are anticipating only a small network of users, it is difficult for new standards to overcome the *start-up problem*, even if the standard might be preferred by everyone, as Arthur (Arthur 1989) notes in his instructive presentation of the battle between two standards.

More information-systems-related approaches analyze the start-up and diffusion of communication standards with network effects by using social science concepts such as social coherence or closeness. Relational closeness between agents in a social system is analyzed by using neural networks simulating a population of agents (Plouraboue et al. 1998) or stochastic simulations (Wendt et al. 2000) analyzing the patterns of diffusion for standards. Where communication between agents or experiences and learning effects with standards are important for the adoption decision, the so-called first-mover-advantage (see, e.g., Hawkins et al. 1999, p. 84) for early standards diminishes if the establishing of an installed base of users due to increasing network effects is important (Katz et al. 1985). Plouraboue et al. (Plouraboue et al. 1998) argue that an early innovation can start a learning process but not necessarily the adoption process itself. After a certain time lag, depending on the structure of the agent network (the number of relations and the intensity of communication), another standard or second-mover might take over the market. Consequently, the diffusion of a network-constituting standard does not necessarily depend on a few early innovators or opinion leaders, but on the experienced maturity or benefit accompanying the adoption of a new technology recognized by a larger group of agents in the same industry or market.

A general coordination problem emerges if not all agents can benefit from a standard in the same way, especially if the private adoption costs for some agents are higher than their individual benefit. This can be the case, if only a fraction of the market adopts the "right" standard which means that the critical mass cannot be reached to gain the full benefit from network effects (David et al. 1990). Farrell and Saloner (Farrell et al. 1986) analyze the underlying coordination problem: only with complete information and only if all agents have the same assessment of the success of a new standard is everyone better off when switching to the new standard. Then the increasing number of agents in the network will start the *bandwagon* process (Rohlfs 2003). The idea is that in anticipation of others' behavior every agent will adopt the new technology, starting with those with the highest private utility. Especially when compared to situations with incomplete information and heterogeneous preferences, Farrell and Saloner emphasize the influence of early standard adopters on the decision calculus of later adopters. A pivotal finding is that uncertainty about other agents' preferences (utility function) can result in excess inertia for early adopters who bear a disproportionate share of "transient incompatibility costs" (Farrell et al. 1985; Farrell et al. 1986). Regardless of others' preferences, there is no incentive to any individual agent to start the bandwagon by himself. This phenomenon is also called the penguin effect in network effect theory: "Penguins who must enter the water to find food often delay doing so because they fear the presence of predators. Each would prefer some other penguin to test the waters first" (Farrell et al. 1986, p. 943).

The original model of Katz and Shapiro (Katz et al. 1985) also shows lock-in effects when expectations are important, because there is a tendency to self-fulfillment. Excess inertia can occur if there is an installed base, even though there may be complete information (Farrell et al. 1986). Generally, the excess inertia property of network effect goods is emphasized by authors stressing the public goods character of standards, which implies that user groups are too small, compared to the collective use of the standard.

6.2.2   Extending the Basic View of Network Effects

The literature on network effect theory offers a collection of phenomena, such as the start-up problem in particular, to explain certain patterns of standard dif-fusion. Based on these findings, there are discussions about whether network effects increase without limit and what remedies to the problems identified are possible. Most notably, if network effects are exhaustible, or if the costs of building a standardized network increase faster than the benefits, there can also be other efficient solutions characterized by the coexistence of multiple standards, thereby eliminating a monopolistic situation (all agents using the same standard) as the only possible efficient solution. For a critical discussion of traditional network effect theory see (Liebowitz et al. 1994a; Liebowitz et al. 1995b; Liebowitz et al. 1995c; Margolis et al. 1998; Weitzel et al. 2000a). In the following, some possible extensions to the basic view of network effects will be analyzed by incorporating the possibility of non-linear value develop-ment based on (a) the costs of network size, (b) the dynamic interplay be-tween direct and indirect network effects, and (c) the impact of heterogeneous preferences on the standardizing agents.

Costs of network size: Communication standards as part of a special form of information goods are characterized by large fixed costs of production (or first-copy costs), but small variable costs of reproduction (Varian 1997). Therefore networks based on communication standards tend to have high up-front and low variable costs (Mauboussin et al. 2000). Additionally, the proposition of indefinitely increasing positive network effects as described in the literature (e.g. (Chou et al. 1996; Farrell et al. 1992a; Katz et al. 1986a; Katz et al. 1986b) implies natural monopolies. Fixed costs, together with constant marginal costs, lead to an inexhaustible economy of large-scale operations. This, in turn, installs an externality if goods are priced at average costs (Liebowitz et al. 1995a).

If optimal networks under network externalities should include the whole population (monopolies), then all networks are too small. If network effects were exhaustible, then multiple efficient networks could coexist. Even though IT might be less subject to the physical limitations that accompany the law of diminishing returns, there might be organizational or managerial problems restraining an optimal network size (Radner 1992). This phenomenon has long been discussed in competition and allocation theories, asking whether diseconomies deriving from sub-additive production functions, organizational complexity costs or increasing costs of market exploitation restrict optimal firm size. This implies a U-shaped development of the (long-term) cost curve. Even if these diseconomies can be reduced by diversification or economies of scope, it is unlikely that they can be reduced in a way that would lead to L-shaped cost curves implying a minimal efficient network size but not a solely efficient monopoly. Thus, the importance shifts from the size of networks to optimal networks. In the context of developing EDI networks, the important result is that the existence of network effects is not sufficient for natural-monopoly-type results, since the average network generation costs are not zero and the mean costs of adding new members are not necessarily constant or falling. However, these costs are largely ignored in the literature on network effects, and most models assume (sometimes implicitly) constant marginal costs of network size with endlessly increasing network effects. Thus, network effects are not sufficient for natural monopoly and one single standard is not a compulsory social optimum. Instead, there can be optimal network sizes below the entire population and different standards can coexist. This finding will be further discussed and applied in the context of EDI diffusion among SMEs, based on the explicit modeling of direct and indirect network effects.

Using the historical debate on externalities, (Liebowitz et al. 1995c) argue that the importance of increasing returns is largely based on anecdotes and suffers from confusing movements along cost curves with movements of cost curves (see also (Ellis et al. 1943; Stigler 1941). One example is the interpretation of the coincidence of (first) enormous price declines and (second) tremendous growths in sales as in the VCR, PC or cellular phone markets. One reason could be increasing returns: bigger is cheaper. Another reason could be technological advances over time shifting the average cost curve downwards. They extend their argument to modern software and find that although it is said to be knowledge-based, with high upfront fixed costs and very small and constant costs per unit sold (even zero) (and thereby indefinitely falling average costs while output increases), a major part of the real costs is not fixed but variable, e.g., all service and sales costs. That is why they expect even software markets to exhibit U-shaped cost curves: with increasing output, the decrease in average fixed costs decreases itself, and is more than set off by increases in (average) variable costs due to management, service, and individualization complexity, among other things.

Direct vs. indirect network effects: The economic impact of direct and indirect effects can vary substantially, contributing to the hypothesis that the value of standardization consists of several elements that need to be understood in their compound dynamic value creation. The distinction between direct and indirect network effects (as introduced by (Katz et al. 1985)) is almost commonplace in the introductions to articles about standards. However, there is very little consideration of these differences in the models. But indirect network externalities may have different economic implications (Katz et al. 1994). One possible reason is that indirect network effects are often pecuniary externalities and therefore should not be internalized (Ellis et al. 1943; Knight 1924; Young 1913): "Indirect network externalities thus appear to be either pecuniary externalities, which require no remediation, or the reflection of conventional market failures in upstream markets" (Liebowitz et al. 1995a). Empirical research shows that direct and indirect network effects are evaluated differently by potential buyers depending on the category of the network effect product. Nevertheless, the distinction has not been adopted in the models, adding to the vagueness of their results. Indirect network effects are very hard to internalize in terms of the many transactions required between all network participants. The simulation model contributes to this research field by explicitly evaluating the changing impact of direct and indirect network effects over time and diffusion process where indirect network effects can not in fact be internalized on a pecuniary basis.

Positive externalities do not always stem from network effects and can emerge simply in prospering markets: Car sellers attract customers, who thus attract more sellers with more varieties of cars, which in return attract more customers. Such two-sided market relations are not characterized by externalities or interactions within the adopter network. Unfortunately, the confusion is pre-assigned if even in network effect theory literature authors confuse common economy of scale and growing demand driven positive feedbacks with network effect externalities. This is the case for Rysman's work on the market for yellow pages, where he describes a simple vertical relation between firms advertising in yellow pages and customers using them (Rysman 2004). According to Economides and White (Economides et al. 1996), one-way networks are indirect networks lacking the reciprocal characteristic of direct networks and are produced for the anonymous market, where customers or nodes cannot be identified.

Heterogeneous preferences and critical mass: Network markets are generally considered to be *tippy*: "When two or more firms compete for a market where there is strong positive feedback, only one may emerge as a winner. Economists say that such a market is tippy, meaning that it can tip in favor of one player or another depending on the different preferences of market participants. It is unlikely that all will survive" (Shapiro et al. 1998, p.176). Hence, the coexistence of incompatible products may be unstable, with a single winning standard dominating the market (Besen et al. 1994). An often-cited example is the battle between VHS and Beta videocassette recorders.

Besen and Farrell (Besen et al. 1994) emphasize the role of expectations about ultimate network size for rapid tipping. Compatibility is an important action variable, especially for firms producing products with network effect properties. If the market "tips" in favor of the firm's product or standard, it will benefit from a most favorable monopolistic market position. On the other hand, fierce competition (before tipping) might be costly, and competitors could agree on standardization, exchanging inter- for intra-technological competition.

Closely related to tipping is the observation of a critical mass of users (due to high fixed upfront costs and positive network effects) that determines when markets tip (Oren et al. 1981). A very early contribution identifying critical mass phenomena as part of a formal analysis of the observation that the value of telecommunications services to a user largely depends on the number of other subscribers is provided by Rohlfs (Rohlfs 1974), sometimes cited as the origin of network economics. This is often called the chicken and egg paradox: "...many consumers are not interested in purchasing the good because the installed base is too small, and the installed base is too small because an insufficiently small number of consumers have purchased the good" (Economides et al. 1995b).

Bridging the argument of exhaustive network effects and threshold phenomena, we propose to model the standardization value, considering an increasing but in parts exhaustive value development. Analogously, Hayashi (Hayashi 1992) introduces the concept of a "second critical mass" that causes network effects to become negative when a certain number of network participants is reached because of complexity costs and increased power of the network owner.

6.2.3 Standards in Corporate Reality: EDI

In an EDI relationship among business partners, the structure of benefit distribution, based on the ability to exchange information and on the advent of having access to current data and processing this data in-house, is often neglected (Beck et al. 2003d). These pivotal elements of benefits are asymmetrically distributed between large EDI-deploying enterprises or champions (in the office supply industry, the suppliers) and their smaller, EDI-using business partners (retailers). Often, the return on investment in an EDI infrastructure is only calculated by the reduction of information transmission costs, forgetting that small firms will hardly reach a level of EDI use that will justify its implementation (see (Suzuki et al. 1998; Williams et al. 1998) for a multidimensional EDI evaluation). In general, small firms have not enough order, invoice or logistic messages to justify the high setup costs, or even lack the ability to process EDI data (Iacovou et al. 1995). On the other hand, they also need proper data to run their business accurately as urgently as large firms do for their enterprise resource planning (ERP) or material management system (MMS). The gap in interest between large firms and SMEs is based on different goals, namely the use of EDI to reduce costs and increase efficiency for EDI champions versus the business process improvements derived from storing permanent data in ERP or MMS systems to increase the efficiency of SMEs. These inconsistent goals have led to EDI standards and diffusion models mainly dominated by large firms ignoring the special interests of SMEs, leading to the premature diffusion and use situation of EDI among SMEs today.

The direct and indirect effects of EDI have been modeled in prior research as important sources of benefit from EDI (see (Iacovou et al. 1995; Lee et al. 1999). This research adapts these models and focuses on the direct and indirect effects from the network effect theory point of view. While direct network effect models are largely discussed to examine the effects of compatibility and competition, as well as incentives for standardization (Farrell et al. 1988a; Farrell et al. 1985; Farrell et al. 1992c; Katz et al. 1985), there has been little research dealing specifically with indirect network effects such as that by Church and Gandal (Church et al. 1992) or Chou and Shy (Chou et al. 1996). An evaluation of both network effects is provided by Clements (Clements 2002; Clements 2004).

For the following simulation model, it is assumed that the value of EDI for each network participant increases with each new adopter of the same EDI standard. In general, an EDI network is not owned by a single firm and not sponsored or dominated (of course, there might be strong players inside an industry forcing smaller ones to adopt "their" EDI standards, but the network itself is not owned, unlike a telephone network). Therefore, it is impossible to make a central decision to adopt a single industry-wide standard. Even for rationally acting enterprises, it seems to be difficult to estimate the diffusion of a standard based on uncertain and incomplete information. Consequently, the risk of being stranded as the only user of a new communication standard is high. To simplify the decision dilemma, a new standard should comprise enough intrinsic incentives to attract adopters. One possible solution is to "enrich" a new technology or standard with enough stand-alone benefits so adopters can gain at least some use from the product in a not yet existing network, e.g., using the FAX machine as a copier. Nevertheless, what is the stand-alone benefit of an EDI-system?

6.2.4   Simulating the Diffusion of EDI

Conforming with the literature, for the following simulation model it is assumed that the value of EDI for each network participant increases with each new adopter of the same EDI standard. In general, an EDI network is not owned by a single firm; of course, there might be strong industry players forcing smaller ones to adopt "their" EDI standards, but the network itself is not owned (i.e. it is unsponsored (Arthur 1983; David et al. 1990)). Since no one is in possession of property rights in the standard at issue, well-known internalization strategies based on, e.g., penetration pricing are not easily available. As a consequence, the adoption decision largely depends on the prospective user's expectation about the standard adoption behavior of peers (Weitzel et al. 2003a). However, even for rationally acting enterprises it is difficult to estimate the diffusion of a standard when relying on uncertain and incomplete information. Consequently, the risk of being stranded as the only user of a new communication standard is high, resulting in the notorious start-up problem. Ideally, a new standard intending to win the market should include enough intrinsic incentives to attract adopters. One possible solution is to "enrich" a new technology or standard with enough quasi stand-alone benefits to overcome some initial adoption thresholds. An instructive example is using the fax machine as a copier. Since we expect indirect network effects in an EDI network that are largely undiscovered at the moment, the following question arises: what are the indirect network effect benefits of an EDI-system and how can they contribute to overcoming the start-up problem together with direct network effects?

Based on the critical discussion of network effect theory in the previous section, in the following the findings are aggregated by combining the considerations of direct and indirect network effects into a single model of EDI diffusion. In doing so, the structural development of the utility components on a micro level and the character and speed of the EDI diffusion on a macro-level can be derived. The resulting welfare benefits strongly depend on the network topology and the communication preferences of each adopter (Wendt et al. 2000).

Based on an empirical survey conducted among retailers and industry partners in the office supply industry in 2000, we distinguish between i independent SME retailers as potential EDI users and j suppliers as large EDI-using enterprises. The German office supply industry is a relatively small part of the retail/wholesale and distribution industry in Germany. The size and the market structure with its large number of SMEs are not the ideal pre-condition for a successful EDI network. With more than 95% SMEs on the retail side, a standardized electronic communication seems to be a difficult venture, as countless unsuccessful approaches in this industry have demonstrated. For the following model, the office supply industry was chosen since the special topology and the history of unsuccessful and successful EDI approaches to integrating SMEs provided an ideal setting for analyzing the assumed network dynamics. Furthermore, in this industry sector an intermediary was established to endorse the UN/EDIFACT subset EANCOM as EDI communication standard, to provide subsidies for SMEs, and to accelerate the diffusion of EDI among 9048 SMEs known in this sector. For the importance of intermediaries as EDI-enablers or door-openers see (Damsgaard et al. 2001).

Setup and maintenance costs: The dominant communication channel in the absence of EDI is the use of fax machines, as a survey conducted in the German office supply industry in 2000 revealed. If SMEs decide to use the EDI standard offered, adopters will have to invest at least in software for the EDI converter. The EDI software for Windows based systems is available for € 1,990. - in the office supply industry for SMEs. Apart from these setup costs, monthly software maintenance fees of € 25. - accrue (15% of the setup costs), as well as monthly service fees of € 40. - for the EANCOM system. For participation in an EANCOM network, an International Location Number (ILN) for each EDI user is necessary for identification reasons (5.40 €/month). Altogether, EDI readiness costs a monthly base fee of € 70.40. According to the survey, on the supplier side, there are 173 large industry partners which have to invest on average € 30,500. - in EDI converter software with monthly maintenance costs of approximately € 5,250.-.

Each SME or agent *i* has to decide whether to transmit orders by fax or to shift by adopting the EDI solution offered. Due to bounded and dynamically adapted information sets, agents will make their EDI adoption decision mainly based on the past technology adoption decisions of their direct business partners and assessment of their future adoption behavior. To benefit from EDI, adopting agents use the possibility of exchanging data actively with their business partners (suppliers). SMEs and suppliers are able to decide anew for or against EDI in each period. According to the bounded and dynamically adapted information available from past technology adoption decisions of i's competitors and suppliers j an SME retailer can adopt EDI in one period and drop it in the next.

The calculus of decision of each retailer is to evaluate the benefit surplus using EDI in comparison to traditional order methods or more abstractly, to estimate the net value of using the standard given the individual preferences and available information.

Direct network effects: Due to the use of electronic messages and depending on the number of orders, the EDI adopter i gains more benefits when communicating with EDI-capable partners j in comparison to fax. Until the critical mass of orders necessary to justify the use of an EDI converter is reached, the use of fax is more effective. Therefore, the EDI standardization or diffusion dilemma among SMEs (a substantial start-up problem) is primarily based on a shortage of sufficient EDI messages.

According to the survey, a typical small retailer sells directly to end-customers and therefore cannot gain benefits from additional EDI transfers on the customer-side. Therefore, only outgoing orders and incoming price and product data, as well as invoices, can be taken into account for the decision whether or not to adopt EDI. The EDI communication costs depend on the telephone communication costs and the costs for the store-and-forward EDI telebox where the incoming and outgoing EDI messages are stored. Furthermore, a data-transmission-based price has to be paid, depending on the number of kilobytes transferred. According to the survey, at least € 0.26 will be charged for submitting a typical EANCOM order message. In addition to these transaction-based payments, further costs are incurred, such as an annual fee for the EANCOM membership necessary to get the ILN and a monthly fee for the EDI-usage of the office supply industry solution. If an EDI-solution is not installed, the conventional communication channel for ordering is based on fax transmission. The traditional ordering process produces marginal material costs and communication costs of approximately 0.65 €/message (without personnel costs) for using fax. Therefore, switching to EDI saves on average € 0.39 per message. Due to the communication channel, automatic update or data transfer between the MMS and the ERP system of the industry partner is not possible when using fax.

Indirect network effects: With the increasing number of retailers adopting EDI it is more and more beneficial for larger industry partners in this sector to offer not only the ability to exchange messages by EDI, but also to provide standardized and high-quality product data and price data for the central EDI data pool hosted by the intermediary. Unlike direct network effects, the indirect network effects are based on the utilization of the master data pool, comprising all the price and article data of suppliers already deploying EDI in the office supply industry. By the downloading of up-to-date and proved high quality data, a retailer can add it to his MMS system, e.g., to automate price calculation, to improve inventory management, to label prices electronically, to stock online stores with product data and pictures, and to automate cashing with point of sale scanners. These positive indirect benefits of EDI increase with each additional supplier offering standardized master data to the industry data pool which is a strong EDI adoption incentive for retailers.

The simulation model in this contribution describes a unique monotonously declining increase correlation between the diffusion of EDI among SMEs and the additional utility offered by available master data from the data pool. This is equivalent to a still positive but marginally increasing additional benefit with each new set of master data available from the data pool. The intensive use of the master data pool will attract further adopters, accompanied by further network effect benefits. In combination with the steadily increasing number of electronically exchanged orders, and invoices as source of direct network effects, a self-perpetuating network effect helix occurs.

While the individual benefits in the early stage of EDI diffusion—or for SMEs in general—might be negative due to the higher costs of communication in comparison with FAX-based communication, EDI diffusion can also be initiated by positive indirect network benefits. The resulting indirect network effect benefits of a central master data pool per period due to EDI can be defined as a function of all adopting SMEs. Therefore, the diffusion of EDI among SME retailers also depends on the availability of master data provided by the industry partners (e.g., in the automobile industry (Webster 1995) or the European retail sector (Jimenez-Martinez et al. 1998)).

Simulation model: To model the standardization behavior of the SMEs within the office supply industry, the suppliers and their adoption behavior also have to be incorporated. The decision whether or not to adopt EDI is by no means as complex for them in comparison with SME retailers due to the large number of EDI messages on the supplier side. As the survey has revealed, the number of incoming orders as a source of direct network effect benefits justifies the usage of EDI systems even without gaining any benefit from indirect network effects on the supplier side. Consequently, the utility and costs structure of the supplier side is incorporated into the computer-based simulation model, based on the empirical survey in the German office supply industry. For the simulation, an adapted and extended standards diffusion approach is used, which is based on the decentralized standardization model (Weitzel 2004). The necessary parameters for retailers and suppliers can be defined as follows:

N^R = Number of retailers
B_0^R = Number of already EDI capable retailers
B_t^R = Number of EDI capable retailers in period t
i = Retailer index

N^S = Number of suppliers
B_0^S = Number of already EDI capable suppliers
B_t^S = Number of EDI capable suppliers in period t
j = Supplier index

In contrast to a frequently used, fully connected network of n agents and $n(n-1)$ relations, in this model there are only communication edges along the supply chain between retailers and suppliers and not within these clusters. To analyze the impact of direct and indirect network effects on the dynamic adoption process of EDI over time, the multi-period model assumes a monthly time unit t with T for the last simulated period.

Due to the nature of an EDI system, the adoption-relevant parameter values are related to the intensity of EDI interaction, apart from the setup costs, EDI use fees, and maintenance costs. One can distinguish two different states: before an agent (retailer or supplier) has adopted an EDI system (state 1) and after the adoption (state 2). After the implementation of an EDI converter in state 2, the decision whether or not to apply it is reduced to just the costs of maintenance and EDI usage fees (the earlier setup investment in the EDI converter is sunk costs).

k_{it}^{R1} = *Decision relevant stand - alone costs of retailer i in state 1 and period t*

k_{it}^{R2} = *Decision relevant stand - alone costs of retailer i in state 2 and period t*

k_{jt}^{S1} = *Decision relevant stand - alone costs of supplier j in state 1 and period t*

k_{jt}^{S2} = *Decision relevant stand - alone costs of suplier j in state 2 and period t*

In this model, the supply chain has only two levels (retailers and suppliers) and EDI is only used by them to communicate with each other. Switching from fax-based messaging to EDI primarily reduces message processing and handling costs as a source of direct network effects. Starting from an average number of messages transferred between retailer *i* and supplier *j* the transmission costs saved per month can be deduced from the underlying survey.

c_{ijt}^{R} = *Communication savings of retailer i in period t, if i and j use EDI*

c_{jit}^{S} = *Communication savings of supplier j in period t, if i and j use EDI*

These possible positive network effects are bilateral communication-based savings *c* and occur on both sides of the communication link between retailer *i* and supplier *j*.

Indirect network effects are based on the availability of master data. If all EDI-capable suppliers provide their data to the data pool because there are an increasing number of EDI-capable retailers, then the utility is a function of the proportion of EDI-capable retailers compared to the underlying population following a monotonously degressively increasing function.

This is equivalent to the investigated marginally or sub-linear increasing benefit of each new industry partner offering master data to SME retailers (Equation 23):

$$INE_{it} = f\left(\frac{B_t^R}{N^R}\right) = u_{it}^I \cdot \left(\frac{B_{t-1}^R}{N^R}\right)^{\beta} = indirect\ network\ effects\ utility\ for\ retailer\ i\ in\ period\ t$$

Equation 23: indirect network effects utility for retailer *i* in period *t*

with $\dfrac{\delta f}{\delta B_{it}} > 0$ and $\dfrac{\delta f^2}{\delta^2 B_{it}} < 0$

u_{it}^I = individual indirect network utility coefficient of actor i in period t

β = constant parameter with $\beta =]0.0;1.0[$

Simulation procedure: The EDI adoption decision dynamics of the business partners in the German office supply industry are simulated as follows: in the initial period t=0 a network of retailers and suppliers is generated. Each retailer is connected to each supplier by communication links with costs of c_{ijt} and c_{jit} for every period t within the simulation horizon. For each agent the stand-alone costs of EDI for state 1 and 2 and the indirect network effect parameter u_{it}^I have to be determined. Afterwards, a specific number of retailers (B_0^R) and suppliers (B_0^S) will be "pre-equipped" with EDI converter software, based on the survey results. In the following periods, each agent has to decide anew in every period whether or not to use EDI, based on the observed standardization decisions and the expected decision behaviors of its business partners. The standardization model used is an improved decision model (Equation 24) based on previous decentral standardization models (Beck et al. 2003c; Weitzel 2004) with the expected utility of EDI for retailers (that are assumed to be risk neutral):

$$E[U_{it}] = \sum_{j=1}^{J} p_{ijt} \cdot c_{ijt}^R - k_{it}^R + E[INE_{it}]$$

Equation 24: adapted decentral standardization model for retailers

with $k_{it}^R = k_{it}^{R1} \vee k_{it}^R = k_{it}^{R2}$ depending on an already existing EDI-solution. The term $E[INE_{it}]$ is the expected utility deriving from indirect network effects. The probability p_{ij} represents i's anticipation of j's adoption decision. The model assumes that each agent knows the state of every business partner. If the business partner is already utilizing an EDI installation, then p_{ijt} is equivalent to one. If this is not the case, an expectation probability has to be estimated (Equation 25).

$$p_{ijt} = \frac{N_R \cdot c_{jit}^S - k_{jt}^S + E[INE_{jt}]}{N_R \cdot c_{jit}^S}$$

Equation 25: adapted individual standard adoption probability for retailers

Analogous to the utility expectation and probability for the retailers, the corresponding equations of the supplier can be described as follows:

$$E[U_{jt}] = \sum_{i=1}^{I} p_{jit} \cdot c_{jit}^{S} - k_{jt}^{S}$$

Equation 26: adapted decentral standardization model for suppliers

$$p_{jit} = \frac{N_S \cdot c_{ijt}^{R} - k_{it}^{R} + E[INE_{it}]}{N_S \cdot c_{ijt}^{R}}$$

Equation 27: adapted individual standard adoption probability for suppliers

The terms $k_{it}^{R} = k_{it}^{R1} \vee k_{it}^{R} = k_{it}^{R2}$ and $k_{jt}^{S} = k_{jt}^{S1} \vee k_{jt}^{S} = k_{jt}^{S2}$ depend on an already existing EDI solution. Furthermore, the utility function of the supplier does not contain indirect network effects. $E[INE_{it}]$ in the probability function p_{jit} is the expected utility from indirect network effects which agent j believes agent i will benefit from. Based on the expected utility, each agent decides for ($E[U_{it}]$ or $E[U_{jt}] > 0$ respectively) or against ($E[U_{it}]$ or $E[U_{jt}] \leq 0$ respectively) EDI. It is assumed that each supplier has complete information about the partners' INE_{it} function (Equation 23) so they can estimate the INE_{it} value of their business partners by observing the market and inserting the number of EDI-using retailers of the previous period (B_{Rt-1} as restrictive estimator) into the function. This is plausible, because the number of EDI-implementing retailers and suppliers is provided by the EDI intermediary in the office supply industry. Observing the adoption behavior of their environment, a retailer can assume that a supplier using EDI in period t will also use it in period $t+1$ and in consequence can set $p_{ijt+1} = 1$. Although an agent has to install the EDI converter software only once, the decision whether to use EDI or not has to be made anew in every period.

The simulation routine itself is implemented in JAVA 1.4. The underlying values are based on the empirical results of a survey in the German office supply industry conducted by the authors. Table 25 summarizes the parameterization of the model. Simulation-relevant parameters such as stand-alone costs or the number of messages (Table 25) are normally distributed (ND) with μ and σ provided in parentheses. Due to the short amortization duration of three years for EDI converter software the model neglects any discount rates for the EDI investment. The setup costs of € 1,990 for retailers and € 30,500 for suppliers are therefore uniformly distributed over 36 months (model periods), corresponding to a 0% interest rate. The mean of k_{it}^{R1} is formed by € 1990.00/36 + € 25.00 + € 70.40.

Table 25: Empirical Parameters for the Computer-based Simulation

	Retailer	Supplier
Network size	N^R = 9048	N^S = 173
Agents already using EDI	B_0^R = 450	B_0^S = 66
Stand alone costs (stage 1): setup + maintenance + fees	$k_{it}^{R1} \sim ND(153.32;30.66)$ in €; Notation: ND(μ,σ)	$k_{jt}^{S1} \sim ND(6097.22;1219.44)$ in €
Stand alone costs (stage 2): maintenance + fees	$k_{it}^{R2} \sim ND(70.40;14.08)$ in €; Notation: ND(μ,σ)	$k_{jt}^{S2} \sim ND(5250.0;1050.0)$ in €
Utility from direct network effects (per message)	$c_{ij}^{message} = 0.39\,EUR$	$c_{ji}^{message} = 5.10\,EUR$
Number of messages sent from i to j	$m_{ijt} \sim ND(1.17;0.234)$ Notation: ND(μ,σ)	
Utility from direct network effects (per link and period)	$c_{ijt}^R = c_{ij}^{message} \cdot m_{ijt}$	$c_{jit}^S = c_{ji}^{message} \cdot m_{ijt}$
Utility from indirect network effects	$u_{it}^I = u_i^I \;\; \forall t$ $u_i^I \sim ND\left(\mu\!\left(u_i^I\right), 0.2 \cdot \mu\!\left(u_i^I\right)\right)$ $\mu\!\left(u_i^I\right)$ varied during the simulation; $\beta = 0.5$; Notation: ND(μ,σ)	

6.2.5 Discussion: The Network Effect Helix

In Figure 32, the cumulative number of EDI adopters is represented in the stationary state (stable equilibrium in the period after the last adoption activities), depending on the indirect network effect coefficient u_i^I. Each data spot represents the result of a single simulation run. For each value of $\mu(u^I)$ 10 simulation runs were calculated. The value then was incremented by about 2.5.

Figure 32 provides the size of the EDI-using SME retailer network (number of adopters) in the stationary state. We find a sigmoid relationship between an increase in the indirect network effect coefficient and the number of adopters. While with rather low utility from indirect network effects only a few retailers adopt EDI, for high values obviously a very large number of retailers implement the standard (an exemplary diffusion process over time is diagramed in Figure 33).

Figure 32: Number of EDI Adopters in the Stationary State, Depending on the Indirect Network Effects Utility

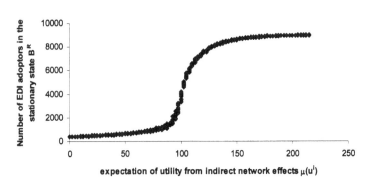

The "tippiness" of the network can be seen in the range of $\mu(u^I) \approx 100$, where the number of adopters reaches a critical mass, and where the majority of the network switches to EDI due to the master data and services additionally offered (indirect network effects) as the result of the EDI diffusion itself. Nevertheless, due to the heterogeneity in the cost and benefit structure of the retailers EDI diffusion does not standardize the whole network, even with very high $\mu(u^I)$. On the supplier side, the number of EDI-deploying enterprises increases immediately from 66 to 173 in the first period (not diagramed). The expected direct network effect utility of EDI is big enough for suppliers to standardize the whole supplier side immediately, even with only a fraction of all retailers as EDI partners.

Figure 33: Occurrence Time of Stationary State t_{stat} for Different u_i

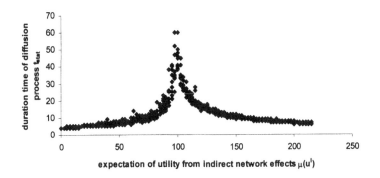

Unlike other network simulations in previous research, the standardization process in this model is quite tedious, due to the more realistic supply chain network structure used (only edges between retailers and suppliers as illustrated in Figure 32) with process duration times of up to 60 periods in the "tippy" area of $\mu(u^I) \sim 100$ (see Figure 33).

Figure 34 provides two different exemplary diffusion paths of EDI among retailers in the office supply industry (with different scales (abscissa, as well as ordinate) in both diagrams). For medium-size values of $\mu(u^I)$ (left diagram) the diffusion path follows a declining function, while at higher values (above $\mu(u^I) \approx 115$) the diffusion path has a sigmoid shape. In the left case, the adoption process takes a long time and standardizes less than half of all agents on the retailer side. In the early periods, only those retailers who have strong individual net benefits from this decision standardize.

In contrast to the right case, this has only marginal consequences for the expected savings of the other retailers. Therefore, a rather small fraction shares the EDI network in the latter periods. In the case depicted on the right diagram, the behavior of the early adopters suffices to provide positive expected net savings to the remaining retailers. Consequently, a large section of retailers follows, resulting in a typical diffusion curve described as imitative diffusion. In contrast to the latter example, the declining diffusion depicted in the left diagram can be described as innovative or exponential diffusion, respectively (Lilien et al. 1983; Mahajan et al. 1985).

Figure 34: Exemplary Diffusion Paths of EDI among Retailers

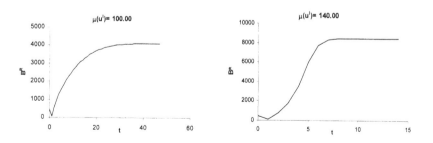

In both examples in Figure 34 the number of EDI-using retailers decreases in the first period because they only take 66 EDI-using suppliers into their forecast according to the underlying survey, where only 66 industry partners were EDI-capable in the first period. In the same first period, the number of EDI-deploying suppliers increases to 173 (100% standardization of all suppliers in the industry under investigation) resulting in increasing direct network effects. But the utility resulting from 100% EDI availability on the supplier side is not enough to accelerate the diffusion process of EDI among retailers significantly (see lower left branch of diffusion curve in Figure 32), equivalent to predominant direct network effects and marginal indirect network effects.

Figure 35: Progression of Average Indirect Network Effects (INE), Communication Savings (sav$_R$), and Overall Utility (U(R)) for SMEs

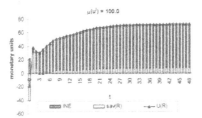 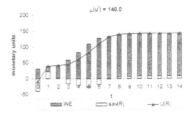

Analogous to Figure 34, where the diffusion of EDI among SME retailers is demonstrated for a given number of EDI messages and indirect network effects, Figure 35 depicts the monetary net utility U^R for retaiilers direct savings and indirect network effects.

Due to the pre-standardization of retailers and suppliers in the first period, all suppliers standardize. On the other hand, due to low expected benefits a number of retailers decide to drop EDI. Thus, the remaining retailers only have to pay k^{R2} while no new ones adopt EDI. In period 1, retailers can observe the standardization behavior of suppliers from period 0 and start to adopt EDI themselves. The bandwagon process starts and an increasing number of retailers adopt EDI by investing k^{R1}, resulting in negative savings during the following standardization phases. Due to the chosen parameter values and the constant number of EDI messages, the chosen level of indirect network benefits is responsible for the resulting EDI network size. Lower levels of indirect network effects lead to no standardization or at least to a longer adoption process (Figure 36).

Figure 36 provides the monetary benefits for retailers in the stationary state. The lower set of data points describes the average monetary net benefit of direct network effects and standardization costs for one retailer (who has decided to adopt EDI sometime in the past). The data points in the upper curve show the sum of the lower set and the (valuated in monetary terms) indirect network effect utility, i.e. the total ex post utility, as shown in equation 2. The level of direct net savings slightly decreases because of the different levels of standardization costs in state 1 and 2. The greater the relative number of adopters deciding to use EDI for the first time in the last period, the higher the average standardization costs and the lower the savings. With higher $\mu(u^I)$ this effect slightly amplifies. Afterwards, EDI-using adopters only have to pay k^{R2} in every subsequent period with completely horizontal progression in the lower set of data points.

Figure 36: Resulting Retailers' Monetary Benefits (avg.) (Net Savings from Direct Network Effects and Standardization Costs (savR) and Overall Utility (UR))

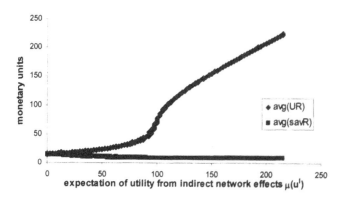

Figure 37 provides the results previously depicted in Figure 32 but with varying network effects: the indirect $\mu(u^I)$, as well as the direct $\mu(m_{ij})$ (i.e. the number of messages exchanged between one retailer and one supplier). The diagram provides an obvious trade-off between direct and indirect network effects influencing the diffusion of EDI among retailers.

Low indirect network effects $\mu(u^I)$ up to approximately 100 hinder the diffusion, resulting in a sticky cluster at the bottom of the diagram, equivalent to many partially standardized networks ($1000 < B^R_{r_{stat}} < 8000$). With higher $\mu(u^I)$ (>100), a marginal number of only $\mu(m_{ij})$=1.16 EDI messages is sufficient to start the diffusion process. Based on correlation analyses, the substitution rate between direct and indirect network effects is equivalent to € 65 for 1 message and vice versa for different $B_{t_{stat}}^R$. If retailers could increase the number of monthly EDI messages to above $\mu(m_{ij})$=3.4, then the diffusion process would be mainly driven by direct network effects as in the case of large suppliers in the office supply industry. Beneath this level, the incorporation of indirect network effects is necessary to start the diffusion process for small EDI-using enterprises. As the EDI-network increases (more EDI messages and/or more participants), the ratio of achievable direct and indirect network benefits grows and varies in an upward process with positive interplay with each other.

Figure 37: Diffusion Process of EDI, Based on Direct ($\mu(m_{ij})$) and Indirect Network Effects ($\mu(u^i)$)

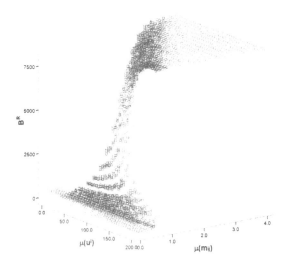

6.2.6   Limitations and Managerial Implications

Without doubt, the adoption of a communication standard with network effects is a far more complex issue than has been modeled here for the case of whether or not to adopt a single EDI standard. That is, e.g., possible strategic behavior of potential adopters is not incorporated. Furthermore, it is assumed that all market participants have full information with regard to the benefits of adoption. Another important issue not discussed in detail is the possible existence of stand-alone benefits of a communication standard. While the authors assume that there is no stand-alone benefit of an EDI standard, it would be possible to internalize such a benefit resulting in a further increasing speed of adoption. A stand-alone benefit could be modeled by reducing the set-up costs of a standard as the equivalent of a higher utility.

Apart from the abovementioned limitations of the model, some relevant implications have to be considered in more detail when dealing with computer-based simulation approaches: the model and the subsequent simulation analysis are used to reveal the dynamics of communication standards diffusion patterns. The simulations prove the assumption that the interplay between direct and indirect network effects has an especially important influence on communication standards diffusion in the modeled supply chain topology. The use of computer simulation has several advantages, since it allows one to handle highly complex, dynamic, and discrete choice problems, as well as to analyze of simultaneous parameter variations. Methodologically, such an approach is known as agent-based computational economics, which studies the emerging economic facets in an evolving system of autonomously interacting agents (Tesfatsion 2002). As applied in this contribution, computational models allow one to simultaneously analyze the impact of a variety of local and global influences on system behavior that is otherwise very difficult to achieve. Consequently, such a methodological approach focuses on how structures *emerge* in decentralized networks rather than being explicitly planned and rationally implemented. However, this comes with the necessity to validate simulation models somehow. Referring to Sargent (Sargent 1998) and Naylor et al. (Naylor et al. 1967) we use a three stage validation approach:

Conceptual model validity: do the model assumptions conform to theory and observations? This stage focuses on internal coherence, in that causal relations are "reasonable" and are consistant with existing theory. The simulation model is a straight implementation of the analytical model that is based on network effect theory and fundamental assumptions about choice and adoption behavior.

Model verification: is the implementation of the conceptual model correct? Besides structured walk-throughs through the program and test runs with extreme values, the simulation model was independently implemented by different persons. All yielded identical results.

Operational validity: are the simulation results reasonable and how do they fit the real world? The simulation results allow one to coherently explain many isolated findings in the literature, which indicates that the "model's output be-havior has the accuracy required for the model's intended purpose over the domain of its intended applicability" (Sargent 1998, p. 125). Concerning exter-nal validity, applying the model to the EDI diffusion in the office supply industry in Germany revealed a corresponding path of diffusion. Therefore, the model has been used successfully to capture and predict standardization problems and phenomena in an appropriate way. One substantial restriction remains, namely that the findings are limited to situations where standard diffusion is explicable solely by direct and indirect network effects. Obviously, the practical application reveals continuously that technology adoption is strongly influ-enced by non-rational factors that can not as yet be captured by economic models.

6.2.7   Implications for the Diffusion of EDI

Analogous to the metaphor of the penguin who moves first, because it has seen the first fish, or a special prey only it prefers while the rest are waiting for the dish of the day, there are also heterogeneous preferences and network market determinations responsible for getting the first-mover to lock into a new standard which are different from the determinants of the subsequent adopt-ers. Given a fixed number of orders, early SMEs adopting EDI need high indi-rect network effect benefits to standardize. Large EDI-using business partners (in this case large suppliers in the office supply industry) adopt EDI immedi-ately, gaining nothing but benefits from direct network effects.

As long as the master data of the data pool is not owned by a single market player who sells it to EDI-deploying SMEs, the value of the master data cannot be quantified in pecuniary terms as having the same value for all users. There-fore, the resulting indirect network effect benefits depend not only on estima-tions of the accessible amount of master data in the future, but also on the in-house usage of this data. Incomplete information hinders single adopters from making a rational decision as efficiently as the decision made by a central planner or intermediary. Intermediaries or providers of EDI solutions in individ-ual industries may use the results of the network effect helix approach pre-sented in this contribution to create improved and more successful standards, standards product bundles, and distribution strategies for the diffusion of stan-dards.

Unlike other highly network-effect-related markets, such as the mobile tele-communication market, which has strong dependencies on direct network effect benefits, the start of the network effect helix to diffuse EDI among small enterprises with little message traffic is closely related to indirect network effect benefits. The adaptation of the network effect helix concept to the battle of mobile standards in the field of short message exchange demonstrated earlier that these markets are significantly influenced by the availability of network effects in the early phase of diffusion. The simulation model has shown that for launching the diffusion process of EDI among SMEs an EDI standard solution should concern itself with the varying importance of direct and indirect network effects during the life cycle of a communication standard. The pivotal adoption reasons driven by indirect improvements in internal business processes will be accompanied at a later stage of EDI use by increasing benefits gained by more intensive exchanges of electronic data. The knowledge about this independent but correlated system of direct and indirect network effects may help to increase the speed of adoption of new standards and may amplify the number of important early adopters, helping to stabilize the ongoing diffusion process.

7 Conclusions

The importance of standards in communication networks cannot be emphasized enough in modern organizations, be it in bidirectional relations among mobile phone networks or in supply chains among enterprises. While technological communication standards are the backbone of machine-to-machine communications, application standards or more general, common agreements are strongly influenced by the social behavior and kind of trust among network participants. The speed of adoption, as well as the nature of the chosen standard depends on the economic efficiencies an adopter can achieve and benefit from. In the case of communication standards, it is mainly network effect benefits related utilities that can be achieved and they are therefore intensely discussed in this contribution. In addition, the internal benefits and impacts of communication standards are important for their adoption, as the empirical results of the application models have shown. Communication standards change the way business is conducted and therefore provide strong evidence of the importance of standards. In the light of network effect theory, the true nature of a communication standard and its characteristics in the form of being partly a public good reveal the nontrivial economic challenge of estimating the value of standards. Consequently, open standards are less diffused and implemented among potential network participants. The application models provided, the WebConverter solution and reputation-based process automation are just two alternative ways of lowering the entrance barrier for potential adopters who do not yet use such standards, or to increase the potential benefits accompanying communication standard. The network effect helix model enables prospective adopters and providers or intermediaries to estimate the potential benefits of a new standard and consequently supports the adoption decision, as the ACE-based simulation models for the mobile phone and EDI-market have shown.

The network helix model has also shown that traditional price theory on rationing goods and services is not sufficient for allocating communication standards, due to their strong public goods property and the increasing returns in growing networks of the same standard users. Since monopolistic pricing or promotion is not possible for open standards, the diffusion is only driven by the experiences of the users and the quality of the underlying standard. The economic adoption decision is therefore more complex, since externalities, incomplete information, direct interdependence in consumption or adoption, and the public goods property of a relevant standard are difficult to internalize in an adoption model. All these limitations and complications have an impact on the diffusion of unsponsored and sponsored communication network standards today and on any future network as well.

Where the market coordination fails to provide a broad base of network participants due to large positive externalities, possible significant economies of scale, the fact that open communication standards are quasi-public goods, and interdependencies among consumers and adopters, the solution discussed above for estimating the very early path of diffusion between the roll-out and the passing of the critical mass of standard users may help to specify the individual value of a standard and also may help to improve standards in the creation phase and to develop new market strategies for providers following the model.

7.1 Diffusion Theory in the Light of Network Effect Theory

Closely related to the diffusion of communication standards is the overcoming of the start-up problem. The discussed special properties of such intangible standards for communication create further difficulties. Most unsponsored communication standards are durable and retain value after they have been used and even more: they are non-rivalry in that others may also use the standards, and they may be nonexclusive in that no market participant can prevent others from using them. Consequently, the technical qualities of communication standards imply that market mechanisms for stand-alone goods often operate imperfectly in distributing those standards since they have a lot in common with the Internet, electric power grids, highway systems, or education systems. None of these networks has been installed without subsidies or governmental regulation. Thus, communication standards have the same properties as other infrastructure goods with quasi-public and private goods properties.

It could be shown that an important characteristic of networks is both direct and indirect network effects. However, these network effects are not given or distributed equally in all networks and are subject to network-specific differences. Consequently, this implies different adoption decision results or different adoption times due to heterogeneous preferences among prospective adopters. Furthermore, it depends on the individual case which network effect is most important in the early phase of diffusion, as the examples of the mobile communication standards and EDI have demonstrated: while direct network effects are more important for mobile phone users in the early phase of diffusion, indirect network effects seem to be more important in the case of EDI diffusion at the time that tool place. These differences have to be addressed when service providers or intermediaries are dealing with communication standards. In the following, the main contributions of this work to the information systems literature are summarized, following the chapters of this thesis:

The decision situation of potential network participants at the time of adoption is specified based on the importance of direct and indirect network effects for communication standards which was discovered. In addition, by using the ideal type approach for network effect goods a systematization in the context of public and private goods is provided by identifying network effect goods as part of the group of public goods. The self-reinforcing interdependences between direct and indirect network effects could be identified as the source of the continuous diffusion process by the inclusion of diffusion-theoretical approaches in the theory of positive network effects. Both effects are considerably responsible for the ongoing diffusion. Based on these findings, an explanatory model is developed, which permits the explicit integration of both effects to support the decision calculus of potential adopters and service providers by evaluating the real value of both network effects in unsponsored networks. For this, two network markets are analyzed and different action alternatives are elaborated on in an exemplary fashion. In addition, the start-up problem and the concept of critical mass received special attention, since both phenomena result from interpersonal differences in the adopter's preference formation which considerably affect the macroeconomic result of diffusion. In accordance with these findings, the explanatory model has been developed, permitting prospective network participants to determine the characteristics of network goods.

The model developed sheds light on the varying and individually receivable direct and indirect network benefits and their composition over time, respectively. Consequently, early adopters of such communication standards have to bear a higher risk due to the underlying consumption externalities. The higher risk of being potentially the only user of a standard but adopting nevertheless can, in particular, be explained by the described model. It is often argued in the literature that this risk is covered by some kind of additional stand-alone benefit accompanying with the network effect good. However, such a work-around is not possible in the case of pure network effect goods such as communication standards in the form of EDI systems or cellular phones supporting special data communication standards. If stand-alone benefits are not achievable and the communication standard is open, traditional market strategies for private goods cannot solve the problem of starting the diffusion process. On the other hand, in pure unsponsored network markets with the absence of quasi-monopolistic providers and market penetration and pricing strategies, the model has shown that there are still some strategies enabling adopters and providers to promote the diffusion of communication standards.

The start-up problem is closely connected with the concept of critical mass. If the critical number of adopters is not reached, then a service or a good cannot establish itself as quasi-standard in the market. As the results of the network effect helix model showed, the critical mass in communication networks depends on the ability of early adopters to determine a positive expected utility value of the network standard and thus the ability to forecast to a certain degree the diffusion result in the future. In order to avoid the disproportionately high risk of making the wrong decision, adopters can now consider the value of direct and indirect network effects for every expansion stage of the network. The ongoing environmental changes in the network can now be predicted, since the total amount and proportion of direct and indirect network effects achievable for each adopter change with each new adopter: if the expansion of a network and therefore the diffusion of a standard is in an immature stage (or has not reached the critical mass yet), then those small networks react particularly sensitively to the changing composition of network effects. The changes are subject to adoption and use, and consequently the reasons for the changing ratio of network effects, which were crucial for early adopters in the choice of a standard, may disappear or at least change during the diffusion process. With more adopters, direct network effects may become the driver of diffusion while it was started due to the availability of indirect network effects and vice versa. By the employment of the network effect helix model, the adopter's lack of information can be reduced, which may result in an increase in diffusion if the net present value of the investment is positive when considering network effects.

7.2 Empirical Cross-Country Analysis of E-Business Diffusion

The survey data showed that the diffusion of "state-of-the-art" e-business communication standards has reached a high level in Germany. Analogous to the widespread use of e-business applications, the importance of factors inhibiting their diffusion is reported to be below the global average. This seems to be an excellent prerequisite for the implementation and use of new communication standards such as in the areas of mobile commerce, next generation Internet, wireless broadband technologies, grid-based web services, etc. to transcend previously manual processes in the direction of more machine-to-machine-based automated services.

Although broad diffusion of all kinds of e-business applications and communication standards is observable, the intensity of their use should be increased in order to make additional manual fax or telephone-based transactions obsolete. The close international trade connections of all the investigated German industries are an important driver for the diffusion of standardized electronic transactions, especially to overcome language barriers.

Moreover, SMEs play an important role in the diffusion of e-business standards at the industry level. Due to the large number of SMEs, especially in the retail/wholesale sector, the benefits deriving from e-business would not be achievable if only large establishments used it. SMEs have shown that they are an innovation-friendly group which implements new applications just as fast as large enterprises. Using the given definition of SME (25 to 249 employees) and large firms (250 employees and more), size does not predetermine the relative efficiency of e-business usage. Thus, in each cluster both "efficient" as well as "inefficient" implementations and use may be observed.

In contrast to the size of firms, the affiliation to a special industry sector strongly influences the diffusion of e-business standards. While the manufacturing industry has been using ERP systems and EDI standards for a couple of years, as has the banking/insurance sector, the availability of Internet-based services opens the way for automated business processes to be used in the retail/wholesale sector for the first time. The implementation of e-business standards to improve internal, as well as external, processes was mentioned as having a significant impact in the retail/wholesale sector, while in the banking sector e-business is seen as part of the current problems.

Furthermore, there is a significant but weak correlation between the number of e-business applications employed in establishments per industry, and the perceived efficiency increases as provided for SMEs. The use of the rank order correlation coefficient reveals a monotone relationship among ordinal-scaled data. While the results are very significant in the manufacturing and banking and insurance industry, the retail and wholesale industry is insignificant in terms of internal processes and staff efficiency, as well as with increasing international sales. Nevertheless, the efficient use of e-business standards seems to be positively correlated with the number of technologies deployed, as has already been revealed by the DEA analysis.

The impacts observed, measured on a five-point scale, revealed that efficient use of e-business-based processes increases with (and depends on) the growing complexity of the successfully integrated e-business standards. Although most firms use e-mail or web advertising, the satisfaction, or level of impact perceived, depends on the implementation of higher-order solutions in order to benefit from communication standards. The DEA analysis showed that the consistent realization of e-business standards, especially to communicate in a standardized way with business partners, is a necessary prerequisite to developing the full benefit of such applications. It may be tempting to cherry-pick certain applications, but true benefits are gained only from the widespread and consistent application of all kinds of e-business standards. Satisfaction with e-business standards and applications as enabling technologies is directly proportional to the complexity of the solutions used.

In summary, many German firms have implemented e-business standards and applications in a consistent way and have benefited from process improvements. The e-business diffusion race has reached a mature and internationally competitive stage, which seems to be an excellent base for subsequent development in the near future.

7.3 Development of E-Business Solutions

Although the two communication solutions developed are not communication standards, they may definitely enable firms and industry sectors to build communication networks with SMEs which could previously not be contacted electronically, as in the case of the WebConverter solution, or to increase the indirect benefits of communication networks, as in the case of the customer complaints and reputation accounts solution. While the latter solution has not proven its serviceability potential since it is still only a model, the former has been implemented successfully in the German office supply industry for a couple of years now.

Both solutions illustrate that the benefits of automated communication channels have not yet been totally exploited, and that more processes could be conducted in a standardized way. Further solutions based on new network standards such as grid technologies in combination with web services or RFID-based seamless information transfers have the potential to promote further e-business-based processes. Technological progress together with sophisticated applications will lower the entrance or adoption barrier for new standards and will enhance the automation benefits, which make their adoption more likely.

It is not necessarily totally new technologies or innovations that are needed to increase the benefits of automated communication, as the WebConverter solution has shown. By the use of simple but common ASCII files in combination with web services to convert ASCII code into another EDI standard, a solution for an old problem is possible, based on existing technologies and standards. In doing so, the special need of SMEs, which are not primarily focused on the data exchanges due to low traffic but on internal improvements of their material management systems based on accurate master data, are addressed. When the number of EDI messages increases, SMEs can not only benefit from indirect network effects by using the electronically provided master data, but also from direct network effects by benefiting from automated messaging and processes.

The other solution discussed is to increase the level of automated processes in the case of customer complaints management. In combination with existing information management systems such as EDI converters, the number of manual, and therefore costly, human interactions can be reduced. Using game-theoretical modeling aimed at the opportunistic behavior of customers who will try to cheat suppliers if no control mechanism is applied, the solution may help to achieve as yet unexploited automation potentials by increasing the number of computer-mediated applications. Apart from the reduction of manual handling and shipping costs, the process quality may be increased for customers and suppliers, resulting in higher customer loyalty.

Such automated decision support systems based on trust and reputation can be used to improve coordination results which would otherwise be less favorable and to create situations where all participants can benefit. Information systems such as EDI can be used in business processes that could not previously be applied successfully because of the threat of opportunistic behavior. The full potential of EDI automation may only be realized if mechanisms that allow the reduction of human control and manual interaction can be applied. Nevertheless, even with a successfully installed reputation mechanism, a random fraction of defective shipments should be checked to improve the quality of production by determining the source of errors.

7.4 ACE-based Diffusion Model of Communication Standards

Through the application of ACE-based simulation models in the area of mobile communication and EDI, possible diffusion paths have been analyzed with different simulation settings to derive the most promising combination of market strategies for providers and intermediary to penetrate the market. Since this is only possible when adopters also can benefit from the adopted communication standard, the potential of "stranding" with a standard can be reduced for providers and adopters at the same time.

The difficulty for successful mobile communication standards can be characterized by the problem of potential adopters to overcome the start-up problem in the early phase of diffusion under imperfect information about the success of a standard. Imponderabilities in the decision making process can be simplified by applying simulation-based models in order to determine the expected net present value, based on the qualitative properties and features of the regarded communication standard.

In general, providers of new communications standards can apply the following strategies, which have to be customized and adjusted to each market and over time. If all or only a few can be applied depends on the network effect market and the public good property of the regarded standard.

- **Standardization strategy**: The regarded communication standard should be developed already from the view of future adopters. Focused on direct and indirect network effects, during standards development both types should be considered in order to serve all potential benefit sources influencing the adoption decision over the life cycle of a standard.

- **Communication strategy**: In order to reduce uncertainties over the success of a new communication standard on the consumer side, communication strategies must be applied purposefully focused on the underlying standard features and properties that are decision relevant for early adopters. As the example of the i-mode introduction in the German mobile phone market has shown, too late or wrong-focused communication activities can hamper the fast diffusion of a solution. The i-mode case is an excellent example of underestimating the impact of direct network effects in the early phase of diffusion.

- **Distribution strategy**: The key problem of the diffusion of new standards in network markets is the start-up phase. As long as no monopolist with sponsored introductory prices prepares the market, and with decentralized decision making on the consumer side, a new communication standard will face a hard time in the early phase of diffusion. Nevertheless, even non-monopolistic providers can reduce market uncertainties, in order to introduce a group of early adopters by using the strategic advice deduced from the network effect helix simulation model. An important factor in the selection of appropriate distribution strategies is the network topology type of the particular market. Therefore, the role of sponsored and unsponsored network markets in particular has to be analyzed by providers in advance.

- **Pricing strategy**: The fixing of prices for communication standards or those based on services in network markets represents a special challenge due to the quasi-characteristic of a public good property. From a providers' viewpoint, the full adopters' willingness to pay can be skimmed only if the network is already established and potential new network participants can realize benefits due to network effects. A successful inter-temporal price discrimination strategy is therefore not possible in oligopolistic markets.

8 Future Research

8.1 Strengthening the Empirical Foundation

Starting from the research results described so far, future research will still be focused on the competition between a new communication standard and an already existing standard (installed base). In contrast to the prior work, what were formerly completely incompatible standards will now be partly compatible. In this extension, we will be analyze how the new setting influences the start-up problem when communication standards are compatible with each other. Using the decentralized standardization model, as well as the network effect helix model, further real-world scenario extensions will be made, in order to explain and forecast the reasons for communication standards diffusion. In doing so, an empirical survey will be conducted in order to validate the simulation results for single markets.

This further research will be more closely focused on mobile and wireless communication standards since the battle between 3rd-generation telecommunication standards and the installed 2.5-generation standards has just started, while the next generation of communication standards has already appeared on the horizon with an already huge installed base of access points for PCs. Therefore, this area seems to be promising for analyzing the dynamics of direct and indirect network effects in more detail.

Wireless local area networks or the fourth generation of telecommunication have already retained a larger section of the wireless world, promising significantly more features for lower prices than GSM or even UMTS. The diffusion of UMTS as the third generation of mobile communication standards and protocols was expected to spread rapidly during the hype in 2000. Although mobile narrowband communication standards existed previously, UMTS in Europe was expected to diffuse even faster, mostly due to new so-called killer applications which would make 3rd-generation standards more attractive. It turned out that the promised applications did not appear and that the additional benefit offered by UMTS was not sufficient to persuade larger groups of market participants to adopt the new standard. One preliminary conclusion is that the suppliers of communication standards underestimate the importance of network effects.

Further research on this topic should reconsider the lessons learned from 3rd-generation to analyze similarities and differences between 3rd-generation and 4th-generation to develop market penetration strategies in order to avoid the same undesired path of diffusion as in the case of 3rd-generation. Based on the developed simulation model, the diffusion of WiFi and WIMAX standards—especially the important diffusion paths until the critical mass of adopters is reached—should be analyzed. The potential diffusion paths derived can help to customize the market penetration instruments of providers in order to solve the so-called start-up problem and to influence certain economically desirable paths of diffusion.

The implicit assumption in economics-oriented diffusion literature in all phases of market diffusion (starting with the market entrance to its saturation) is that the strength of direct and indirect network effects of communication standards is identical. Since network externalities increase with each new network adopter, the direct and indirect network effects must also increase. Since developing networks have to cope with a growing but oscillating number of network participants due to fluctuation, this is consequently equivalent (1) to changing overall available network effects and (2) to changing the ratios or composition of direct and indirect network effects over time.

Astonishingly, these two aspects are almost totally disregarded in existing research approaches although they are extremely important for understanding not only the diffusion of wireless communication standards, but all types of adopter-networks. Therefore, this seems to be a suitable application area for the network effect helix model, since further research in this area seems to be necessary, explicitly to capture the benefit of standards distribution on the micro- and the macroeconomic level.

8.2 Next Generation Mobile Communication Standards

Competitive industries and underlying infrastructures drive economic growth and raise standards of living. Understanding economic competitiveness requires the continual assessment of economic data in order to identify important IS-related drivers or trends as early as possible. Industry standards—how they are developed, agreed upon and how they are deployed—play an important role in making industries competitive and, in turn, improving the economic welfare of nations. The seamless and smooth interaction of communication standards, in particular, significantly reduces frictions and transaction costs that would otherwise exist within the economy, between industries, and between individual end-users. Investment in standards and standards development is critical to prosperity in an advanced economy and boosts the productivity growth that underpins a continually rising standard of living.

The increasingly complex relationships and number of communication standards present a continuing challenge for standards development and standards diffusion (as well as related issues surrounding the rapid pace of technological change, Internet application development, and globalization) for industry and company-level decision makers. Thus the careful development and design of standards, as well as a predictable and successfully anticipated path of diffusion is pivotal to international competitiveness in cutting-edge markets. The potential contribution of IPv6, WiFi, and MobileFi standards to economic prosperity makes it a highly important and relevant research area.

Potential research projects will provide new knowledge about the ways in which broadband communication standards can be established, promoted, and successfully distributed. Moreover, further research will provide a fundamental understanding of the influence of individual end-users and industry players on the emergence of standards, start-up, and subsequent diffusion of such WiFi and next generation Internet standards from a network effect theory point of view. An advanced research project on standardization will enable researchers to analyze the social, business, and economic aspects of IT, as well as their respective implications for public and business policy. From a broader perspective, such a project will advance the state of knowledge in several fields, including information technology, management, economics, social systems, and computation science.

The importance of ubiquitous and reliable broadband Internet access as the virtual infrastructure for ad-hoc access to computing and data resources cannot be overestimated as an important economic potential factor. While in the past physical connections and infrastructure, e.g. telephone, railway or power-grid networks, were crucial, nowadays these infrastructure networks are complemented by wireless networks, as the mobile phone networks have already proven.

8.3 Investigation of Wireless Broadband Standards Development

As mentioned above, developing a standard that meets the needs of all market participants requires a fundamental understanding of their heterogeneous preferences to enable the successful development and promotion of a WIFI solution. Participation may be difficult because standards have public goods characteristics: companies that do not participate in standards development cannot be prevented from enjoying the benefits of the standard (Flanagin et al. 2001; Monge et al. 1998).

Additional complications arise when one or more of the participants in a standardization effort believe that they should not take part in this effort because they will gain greater advantage by doing it alone or by developing a proprietary approach that they hope will become a de facto standard. Even organizations that are willing in principle to participate in standards development may need to be reassured that the effort will be worth their while. Specifically, most participants would balance the costs of adoption against the reasonable likelihood that the outcome of the standardization effort would in fact meet their needs, at least in the long run. Therefore, the standardization process would have to be set up in such a way that a few interests could not easily dominate it.

In this context, the emergence and diffusion of wireless communication standards and related economic implications such as the start-up problem, the critical mass phenomenon and the avalanche or bandwagon phenomenon should be analyzed. Interpersonal differences and heterogeneous preferences will be considered especially important for the successful diffusion of public networks. One important goal is the incorporation of public goods theory into the diffusion model for wireless communication standards in order to integrate the special network effect property of standards into existing diffusion models. Diffusion problems occuring in the start-up phase, such as switching costs when adopting a new but incompatible communication standard, result in negative benefits due to the lack of an installed base of standards adopters (Farrell et al. 2001; Grilli 2002; Klemperer 1987; Rohlfs 1974). Such a "standardization gap" can be an important barrier, if existing hard- and software components are incompatible with a new standard. Therefore the wireless communication standards properties will be analyzed and suitable standardization strategies with regard to existing standards and infrastructure settings will be developed.

a) How can adopters and users of a new WiFi or WiMAX standard contribute to overcoming diffusion barriers or even to dislodging existing wireless standards from the market? (Overcoming the lock-in problem in other standards)

b) Which influence has compatibility (completely or partly) with existing wireless standards? Which interfaces are mandatory to attract switching users from other networks? (Impact of backwards compatibility)

c) Furthermore, this working package will provide new knowledge about the ways in which IT and IT-driven market mechanisms and business practices are diffused, based on different influences of national environments on the diffusion process and on the impacts of such diffusion on firms and end-users. The findings will advance the state of academic knowledge in the fields of information technology, management, economics, and computation and social systems.

8.4 Development of Economic Models to explain the Diffusion of Wireless Broadband Standards

The development of a standard does not ensure its adoption, even by the organizations that participate in the process. It is important to consider adoption from the adopters' perspectives: what their major reasons are for choosing to use a standard, or, conversely, what barriers firms and end-users face when adopting. Adopters must know about the standards and have the knowledge and skills they need to adopt them. Moreover, in many cases, complementary resources must be made available before would-be adopters are in fact able to adopt the standard. In addition, for adoption to be likely, the standard finally agreed upon must in fact meet adopters' needs.

Standards-writing committees emphasize consensus to ensure broad participation and to satisfy participants' needs, encouraging them to adopt. However, these very strengths can include some weaknesses. Committees are said to take longer than markets to arrive at standards and the standards they produce are said to be less innovative, in part owing to the need to preserve the competitiveness of industry participants (David et al. 1990). In addition, they are said to produce technically more complicated standards, although the rationale for this assertion is unclear. (If accurate, it would seem to work against the adoption of the standards.) Specifically, we examine the technical complexity of each WiFi-standard and how they reflect firms' and end-users preferences' and interests.

a) What kind of strategic instruments do providers and intermediaries of WiFi-standards and applications have to promote the adoption of a standard?

b) What strategic instruments exist to enable suppliers and providers of such public networks to manipulate the adoption decisions of potential users? Which features of the wireless standard are of pivotal importance for successful market penetration and does the level of importance shift between different features or is it subject to changes at all over time? (Overcoming the start-up problem)

c) What are the major reasons why firms and end-users adopt an integration standard? What barriers to adoption exist?

d) Does the nature of particular standards help to increase process efficiency and thereby one's competitive position?

8.5 Developing Mobile Business Models and Market Strategies

The work of standards developers and promoters does not end even when widespread adoption of the standard has been achieved. Although the nature of post-adoption processes will vary with circumstances, the activities required can include routine administration, updating or extending the standard as technology or needs change, and defending the standard against threats to its existence or success. This is especially the case when the critical mass of users has not yet been reached or further standards battle to dominate the market. Moreover, adoption does not end challenges for the adopting organizations, either. They still need to work to ensure that business processes are changed and that benefits from using the new approaches are acquired. We are particularly interested in the benefits (or lack thereof) that companies perceive themselves to have realized from standards adoption.

Based on the findings of the abovementioned research packages and economic models, m-business models will be developed incorporating the external network effect dynamics in developing wireless adopter networks. By the application of ACE-based simulation models, possible diffusion paths will be analyzed with different simulation settings to derive the most promising combination of market strategies for vendors and intermediaries to penetrate the market. Since this is only possible when adopters can also benefit from a wireless communication standard, the potential of "being stranded" with a standard can be reduced for vendors and adopters at the same time.

The starting point of the research will be the competition between wireless communication standards and m-business solutions, an already existing standard (installed base), and a new standard, which are incompatible with each other. In an extension to the research we will analyze how the start-up problem changes if the communication standards are compatible to each other. Using the decentralized standardization model (Weitzel 2004), as well as simulated network development, further real-world scenario extensions will be made, in order to explain and prognosticate the reasons for standards and m-business models diffusion. The following tasks will be treated in detail:

a) What are the impacts of the use of integration standards on firms or segments in an industry? Which relevant network effect components should be addressed in a demonstration model? How do firms acquire the benefits from adoption and use of WiFi-standards?

b) How can potential adopters, but also existing network participants or providers, estimate the net present value of a standard when external network effects, uncertainties, and incomplete information influence their decision-making? (Overcoming information asymmetries as far as possible.)

c) How can the diffusion process be fueled until the critical mass of adopters is reached to avoid excess inertia? (Overcoming the critical mass barrier and stimulating the bandwagon effect.)

d) To what extent are the processes of the emergence, adoption, and use of WiFi-standards' different across industries and end-users?

8.6 Grid-Economic Perspectives

Another important application area of the network effect helix discussed which will enable us to analyze dynamics of adoption and diffusion in networks can be seen in so-called Grid economic environments. Based on syntactically and partly semantically defined communication standards as provided by open grid services architecture (OGSA), business partners can spontaneously create a virtual enterprise to work together on a certain project by sharing knowledge, processor capacity, and business models. Since the research, development and deployment of large-scale computation grids for business environments is just starting, the emerging network externalities have also not yet been identified and analyzed. The major application drivers, the grid services offered, and the grid technology itself will greatly change and adjust business requirements. The grid environment will expand existing technologies and integrate new suitable technologies and standards to bring forward the current business IT infrastructure. The accomplishment of technical and economic achievements will still require an immense research, development, and deployment effort.

A grid environment is a decentralized infrastructure, in which the participants are organized independently. Such a decentralized solution has different macro- and microeconomic effects, which have to be analyzed. Currently available grid solutions do not completely support the monitoring and controlling of grid-based business transactions. In particular, the monitoring phase ensures a permanent control of the services offered and reveals whether participants perform and complete their services according to the contract. Furthermore, the trust problem in the grid context currently only considers the identity trust of the users. In this respect, it is necessary for future developments to tackle behavior trust and reputation, which will lead to increasing mutual trust and respectively decreasing transaction costs.

As already mentioned, the commercialization of grid services cannot currently fulfill the accumulating requirements of an efficient grid market. In particular, grid systems need to address the demand and supply of virtual resources to create a computational exchange. Researchers are still looking for a suitable market model for the grid environment and a price model for grid services (resources). Furthermore, national borders and different pricing policies within different countries need to be considered when an economic model is formed for a future grid environment.

The possible adoption of commonly accepted grid standards or compatible systems constituting a network will definitely bridge the currently observable standardization problem. Since it is very likely that in grid environments strong network effects will appear, compatibility and open communication standards are an important issue. The solution of these problems may help to achieve the next level of cooperation from a networked towards a network economy.

References

A

Adams, M. "Norms, standards, rights," *European Journal of Political Economy* (12:2) 1996, pp 363-375.

Adams, R.D., and McCormick, K. "The Traditional Distinction Between Public and Private Goods Needs to be Expanded, Not Abandoned," *Journal of Theoretical Politics* (5:1) 1993, pp 109-116.

Adler, S. "The birth of a standard," *Journal of the American Society for Information Science* (43:8) 1992, pp 556-558.

Agliardi, E. "Discontinuous Adoption Paths with Dynamic Scale Economies," *Economica* (62:248) 1995, pp 541-549.

Andel, N. *Finanzwissenschaften*, (3 ed.) J.C.B. Mohr (Paul Siebeck), Tübingen, 1992.

Andersen, K.V., Beck, R., Wigand, R.T., Brousseau, E., and Bjorn-Andersen, N. "European E-Commerce Policies in the Pioneering Days, the Gold Rush and the post-hype Era," *Information Polity* (9:3/4) 2005, pp 217-232.

Andersen, K.V., Beck, R., Wigand, R.T., Brousseau, E., Grunge, E., and Bjorn-Andersen, N. "Agile Government and Global Market-Driven E-Commerce: The Cases of Denmark, France, and Germany," International Conference on Information Systems (ICIS 2003), Association for Information Systems, Seattle, 2003, pp. 167-180.

Angeles, R., Corritore, C.L., Basu, S.C., and Nath, R. "Success factors for domestic and international electronic data interchange (EDI) implementation for US firms," *International Journal of Information Management* (21:5) 2001, pp 329–347.

Arrow, K.J. "The Economic Implications of Learning by Doing," *Review of Economic Studies* (29:3) 1962, pp 155-173.

Arrow, K.J. "The Organization of Economic Activity: Issues Pertinent to the Choice of Market Versus Nonmarket Allocation," in: *Public Expenditure and Policy Analysis*, R. Haveman and J. Margolis (eds.), Houghton Mifflin, Dallas, 1977, pp. 67-81.

Arthur, B.W. "Competing technologies and lock-in by historical small events: the dynamics of allocation under increasing returns," International Institute for Applied Systems Analysis Working Paper WP-83-92, Laxenburg, Austria, 1983.

Arthur, B.W. "Competing Technologies, Increasing Returns, and Lock-In by Historical Events," *The Economic Journal* (99:394) 1989, pp 116-131.

Arthur, B.W. "Positive Feedbacks in the Economy," *Scientific American* (262:2) 1990, pp 92-99.

Arthur, B.W. "Increasing Returns and the New World of Business," *Harvard Business Review* (74:4) 1996, pp 100-109.

Artle, R., and Averous, C. "The Telephone System as a Public Good: Static and Dynamic Aspects," *The Bell Journal of Economics and Management Science* (4:1) 1973, pp 89-100.

B

Bailey, J.E., and Pearson, S.W. "Development of a Tool for Measuring and Analyzing Computer User Satisfaction," *Management Science* (29:5) 1983, pp 530-545.

Bala, K., and Cook, W.D. "Performance measurement with classification information: an enhanced additive DEA model," *OMEGA International Journal of Management Science* (31:6) 2003, pp 439-450.

Barnes, S.J., and Huff, S.L. "Rising sun: iMode and the wireless Internet," *Communications of The ACM* (46:11) 2003, pp 79-84.

Barr, R.S., Killgo, K.A., Siems, T.F., and Zimmel, S. "Evaluating the Productive Efficiency and Performance of U.S. Commercial Banks," *Managerial Finance* (28:8) 2002, pp 3-25.

Barua, A., and Lee, B. "An economic analysis of the introduction of an electronic data interchange system," *Information Systems Research* (8:4) 1997, pp 398-422.

Beck, R. "Empirische Untersuchung über Einsatz und Nutzung von EC/EDI, M-Commerce, elektronischen Marktplätzen und Wissensmanagement," in: *eBusiness aktuell 2002*, H. Rautenkranz (ed.), DEDIG Deutsche EC/EDI-Gesellschaft, Berlin, 2002.

Beck, R., Beimborn, D., and Weitzel, T. "The German Mobile Standards Battle," 36th Hawaii International Conference on Systems Sciences (HICSS-36), Big Island, Hawaii, 2003a.

Beck, R., Franke, J., König, W., and Wigand, R.T. "Globalization and E-Business Application Adoption and Usage: Comparing Germany in a Global Context," Proceedings of Americas Conference on Information Systems (AMCIS 2005), Omaha, Nebraska, USA, 2005a.

Beck, R., König, W., and Wigand, R.T. "Creating Value in E-Banking: Efficient Usage of E-Commerce Applications and Technologies," Proceedings of the 7th Pacific-Asia Conference on Information Systems (PACIS), Adelaide, Australia, 2003b.

Beck, R., Weitzel, T., Beimborn, D., and König, W. "The Network Effect Helix," MISQ Academic Workshop on ICT standardization, Seattle, USA, 2003c, pp. 120-134.

Beck, R., Weitzel, T., and König, W. "Promises and pitfalls of SME integration," 15th Bled Electronic Commerce Conference "E-Reality", Bled, Slovenia, 2002.

Beck, R., Weitzel, T., and König, W. "The Myth of WebEDI," in: *Towards the Knowledge Society*, J.L. Monteiro, P.M.C. Swatman and L.V. Tavares (eds.), Kluwer Academic Publisher, Boston/Dordrecht/London, 2003d, pp. 585-599.

Beck, R., Wigand, R.T., and König, W. "Beyond the Electronic Commerce Diffusion Race: Efficiency Prevails," Proceedings of the 11th European Conference on Information Systems (ECIS), Naples, Italy, 2003e.

Beck, R., Wigand, R.T., and König, W. "The Diffusion and Efficient Use of Electronic Commerce in Small and Medium-sized Enterprises: An International Three-Industry Survey," *Electronic Markets* (15:1) 2005b, pp 38-52.

Beck, R., Wigand, R.T., and König, W. "Integration of E-Commerce by SMEs in the Manufacturing Sector: A Data Envelopment Analysis Approach," *Journal of Global Information Management* (13:3) 2005c, pp 20-32.

Bendoly, E., and Kaefer, F. "Linking Technological Compatibility and Operational Capacity Constraints to Communication Technology Adoption," *Journal of Electronic Commerce in Organizations* (1:2) 2003, pp 1-13.

Bental, B., and Spiegel, M. "Network Competition, Product Quality, and Market Coverage in the Presence of Network Externalities," *Journal of Industrial Economics* (43:2) 1995, pp 197-208.

Bernstein, J.I., and Nadiri, M.I. "Interindustry R&D Spillovers, Rates and Return, and Production in High-Tech Industries," *American Economic Review* (78:2) 1988, pp 429-434.

Besen, S.M., and Farrell, J. "Choosing How to Compete: Strategies and Tactics in Standardization," *The Journal of Economic Perspectives* (8:2) 1994, pp 117-131.

Biddle, J. "A Bandwagon Effect in Personalized License Plates?," *Economic Inquiry* (29:2) 1991, pp 375-388.

Biehl, D. *The Contribution of Infrastructure to Regional Development* Office for Official Publications of the European Communities, Luxembourg, 1986.

Biehl, D. "Infrastruktur als Bestimmungsfaktor regionaler Entwicklungspotentiale in der Europäischen Union," in: *Regionalentwicklung im Prozess der Europäischen Integration*, H. Karl and W. Henrichsmeyer (eds.), Bonner Schriften zur Integration Europas, Bonn, 1995, pp. 53-86.

Biehl, D., and Münzer, U.A. "Agglomerationsoptima und Agglomerationsbesteuerung - Finanzpolitische Konsequenzen aus der Existenz agglomerationsbedingter sozialer Kosten," in: *Forschungs- und Sitzungsberichte der Akademie für Raumforschung und Landesplanung: Ballung und öffentliche Finanzen*, Akademie für Raumforschung und Landesplanung, Hannover, 1980, pp. 113-150.

Bierfelder, W. *Innovationsmanagement: Prozessorientierte Einführung*, (3 ed.) Oldenbourg Verlag, München Wien, 1994.

Biesheuvel-Roosenburg, S. "Convergence of infrastructure, competition and rights of way: new challenges for infrastructure regulation," in: *Critical Infrastructures,* W.A.H. Thissen and P.M. Herder (eds.), Kluwer Academic Publishers, Delft, 2001, pp. 1-13.

Bikhchandani, S., Hirshleifer, D., and Welch, I. "A Theory of Fads, Fashion, Custom, and Cultural Change as Informational Cascades," *Journal of Political Economy* (100:5) 1992, pp 992-1026.

Bornholdt, S., and Ebel, H. "World Wide Web scaling exponent from Simon's 1955 model," *Physical Review E* (64:035104(R)) 2001.

Borowicz, F., and Scherm, E. "Standardisierungsstrategien: Eine erweiterte Betrachtung des Wettbewerbs auf Netzeffektmärkten," *Zeitschrift für betriebswirtschaftliche Forschung* (53) 2001, pp 391-416.

Brancheu, J.C., and Wetherbe, J.C. "The Adoption of Spreadsheet Software: Testing Innovation Diffusion Theory in Context of End-User Computing," *Information Systems Research* (1:2) 1990, pp 115-143.

Brousseau, E. "EDI and Inter-Firm Relationships: Towards a Standardization of Coordination Processes?," *Information Economics and Policy* (6:3/4) 1994, pp 319-347.

Brown, L.A. *Innovation Diffusion: A new Perspective* Methuen, London/ New York, 1981.

Brynjolfsson, E. "The Productivity Paradox of Information Technology," *Communications of The ACM* (36:12) 1993, pp 66-77.

Brynjolfsson, E. "Information Assets, Technology, and Organization," *Management Science* (40:12) 1994, pp 1645-1662.

Brynjolfsson, E., and Hitt, L. "Paradox Lost? Firm-level Evidence on the Returns to Information Systems Spending," *Management Science* (42:4) 1996a, pp 541-558.

Brynjolfsson, E., and Kemerer, C.F. "Network Externalities in Microcomputer Software: An Econometric Analysis of the Spreadsheet Market," *Management Science* (42:12) 1996b, pp 1627-1648.

Brynjolfsson, E., and Mendelson, H. "Information Systems and the Organization of Modern Enterprise," *Journal of Organizational Computing & Electronic Commerce* (3:3) 1993, pp 245-255.

Buchanan, J.M. "An Economic Theory of Clubs," *Economica* (32:125) 1965, pp 1-14.

Buxmann, P., Weitzel, T., and König, W. "Auswirkung alternativer Koordinationsmechanismen auf die Auswahl von Kommunikationsstandards," *Zeitschrift für Betriebswirtschaft* (Ergänzungsheft Innovation und Absatz) 1999a, pp 133-151.

Buxmann, P., Weitzel, T., Westarp, F.v., and König, W. "The Standardization Problem : An Economic Analysis of Standards in Information Systems,"

1st IEEE Conference on Standardization and Innovation in Information Technology, SIIT 1999, IEEE, Boulder, CO, USA, 1999b.

C

Cabral, L., Salant, D., and Woroch, G.A. "Monopoly pricing with network externalities," *International Journal of Industrial Organization* (17:2) 1999, pp 199-214.

Callon, M. "Techno-economic networks and irreversibility," in: *A Sociology of Monsters: Essays on Power, Technology and Domination*, J. Law (ed.), Routledge, London, 1991.

Cantwell, J. "Innovation, Profits and Growth: Schumpeter and Penrose," DP No. 427, Vol. XIII (2000/2001), University of Reading, Department of Economics, Reading, UK.

Carr, N.G. "IT Doesn't Matter," *Harvard Business Review* (81:5) 2003, pp 41-49.

Carter, J., Bitting, E., and Ghorbani, A.A. "Reputation Formalization within Information Sharing Multiagent Architectures," *Computational Intelligence* (18) 2002, pp 45-64.

Caselli, F., and Coleman, W.J. "Cross country technology diffusion: The case of computers," *The American Economic Review* (91:2) 2001, pp 328-335.

Castells, M. "Information Technology, Globalization and Social Development," in: *UNRISD Discussion Paper 114*, Geneva, Switzerland, 1999.

Ceci, S.J., and Kain, E.L. "Jumping on the Bandwagon: The impact of attitude polls on polling behaviour," *Journal of Opinion Quarterly* (46) 1982, pp 228-242.

Charnes, A., Cooper, W., and Rhodes, E. "A Data Envelopment Analysis Approach to Evaluation of the Program Follow Through Experiments in U.S. Public School Education," 331, University of Texas at Austin Center for Cybernetic Studies, Austin, Texas.

Chau, P.Y.K., and Hui, K.-L. "Determinants of Small Business EDI Adoption: An Empirical Investigation," *Journal of Organizational Computing and Electronic Commerce* (11:4) 2001, pp 229–252.

Chen, J.-C., and Williams, B.C. "The Impact of Electronic Data Interchange (EDI) on SMEs: Summary of Eight British Case Studies," *Journal of Small Business Management* (36:4) 1998, pp 68-72.

Choi, J.P. "Irreversible Choice of Uncertain Technologies with Network Externalities," *The RAND Journal of Economics* (25:3) 1994, pp 382-401.

Choi, J.P. "Standardization and experimentation: Ex ante vs. ex post standardization," *European Journal of Political Economy* (12:2) 1996, pp 273-290.

Choi, J.P. "Herd behavior, the penguin effect, and the suppression of informational diffusion: An analysis of informational externalities and payoff interdependency," *The RAND Journal of Economics* (28:3) 1997, pp 407-425.

Choi, J.P., and Thum, M. "Market structure and the timing of technology adoption with network externalities," *European Economic Review* (42) 1998, pp 225-244.

Choi, S.-Y., Stahl, D.O., and Whinston, A.B. *The Economics of Electronic Commerce* MacMillan Technical Publishing, Indianapolis, 1997.

Chou, C.-f., and Shy, O. "Network Effects Without Network Externalities," *International Journal of Industrial Organization* (8:2) 1990, pp 259-270.

Chou, C.-f., and Shy, O. "Do consumers gain or lose when more people buy the same brand," *European Journal of Political Economy* (12:2) 1996, pp 309-330.

Christmann, R. "Books into bytes: Jacob and Wilhelm Grimm's Deutsches Wörterbuch on CD-ROM and on the Internet," *Literary and Linguistic Computing* (16:2) 2001, pp 121-133.

Church, J., and Gandal, N. "Network Effects, Software Provision, and Standardization," *Journal of Industrial Economics* (40:1) 1992, pp 85-103.

Church, J., and Gandal, N. "Strategic entry deterrence: Complementary products as installed base," *European Journal of Political Economy* (12:2) 1996, pp 331-354.

Church, J., Gandal, N., and Krause, D. "Indirect Network Effects and Adoption Externalities," in: *Discussion Paper 2001-30 (2001)*, Department of Economics, University of Calgary, Alberta, Canada, 2002.

Church, J., and King, I. "Bilingualism and Network Externalities," *The Canadian Journal of Economics* (26:2) 1993, pp 337-345.

Clark, T., and Lee, H.G. "Performance, interdependence and coordination in business-to-business electronic commerce and supply chain management," *Information Technology and Management* (1:1/2) 2000, pp 85-105.

Clements, M.T. "System Components, Network Effects, and Bundling," *Topics in Economic Analysis & Policy* (2:1) 2002, p Article 7.

Clements, M.T. "Direct and Indirect Network Effects: Are They Equivalent?," *International Journal of Industrial Organization* (22:5) 2004, pp 633-645.

Coase, R.H. "The nature of the firm," *Economica* (4:16) 1937, pp 386-405.

Coase, R.H. "The Problem of Social Cost," *Journal of Law and Economics* (3:1) 1960, pp 1-44.

Coleman, J., Menzel, H., and Katz, E. "The diffusion of an innovation among physicians," *Sociometry* (20) 1957, pp 253-270.

Cowan, R. "Nuclear Power Reactors: A Study in Technological Lock-in," *The Journal of Economic History* (50:3) 1990, pp 541-567.

Cowan, R. "High Technology and the Economics of Standardization," in: *New Technology at the Outset. Social Forces in the Shaping of Technological Innovations,* U. Hoffmann and M. Dierkes (eds.), Campus Verlag, 1992, pp. 279-300.

Cowan, R., and Miller, J.H. "Technological standards with local externalities and decentralized behaviour," *Journal of Evolutionary Economics* (8:3) 1998, pp 285-296.

Crawford, D.W. "Pricing Network Usage: A Market for Bandwidth or Market for Communication?," *The Journal of Electronic Publishing* (2:1) 1996.

Crocker, D. "Making Standards the IETF Way," *StandardView* (1:1) 1993, pp 48-54.

Csorba, G. "Read-only Versions for Free and for Profit: Functional Quality Differentiation Strategies of a Software Producing Monopoly," *Central European University Working Paper No. 2/2002)* 2002.

D

Dahlstrom, R., and Nygaard, A. "An Empirical Investigation of Ex Post Transaction Costs in Franchised Distribution Channels," *Journal of Marketing Research* (36:2), May 1999, pp 160-171.

Damsgaard, J., and Lyytinen, K. "The Role of Intermediating Institutions in the Diffusion of Electronic Data Interchange (EDI): How Industry Associations Intervened in Denmark, Finland, and Hong Kong," *The Information Society* (17:3) 2001, pp 195-210.

Das, T.K., and Teng, B.-S. "Between trust and control: Developing confidence in partner cooperation in alliances," *Academy of Management Review* (23:3) 1998, pp 491-512.

David, P.A. "Clio and the Economics of QWERTY," *The American Economic Review* (75:2) 1985, pp 332-337.

David, P.A. "Understanding the Economics of QWERTY: The Necessity of History," in: *Economic History and the Modern Economist,* W.N. Parker (ed.), Blackwell, Oxford, 1986, pp. 30-49.

David, P.A. "Positive Feedbacks and Research Productivity in Science: Reopening another Black Box," in: *Economics of Technology,* O. Grandstrand (ed.), Elsevier, Amsterdam, 1994.

David, P.A. "Standardization policies for network technologies: The flux between freedom and order revisited," in: *Standards, Innovation and Competitiveness: The Politics and Economics of Standards in Natural and Technical Environments,* H. R., R. Mansell and J. Skea (eds.), Edward Elgar Publisher, 1995.

David, P.A., and Greenstein, S.M. "The Economics of Compatibility Standards: An Introduction to Recent Research," *Economics of Innovation and New Technology* (1:1) 1990, pp 3-41.

David, P.A., and Rothwell, G.S. "Measuring standardization: An application to the American and French nuclear power industries," *European Journal of Political Economy* (12:2) 1996a, pp 291-308.

David, P.A., and Rothwell, G.S. "Standardization, diversity and learning: Strategies for the coevolution of technology and industrial capacity," *International Journal of Industrial Organization* (14) 1996b, pp 181-201.

David, P.A., and Steinmueller, W.E. "Standards, trade and competition in the emerging Global Information Infrastructure environment," *Telecommunications Policy* (20:10) 1996c, pp 817-830.

Davis, F.D. "Perceived Usefulness, Perceived Ease of Use, and User Acceptance of Information Technology," *MIS Quarterly* (13:3) 1989, pp 318-340.

Davis, F.D., Bagozzi, R.P., and Warshaw, P.R. "User Acceptance of Computer Technology: A Comparison of Two Theoretical Models," *Management Science* (35:8) 1989, pp 982-1003.

Deutsch, M. *Unternehmenserfolg durch EDI - Strategie und Realisierung des elektronischen Datenaustausches* Vieweg Verlag, Braunschweig, Germany, 1994.

Dranove, D., and Gandal, N. "The DVD-vs.-DIVX Standard War: Empirical Evidence of Network Effects and Preannouncement Effects," *Journal of Economics & Management Strategy* (12:3) 2003, pp 363–386.

Dutta, S., Kwan, S., and Segev, A. "Business Transformation in Electronic Commerce: A Study of Sectoral und Regional Trends," *European Management Journal* (16:5) 1998, pp 540-551.

E

Ebel, H., Davidsen, J., and Bornholdt, S. "Dynamics of Social Networks," *Willey Periodicals* (8:2) 2003, pp 24-27.

Economides, N. "Desirability of Compatibility in the Absence of Network Externalities," *The American Economic Review* (79:5) 1989, pp 1165-1181.

Economides, N. "Compatibility and Market Structure," *Discussion Paper EC-91-16*) 1991a.

Economides, N. "Compatibility and the Creation of Shared Networks," in: *Electronic Services Networks,* M.E. Guerrin-Calvert and S.S. Wildman (eds.), Praeger, New York, 1991b.

Economides, N. "The Economics of Networks," *International Journal of Industrial Organization* (14:6) 1996a, pp 673-699.

Economides, N. "Network Externalities, Complementarities, and Invitations to Enter," *The European Journal of Political Economy* (12:2) 1996b, pp 211-233.

Economides, N. "Compatibility and Market Structure for Network Goods," *Discussion Paper EC-98-02)* 1998.

Economides, N. "Quality Choice and Vertical Integration," *International Journal of Industrial Organization* (17:6) 1999, pp 903-914.

Economides, N. "Durable Goods Monopoly with Network Externalities with Application to the PC Operating Systems Market," *Quarterly Journal of Electronic Commerce* (1:3) 2000.

Economides, N., and Himmelberg, C. "Critical Mass and Network Evolution in Telecommunications," in: *Toward a Competitive Telecommunications Industry: Selected Papers from the 1994 Telecommunications Policy Research Conference,* G. Brock (ed.), Lawrence Erlbaum Association, 1995a.

Economides, N., and Himmelberg, C. "Critical Mass and Network Size with Application to the US FAX Market," *Discussion Paper no. EC-95-11)* 1995b.

Economides, N., and Salop, S.C. "Competition And Integration Among Complements, And Network Market Structure," *The Journal Of Industrial Economics* (40:1) 1992, pp 105-123.

Economides, N., and White, L.J. "One-Way Networks, Two-Way Networks, Compatibility, and Public Policy," in: *Opening Networks to Competition: The Regulation and Pricing of Access,* D. Gabel and D. Weiman (eds.), Kluwer Academic Publisher, Boston Dortrecht London, 1996.

Economides, N., and White, L.J. "The Inefficiency of the ECPR Yet Again: A Reply to Larson," *The Antitrust Bulletin* (43:2) 1998, pp 429-444.

Ehrhardt, M. "Network effects, standardisation and competitive strategy: how companies influence the emergence of dominant designs," *International Journal of Technology Management* (27:2/3) 2004, pp 272-294.

Ellis, H.S., and Fellner, W. "External Economies and Diseconomies," *The American Economic Review* (33:3) 1943, pp 493-511.

Emmelhainz, M.A. *Electronic Data Interchange: A Total Management Guide,* (2 ed.) Van Nostrand Reinhold, New York, 1993.

F

Farrell, J. "Rigidity vs. License," *American Economic Review* (77:1) 1987, pp 195-197.

Farrell, J. "Choosing the Rules for Formal Standardization," *Working Paper)* 1993.

Farrell, J. "Arguments for Weaker Intellectual Property Protection in Network Industries," *StandardView* (3:2) 1995, pp 46-49.

Farrell, J. "Harnesses and Muzzles: Greed as Engine and Threat in the Standards Process," *StandardView* (4:1) 1996, pp 29-31.

Farrell, J., and Gallini, N. "Second-Sourcing as a Commitment: Monopoly Incentives to Attract Competition," *The Quarterly Journal of Economics* (103:4) 1988a, pp 673-694.

Farrell, J., and Klemperer, P. "Coordination and Lock-in: Competition with Switching Costs and Network Effects," *Working Paper)* 2001.

Farrell, J., Monroe, H.K., and Saloner, G. "The Vertical Organization of Industry: Systems Competition versus Component Competition," *Journal of Economics and Management Strategy* (7:2) 1998, pp 143-182.

Farrell, J., and Saloner, G. "Standardization, Compatibility and Innovation," *The RAND Journal of Economics* (16:1) 1985, pp 70-83.

Farrell, J., and Saloner, G. "Installed Base and Compatibility: Innovation, Product Preannouncements, and Predation," *The American Economic Review* (76:5) 1986, pp 940-955.

Farrell, J., and Saloner, G. "Coordination through committees and markets," *The RAND Journal of Economics* (19:2) 1988b, pp 235-252.

Farrell, J., and Saloner, G. "Converters, Compatibility, and the Control of Interfaces," *Journal of Industrial Economics* (40:1) 1992a, pp 9-35.

Farrell, J., and Shapiro, C. "Dynamic Competition with Switching Costs," *The RAND Journal of Economics* (19:1) 1988c, pp 123-137.

Farrell, J., and Shapiro, C. "Optimal Contracts with Lock-In," *The American Economic Review* (79:1) 1989, pp 51-68.

Farrell, J., and Shapiro, C. "Standard Setting in High-Definition Television," *Brookings Papers on Economic Activity. Microeconomics* (1992) 1992b, pp 1-77.

Farrell, J., and Shapiro, C. "Standard Setting in High-Definition Television," *Brookings Papers on Economic Activity. Microeconomics* (1992) 1992c, pp 1-77.

Fearon, C., and Philip, G. "An empirical study of the use of EDI in supermarket chains using a new conceptual framework," *Journal of Information Technology* (14:1) 1999, pp 3-21.

Felten, C. *Adoption und Diffusion von Innovationen* Deutscher Universitätsverlag, Wiesbaden, 2001.

Fink, D. "Guidelines for the Successful Adoption of Information Technology in Small and Medium Enterprises," *International Journal of Information Management* (18:4) 1998, pp 243-253.

Flanagin, A.J., Monge, P., and Fulk, J. "The value of formative investment in organizational federations," *Human Communication Research* (27:1) 2001, pp 69-93.

Fornell, C., and Wernerfelt, B. "Defensive Marketing Strategy by Customer Complaint Management: A Theoretical Analysis," *Journal of Marketing Research* (24:4) 1987, pp 337-346.

Fricke, M. *Information Logistics in Supply Chain Networks - Concept, Empirical Analysis, and Design* ibidem Verlag, Stuttgart, 2003.

Fudenberg, D., and Tirole, J. "Preemption and Rent Equalization in the Adoption of New Technology," *Review of Economic Studies* (52:170) 1985, pp 383-401.

Funk, J.L. "Competition between regional standards and the success and failure of firms in the world-wide mobile communication market," *Telecommunications Policy* (22:4/5) 1998, pp 419-441.

G

Gandal, N. "Hedonic Price Indexes for Spreadsheets and an Empirical Test for Network Externalities," *The RAND Journal of Economics* (25:1) 1994, pp 160-170.

Gandal, N. "Competing Compatibility Standards and Network Externalities in the PC Software Market," *The Review of Economics and Statistics* (77:4) 1995, pp 599-608.

Gandal, N. "Compatibility, Standardization, and Network Effects: some Policy Implications," *Oxford Review of Economic Policy* (18:1) 2002, pp 80-91.

Gandal, N., Greenstein, S.M., and Salant, D. "Adoptions and Orphans in the Early Microcomputer Market," *Working Paper)* 1995.

Gandal, N., Kende, M., and Rob, R. "The dynamics of technological adoption in hardware/software systems: the case of compact disc players," *The RAND Journal of Economics* (31:1) 2000, pp 43-61.

Garud, R., and Kumaraswamy, A. "Changing Competitive Dynamics in Network Industries: An Exploration of Sun Microsystems' Open Systems Strategy," *Strategic Management Journal* (14:5) 1993, pp 351-369.

Gavious, A., and Mizrahi, S. "A continuous time model of the bandwagon effect in collective action," *Social Choice and Welfare* (18) 2001, pp 91-105.

Gaynor, M., and Bradner, S. "The Real Options Approach to Standardization," Proceedings of the 34th Hawaii International Conference on Systems Sciences, IEEE, Maui, Hawaii, 2001.

Gierl, H. *Die Erklärung der Diffusion technischer Produkte* Duncker & Humblot, Berlin, 1987.

Gilbert, R. "Symposium on Compatibility: Incentives and Market Structure," *Journal of Industrial Economics* (40:1) 1992, pp 1-8.

Golany, B., and Roll, Y. "An Application Procedure for DEA," *OMEGA International Journal of Management Science* (17:3) 1989, pp 237-250.

Goodhue, D.L., and Thompson, R.L. "Task-Technology Fit and Individual Performance," *MIS Quarterly* (19:2) 1995, pp 213-236.

Goolsbee, A., and Klenow, P.J. "Evidence on Learning and Network Externalities in the Diffusion of Home Computers," *NBER Working Paper No. W7329)* 2000.

Gordon, R.J. "Does the New Economy Measure Up to the Great Inventions of the Past?," *Journal of Economic Perspectives* (4:14) 2000, pp 49-74.

Gowrisankaran, G., and Stavins, J. "Network externalities and technology adoption: lessons from electronic payments," *The RAND Journal of Economics* (35:2) 2004, pp 260-276.

Granovetter, M. "The Strength of Weak Ties," *The American Journal of Sociology* (78:6) 1973, pp 1360-1380.

Granovetter, M. "Threshold Models for Collective Behavior," *The American Journal of Sociology* (83:6) 1978, pp 1420-1443.

Greenstein, S.M. "Invisible Hands and Visible Advisors: An Economic Interpretation of Standardization," *Journal of the American Society for Information Science* (43:8) 1992, pp 538-549.

Greenstein, S.M. "Did Installed Base Give an Incumbent any (Measurable) Advantages in Federal Computer Procurement?," *The RAND Journal of Economics* (24:1) 1993, pp 19-39.

Greenstein, S.M. "Invisible Hand versus Invisible Advisors: Coordination Mechanisms in Economic Networks," *Working Paper: University of Illinois, Urbana/Champaign)* 1994.

Grilli, L. "Start up Problem in a Network Good Market: The Use of Advertising by a Monopolist Provider," University of Siena, Department of Economics Working Paper 345, Siena, 2002.

Gröhn, A. "Network Effects in PC- Software: An Empirical Analysis," in: *NBER working paper*, 1999.

Gupta, S., Sawhney, M.S., and Jain, D.C. "Modeling the Evolution of Markets with Indirect Network Externalities: An Application to Digital Television," *Marketing Science* (18:3) 1999, pp 396-416.

H

Haj Bakry, S., and Al-Dhelaan, A. "Planning Information Networks: The Scope and the Customer Issues," *International Journal of Network Management* (9) 1999, pp 28-37.

Hallen, G., and Latino, R.J. "Eastman Chemical's Success Story," *Quality Progress* (June) 2003, pp 50-54.

Harhoff, D., and Moch, D. "Price indexes for PC database software and the value of code compatibility," *Research Policy* (26:4/5) 1995, pp 509-520.

Hart, P.J., and Saunders, C.S. "Power and Trust: Critical Factors in the Adoption and Use of Electronic Data Interchange," *Organization Science* (8:1) 1997, pp 23-42.

Hart, P.J., and Saunders, C.S. "Emerging electronic partnerships: Antecedents and dimensions of EDI use from the supplier's perspective," *Journal of Management Information Systems* (14:4) 1998, pp 87-111.

Hartmann, R.S., and Teece, D.J. "Product emulation strategies in the presence of reputation effects and network externalities: some evidence from the minicomputer industry," *Economics of Innovation and New Technology* (1-2) 1990, pp 157-182.

Hausman, A., and Stock, J.R. "Adoption and implementation of technological innovations within long-term relationships," *Journal of Business Research* (56:8) 2003, pp 681-686.

Hawkins, R., Mansell, R., and Swan, P. "The Economic and Social Impact of Electronic Commerce: Preliminary Findings and Research Agenda," OECD, Paris.

Hayashi, K. "From network externalities to interconnection: the changing nature of networks and economy," in: *The Economics of Information Networks*, C. Antonelli (ed.), North-Holland, Amsterdam, 1992, pp. 195-216.

Hecker, F. "Die Akzeptanz und Durchsetzung von Systemtechnologien: Marktbearbeitung und Diffusion am Beispiel der Verkehrstelematik," University of the Saarland, Saarbrücken, 1997, p. 257.

Held, D., McGrew, A., D., G., and Perraton, J. *Global transformations: Politics, economics and culture* Stanford University Press, Stanford, California, 1999.

Hildebrand, W. *Introduction to equilibrium analysis: variations on themes by Edgeworth and Walras* Elsevier Science, Amsterdam, 1976.

Hirschman, A.O. *Exit Voice and Loyalty: Responses to Decline in Firms, Organizations, and States* Harvard University Press, Cambridge, MA, 1970.

Hitt, L., and Brynjolfsson, E. "Productivity, Business Profitability, and Consumer Surplus: Three Different Measures of Information Technology Value," *MIS Quarterly* (20:2) 1996, pp 121-142.

Hoppen, N., Fricke, M., König, W., and Pfitzer, D. "The Role of Bilateral B2B e-Procurement in the European Automotive Industry - Results from an Empirical Survey," Proceedings of Americas Conference on Information Systems (AMCIS), Dallas, USA, 2002.

Howells, J., and Wood, M. "Diffusion and Management of Electronic Data Interchange: Barriers and Opportunities in the UK Pharmaceutical and

Healthcare Industry," *Technology Analysis & Strategic Management* (7:4) 1995, pp 371-386.

I

Iacovou, C.L., Benbasat, I., and Dexter, A.S. "Electronic Data Interchange and Small Organizations: Adoption and Impact of Technology," *MIS Quarterly* (19:4) 1995, pp 465-485.

Ives, B., Baroudi, J.J., and Olson, M.H. "The Measurement of User Satisfaction," *Communications of the ACM* (26:10) 1983, pp 785-793.

J

Jalava, J., and Pohjola, M. "Economic growth in the New Economy: Evidence from advanced economies," *Information Economics and Policy* (14:2) 2002, pp 189-210.

Jarillo, J.C. "On Strategic Networks," *Strategic Management Journal* (9:1) 1988, pp 31-41.

Jimenez-Martinez, J., and Polo-Redondo, Y. "International Diffusion of a new Tool: the case of Electronic Data Interchange (EDI) in the Retail Sector," *Research Policy* (26) 1998, pp 811-827.

K

Kalakota, R., and Whinston, A.B. *Frontiers of Electronic Commerce* Addison-Wesley, Reading, MA, 1996.

Karahanna, E., and Straub, D.W. "Information Technology Adoption Across Time: A Cross-Sectional Comparison of Pre-Adoption and Post-Adoption Beliefs," *MIS Quarterly* (23:2) 1999, pp 183-213.

Katz, M.L., and Shapiro, C. "Network Externalities, Competition and Compatibility," *The American Economic Review* (75:3) 1985, pp 424-440.

Katz, M.L., and Shapiro, C. "Product Compatibility Choice in a Market with Technological Progress," *Oxford Economic Papers* (38:Supplement: Strategic Behaviour and Industrial Competition) 1986a, pp 146-165.

Katz, M.L., and Shapiro, C. "Technology Adoption in the Presence of Network Externalities," *The Journal of Political Economy* (94:4) 1986b, pp 822-841.

Katz, M.L., and Shapiro, C. "R&D Rivalry with Licensing or Imitation," *American Economic Review* (77:3) 1987, pp 402-420.

Katz, M.L., and Shapiro, C. "Product Introduction with Network Externalities," *Journal of Industrial Economics* (40:1) 1992, pp 55-83.

Katz, M.L., and Shapiro, C. "Systems Competition and Network Effects," *The Journal of Economic Perspectives* (8:2) 1994, pp 93-115.

Keil, T. "De-facto standardization through alliances—lessons from Bluetooth," *Telecommunications Policy* (26:3/4) 2002, pp 205-213.

Keppler, J.H. "Externalities, Fixed Costs and Information," *Kyklos - International Review of Social Sciences* (51:4) 1998, pp 547-563.

Ketler, K., Willems, J.R., and Hampton, V. "The EDI implementation decision: a small business perspective," Proceedings of the 1997 ACM SIGCPR conference on computer personnel research, ACM Press, San Francisco, 1997, pp. 70-76.

Kiiski, S., and Pohjola, M. "Cross-country diffusion of the Internet," *Information Economics and Policy* (14:2) 2002, pp 297-310.

Kilian, W., Picot, A., Neuburger, R., Niggl, J., Scholtes, K.L., and Seiler, W. *Electronic Data Interchange (EDI): Aus ökonomischer und juristischer Sicht* Nomos Verlagsgesellschaft, Baden-Baden, 1994.

Kindleberger, C.P. "Standards as Public, Collective and Private Goods," *Kyklos - International Review of Social Sciences* (36:3) 1983, pp 377-396.

Kleinemeyer, J. *Standardisierung zwischen Kooperation und Wettbewerb* Peter Lang, Frankfurt, 1998.

Klemperer, P. "Markets with Consumer Switching Costs," *The Quarterly Journal of Economics* (102:2) 1987, pp 375-394.

Klemperer, P. "Price Wars Caused by Switching Costs," *The Review of Economic Studies* (56:3) 1989, pp 405-420.

Knight, F.H. "Some Fallacies in the Interpretation of Social Cost," *The Quarterly Journal of Economics* (38:4) 1924, pp 582-606.

König, W., Wigand, R.T., and Beck, R. "Globalization and E-Commerce II: Environment and Policy in Germany," *Communications of the Association for Information Systems* (10:Article 3) 2003, pp 33-72.

Korilis, Y.A., Lazar, A.A., and Orda, A. "Achieving network optima using Stackelberg routing strategies," *IEEE/ACM Transactions on Networking* (5:1) 1997, pp 161-173.

Kortmann, W. "Diffusion, Marktentwicklung und Wettbewerb," Universität Dortmund, Dortmund, 1995.

Köster, D. *Wettbewerb in Netzproduktmärkten* Gabler Deutscher Universitäts-Verlag, Wiesbaden, 1998.

Kraemer, K.L., Dedrick, J., and Dunkle, D. "EC in the United States: Leader or One of the Pack?," CRITO, University of California at Irvine, Irvine.

Kreikebaum, H. *Organisationsmanagement internationaler Unternehmen: Grundlagen und neue Strukturen* Gabler Verlag, Wiesbaden, Germany, 1998.

Kubicek, H., and Reimers, K. "Hauptdeterminanten der Nachfrage nach Datenkommunikationsdiensten - Abstimmungsprozesse vs. kritische Masse," *Marketing ZFP* (18:1) 1996, pp 55-67.

Kubicek, H., and Thom, N. "Das betriebliche Umsystem," in: *Handwörterbuch der Betriebswirtschaft*, E. Grochla and W. Wittmann (eds.), Schäffer-Poeschel Verlag, Stuttgart, Germany, 1976.

L

Lane, C., and Bachmann, R. "The Social Constitution of Trust: Supplier Relations in Britain and Germany," *Organization Studies* (17:3) 1996, pp 365-395.

Lee, C.-S., and Vonortas, N.S. "Toward an integrated model of strategy formulation for strategic technical alliances," *International Journal of Technology Transfer and Commercialisation* (1:3) 2002, pp 292-312.

Lee, H.G., Clark, T., and Tam, K.Y. "Research Report: Can EDI Benefit Adopters," *Information Systems Research* (10:2) 1999, pp 186-197.

Leibenstein, H. "Bandwagon, Snob, and Veblen Effects in the Theory of Consumers' Demand," *The Quarterly Journal of Economics* (64:2) 1950, pp 183-207.

Liebowitz, S.J. *Rethinking the Network Economy* American Management Association, New York, 2002.

Liebowitz, S.J., and Margolis, S. "Network Externality: An Uncommon Tragedy," *The Journal of Economic Perspectives* (8:2) 1994a, pp 131-150.

Liebowitz, S.J., and Margolis, S. "Are Network Externalities A New Source of Market Failure?," *Research in Law and Economics* (17) 1995a, pp 1-22.

Liebowitz, S.J., and Margolis, S.E. "The fable of the keys," *Journal of Law and Economics* (33) 1990, pp 1-25.

Liebowitz, S.J., and Margolis, S.E. "Network Externality: An Uncommon Tragedy," *The Journal of Economic Perspectives* (8:2) 1994b, pp 131-150.

Liebowitz, S.J., and Margolis, S.E. "Are Network Externalities A New Source of Market Failure?," *Research in Law and Economics* (17) 1995b, pp 1-22.

Liebowitz, S.J., and Margolis, S.E. "Path Dependence, Lock-in and History," *Journal of Law, Economics and Organization* (11:1) 1995c, pp 205-226.

Liebowitz, S.J., and Margolis, S.E. "Reply to Comments by Regibeau and Gandal," *Research in Law and Economics* (17) 1995d, pp 41-46.

Liebowitz, S.J., and Margolis, S.E. "Should technology choice be a concern of antitrust policy?," *Harvard Journal of Law and Technology* (9:2) 1996, pp 283-318.

Liebowitz, S.J., and Margolis, S.E. *Winners, Losers & Microsoft* The Independent Institute, Oakland, California, 1999.

Lilien, G.L., and Kotler, P. *Marketing Decision Making. A Model Building Approach* Harper & Row, New York, 1983.

Loch, C.H., and Huberman, B.A. "A Punctuated-Equilibrium Model of Technology Diffusion, Management Science," *Management Science* (45:2) 1999, pp 160-177.

M

Mackay, D., and Rosier, M. "Measuring organizational benefits of EDI diffusion: A case of the Australian automotive industry," *International Journal of Physical Distribution & Logistics Management* (26:10) 1996, pp 60-78.

MacKie-Mason, J.K., and Varian, H.R. "Economic FAQs about the Internet," *Journal of Economic Perspectives* (8:3) 1994, pp 75-96.

Mahajan, V., and Peterson, R.A. *Models for Innovation Diffusion* Sage Publications, Thousand Oaks, CA, 1985.

Mahler, A., and Stoetzer, M.-W. "Einführung: Die Diffusion von Innovationen in der Telekommunikation," in: *Die Diffusion von Innovationen in der Telekommunikation,* A. Mahler and M.-W. Stoetzer (eds.), Springer, Berlin, 1995, pp. 1-24.

Malerba, F., and Orsenigo, L. "Schumpeterian patterns of innovation are technology-specific," *Research Policy* (25:3) 1996, pp 451-478.

Malone, T.W., and Crowston, K. "The interdisciplinary study of coordination," *ACM Computing Survey* (26:1) 1994, pp 87-119.

Malone, T.W., Yates, J., and Benjamin, R.I. "Electronic Markets and Electronic Hierarchies," *Communications of the ACM* (30:6) 1987, pp 484-497.

Margolis, S.E., and Liebowitz, S.J. "Path Dependence," in: *The New Palgraves Dictionary of Economics and the Law*, Palgrave Macmillan, 1998.

Marsh, S. "Trust and Reliance in Multi-Agent-Systems: A Preliminary Report," Department of Computer Science and Mathematics, University of Stirling.

Marwell, G., Oliver, P.E., and Prahl, R. "Social Networks and Collective Action: A Theory of the Critical Mass," *American Journal of Sociology* (94:3) 1988, pp 502-534.

Massetti, B., and Zmud, R.W. "Measuring the Extent of EDI Usage in Complex Organizations: Strategies and Illustrative Examples," *MIS Quarterly* (20:3) 1996, pp 331-345.

Matutes, C., and Regibeau, P. "Compatibility and Bundling of Complementary Goods in a Duopoly," *The Journal of Industrial Economics* (40:1) 1992, pp 37-54.

Mauboussin, M.J., Schay, A., and Kawaja "Network to Net Worth: Exploring Network Dynamics," *Credit Suisse First Boston*:5) 2000.

Mayer, C., and Sinai, T. "Network Effects, Congestion Externalities, and Air Traffic Delays: or why all Delays are not Evil," in: *NBER working paper series 8701*, 2002.

Meffert, H. *Internationales Marketing*, (14 ed.) Gabler, Wiesbaden, Germany, 1997, pp. 1980-1989.

Melone, N.P. "A Theoretical Assessment of User Satisfaction Construct in IS Research," *Management Science* (36:1) 1990, pp 76-91.

Mohr, H.-W. *Bestimmungsgründe für die Verbreitung von neuen Technologien* Duncker & Humblodt, Berlin, 1977.

Molka, J.A. "Surrounded by Standards, There is a Simpler View," *Journal of the American Society for Information Science* (43:8) 1992, pp 526-530.

Momberg, R. *Theorie und Politik der Infrastruktur unter Berücksichtigung institutionen- und polit-ökonomischer Einflussfaktoren : Eine Analyse am Beispiel der Bereiche Eisenbahn und Hochschule* Peter Lang GmbH, Frankfurt am Main, 2000.

Monge, P., Fulk, J., Kalman, M.E., Flanagin, A.J., Parnassa, C., and Rumsey, S. "Production of Collective Action in Alliance-Based Interorganizational Communication and Information Systems," *Organization Science* (9:3) 1998, pp 411-433.

Moorman, C., Zaltman, G., and Deshpande, R. "Relationships between providers and users of market research: The dynamics of trust within and between organizations," *Journal of Marketing Research* (29) 1992, pp 314-328.

Mui, L., Halberstadt, A., and Mohtashemi, M. "Notions of reputation in multi-agents systems: a review," Proceedings of the First International Joint Conference on Autonomous Agents and Multiagent Systems, ACM Press New York, Bologna, Italy, 2002a, pp. 280-287.

Mui, L., Mohtashemi, M., and Halberstadt, A. "A Computational Model of Trust and Reputation," Proceedings of the 35th Hawaii International Conference on System Science (HICSS), Big Island, Hawaii, USA, 2002b, p. 188.

Mukhopadhyay, T., Kekre, S., and Kalathur, S. "Business Value of Information Technology: A Study of Electronic Data Interchange," *MIS Quarterly* (19:2) 1995, pp 137-156.

Muller, N.J. "How the Internet is breaking down barriers to EDI," *Information Systems Management* (15:3) 1998, pp 78-81.

Musgrave, R.A. *The Theory of Public Finance - A Study in Public Economy* McGraw-Hill Book Company, New York, Toronto, London, 1959.

N

Naylor, T.H., Finger, J.M., McKenney, J.L., Schrank, W.E., and Holt, C.C. "Verification of Computer Simulation Models," *Management Science* (14:2) 1967, pp B92-B106.

Nelson, R.R. "How Is New Growth Theory?," *Challenge* (40:5) 1997, pp 29-58.

Nicholson, W. *Microeconomic Theory - Basic Principles and Extensions*, (5 ed.) The Dryden Press, Fort Worth, 1992.

Niggl, J. *Die Entstehung von Electronic Data Interchange Standards* Gabler Edition Wissenschaft Deutscher Universitäts Verlag, Wiesbaden, 1994.

Noordewier, T.G., George, J., and Nevin, J.R. "Performance Outcomes of Purchasing Arrangements in Industrial Buy-Vendor Relationships," *Journal of Marketing* (54), October 1990, pp 80-93.

O

Ohashi, H. "The Role of Network Externalities in the U.S. VCR Market in 1978-86," *Working Paper*) 2001.

Oren, S.S., and Smith, S.A. "Critical Mass and Tariff Structure in Electronic Communications Markets," *The Bell Journal of Economics* (12:2) 1981, pp 467-487.

Otto, B., Beckmann, H., Kelkar, O., and Müller, S. *E-Business-Standards - Verbreitung und Akzeptanz* Frauenhofer IRB Verlag, Stuttgart, 2002.

P

Parsons, L.J. "Productivity Versus Relative Efficiency In Marketing: Past And Future?," in: *Research Traditions in Marketing (Recent Economic Thought)*, G. Lilien, G. Laurent and B. Pras (eds.), Kluwer Academic Publisher, Amsterdam, 1992, pp. 169-196.

Peffers, K., Dos Santos, B.L., and Thurner, P.F. "Motivation, implementation, and impact of electronic data interchange among US and German firms," *Information Services & Use* (18:3) 1998, pp 177-189.

Penrose, E.T. "Foreign Investment and the Growth of the Firm," *The Economic Journal* (66:262) 1956, pp 220-235.

Picot, A., and Heger, D.K. "Does The Internet Need A New Competition Policy?," International Conference on Convergence in Communications Industries, University of Warwick, UK, 2002.

Picot, A., Ripperger, T., and Wolff, B. "The Fading Boundaries of the Firm: The Role of Information and Communication Technology," *Journal of Institutional and Theoretical Economics* (152:1) 1996, pp 65-88.

Plouraboue, F., Steyer, A., and Zimmermann, J.-B. "Learning Induced Criticality in Consumers´ Adoption Pattern: A Neural Network Approach," *Economics of Innovation and New Technology* (6:1) 1998, pp 73-90.

Pohjola, M. "The New Economy: facts, impacts and policies," *Information Economics and Policy* (14:2) 2002, pp 133-144.

Postrel, S.R. "Competing Networks and Proprietary Standards: The Case of Quadraphonic Sound," *The Journal of Industrial Economics* (39:2) 1990, pp 169-185.

Powell, P., and Levy, M. "Information systems strategy for small and medium sized enterprises: an organisational perspective," *Journal of Strategic Information Systems* (9:1) 2000, pp 63-84.

R

Radner, R. "Hierarchy: The Economics of Managing," *Journal of Economic Literature* (30:3) 1992, pp 1382-1415.

Raymond, L., and Blili, S. "Adopting EDI in a network enterprise: the case of subcontracting SMEs," *European Journal of Purchasing & Supply Management* (3:3) 1997, pp 165-175.

Riggins, F.J., Kriebel, C.H., and Mukhopadhyay, T. "The Growth of Interorganizational Systems in the Presence of Network Externalities," *Management Science* (40:8) 1994, pp 984-998.

Röck, C. *Die Diffusion von innovativen netzgebundenen Gütern bei unterschiedlichen Interaktionsnetzen* Lang, Peter, GmbH, Europäischer Verlag der Wissenschaften, Frankfurt, 2000.

Rogers, E.M. *Diffusion of Innovations*, (5 ed.) Free Press, New York, 2003.

Rogers, E.M., and Scott, K.L. "The Diffusion of Innovations Model and Outreach from National Network of Libraries of Medicine to Native American Communities," University of New Mexico, Albuquerque.

Rohlfs, J. "A Theory of Interdependent Demand for a Communications Service," *The Bell Journal of Economics and Management Science* (5:1) 1974, pp 16-37.

Rohlfs, J. *Bandwagon Effects in High-Technology Industries* The MIT Press, Cambridge, 2003.

Rose, G., Khoo, H., and Straub, D.W. "Current Technological Impediments to Business-to-Consumer Electonic Commerce," *Communications of the AIS* (1:16) 1999.

Rosenberg, N. *Inside the Black Box : Technology and Economics* Cambridge University Press, New York Melbourne Madrid, 1982.

Rust, R.T., Subramanian, B., and Wells, M. "Making complaints a management tool," *Marketing Management* (1:3) 1992, pp 40-45.

Rysman, M. "Competition Between Networks: A Study of the Market for Yellow Pages," *Review of Economic Studies* (71:2) 2004, pp 483-512.

S

Sabater, J., and Sierra, C. "REGRET: A reputation model for gregarious societies," Proceedings of the fourth Workshop on Deception Fraud and Trust in Agent Societies, Montreal, Canada, 2001, pp. 61-70.

Sabater, J., and Sierra, C. "Reputation and social network analysis in multi-agent systems," Proceedings of the First International Joint Conference on Autonomous Agents and Multiagent Systems, ACM Press New York, Bologna, Italy, 2002, pp. 475-482.

Saloner, G., and Shepard, A. "Adoption of Technologies with Network Effects: An Empirical Examination of the Adoption of Automated Teller Machines," *The RAND Journal of Economics* (26:3) 1995, pp 479-501.

Samuelson, P.A. "The Pure Theory of Public Expenditure," *The Review of Economic Studies* (36:4) 1954, pp 387-389.

Sargent, R.G. "Verification and Validation of Simulation Models," Proceedings of the 1998 Winter Simulation Conference, SCS International, Washington, DC, USA, 1998, pp. 121-130.

Saunders, C.S., Boyette, D., Courtney, J.F., Elgarah, W., Falaleeva, N., Ilie, V., and Shim, J.T. "Viewing EDI-Enabled Interorganizational Relationships Through Multiple Conceptual Lenses," Eighth Americas Conference on Information Systems, Dallas, 2002, pp. 400-409.

Scheel, H. "EMS: Efficiency Measurement System Software and Documentation," University of Dortmund, Operations Research und Wirtschaftsinformatik, Dortmund, Germany.

Schilling, M.A. "Winning the Standards Race: Building Installed Base and the Availability of Complementary Goods," *European Management Journal* (17:3) 1999, pp 265-274.

Schilling, V., and Sobotta, A. "Prozesskostenrechnung der mittelständischen Industrie," Betriebswirtschaftliches Forschungszentrum für Fragen der mittelständischen Wirtschaft e.V., Bayreuth, Germany.

Schmied, G. *High Quality Messaging and Electronic Commerce. Technical Foundations, Standards and Protocols* Springer Verlag, Heidelberg, 1998.

Schumpeter, J.A. *Capitalism, Socialsim, and Democracy* Harper, New York, 1942.

Schumpeter, J.A. "The Creative Response in Economic History," *The Journal of Economic History* (7:2) 1947, pp 149-159.

Schumpeter, J.A. *The Theory of Economic Development* Transaction Publishers, New Brunswick, London, 1983.

Segev, A., Porra, J., and Roldan, M. "Internet-Based EDI Strategy," *Decision Support Systems* (21:3) 1997, pp 157-170.

Senn, J.A. "Expanding the reach of electronic commerce," *Information Systems Management* (15:3) 1998, pp 7-15.

Shapiro, C. "Exclusivity in Network Industries," *George Mason Law Review* (7:3) 1999, pp 1-11.

Shapiro, C., and Varian, H.R. *Information Rules: A Strategic Guide to the Network Economy* Harvard Business School Press, Boston, 1998.

Shih, E., Dedrick, J., and Kraemer, K.L. "Determinations of IT spending at the country level," CRITO, University of California at Irvine, Irvine, California, 2000.

Shurmer, M., and Swann, P. "An Analysis of the Process Generating De Facto Standards in the PC Spreadsheet Software Market," *Journal of Evolutionary Economics* (5:2) 1995, pp 119-132.

Shy, O. "The Economics of Copy Protection in Software and other Media," in: *Internet Publishing and Beyond: The Economics of Digital Information and Intellectual Property*, B. Kahin and H.R. Varian (eds.), MIT Press, Cambridge, 2000, pp. 97-113.

Shy, O. *The Economics of Network Industries* Cambridge University Press, Cambridge New York, 2001.

Siau, K., Lim, E.-P., and Shen, Z. "Mobile Commerce: Promises, Challenges, and Research Agenda," *Journal of Database Management* (12:3) 2001, pp 4-13.

Steinfield, C., and Klein, S. "Local versus global issues in electronic commerce," *Electronic Markets* (9:2) 1999, pp 1-16.

Stigler, G.J. *Production and Distribution Theories*, New York, 1941.

Strassmann, P.A. *Information Productivity: Assessing Information Management Costs of U. S. Corporations* Information Economics Press, New Canaan, CT, 1999.

Suzuki, Y., and Williams, L.R. "Analysis of EDI Resistance Behavior," *Transportation Journal* (37:4) 1998, pp 36-44.

Swaminathan, J.M., Smith, F.S., and Sadeh, N.M. "Modelling Supply Chain Dynamics: a multiagent approach," *Decision Support Systems* (29:3) 1998, pp 607-632.

Swanson, E.B. "Information Systems Innovation Among Organizations," *Management Science* (40:9) 1994, pp 1069-1092.

Swatman, P.M.C., and Swatman, P.A. "Electronic Data Interchange: Organisational Opportunity, Not Technical Problem," in: *Databases in the 1990's*, B. Srinivasan and J. Zeleznikow (eds.), World Scientific Press, Singapore, 1991, pp. 354-374.

Szajna, B. "Empirical evaluation of the revised technology acceptance model," *Management Science* (42:1) 1996, pp 85-92.

T

Tax, S.S., and Brown, S.W. "Recovering and Learning from Service Failure," *Sloan Management Review* (40:1) 1998, pp 75-88.

Teece, D.J. "Capturing value from technological innovation: Integration, strategic partnering, and licensing decisions," in: *Technology and Global Industry: Companies and Nations in the World Economy*, B.R. Guile and H. Brooks (eds.), National Academy Press, Washington, DC, 1987.

Tesfatsion, L.S. "Agent-Based Computational Economics: Growing Economies from the Bottom Up," *Artificial Life* (8) 2002, pp 55-82.

Thum, M. *Netzwerkeffekte, Standardisierung und staatlicher Regulierungsbedarf* J.C.B. Mohr (Paul Siebeck), Tübingen, Germany, 1995.

Tornatzky, L.G., and Fleischer, M. *The Processes of Technological Innovation* Lexington Books, Lexingtion, MA, 1990.

Toth, B. "Putting the U.S. Standardization System into Perspective: New Insights," *StandardView* (4:4) 1996, pp 169-178.

Triplett, J.E. "The Solow Productivity Paradox: What do Computers do to Productivity?," *Canadian Journal of Economics* (32:2) 1999, pp 309-334.

V

Valente, T.W. *Network Models of the Diffusion of Innovations* Hampton Press, Cresskill, New York, 1995.

van de Nouweland, A., Tijs, S., and Wooders, M.H. "Axiomatization of ratio equilibria in public good economies," *Social Choice and Welfare* (19:3) 2002, pp 627-636.

Varian, H.R. "Versioning Information Goods," *Working paper)* 1997.

Varian, H.R., Farrell, J., and Shapiro, C. *The Economics of Information Technology* Cambridge University Press, Cambridge, New York, 2004.

Vijayasarathy, L.R., and Tyler, M.L. "Adoption factors and electronic data interchange use: a survey of retail companies," *International Journal of Retail & Distribution Management* (25:9) 1997, pp 286-292.

von Rabenau, B., and Stahl, K. "Dynamic Aspects of Public Goods: A Further Analysis of the Telephone System," *The Bell Journal of Economics and Management Science* (5:2) 1974, pp 651-669.

von Schelting, A. "Die logische Theorie der historischen Kulturwissenschaft von Max Weber und im besonderen sein Begriff des Idealtypus," *Archiv für Sozialwissenschaft und Sozialpolitik* (49) 1922, pp 623-752.

Vriend, N.J. "Was Hayek an Ace?," Society for Computational Economics.

W

Wade, J. "Dynamics of Organizational Communities and Technological Bandwagons: An Empirical Investigation of Community Evolution in the Microprocessor Market," *Strategic Management Journal* (16:Special Issue: Technological Transformation and the New Competitive Landscape) 1995, pp 111-133.

Warren-Boulton, F.R., Baseman, K.C., and Woroch, G.A. "Economics of Intellectual Property Protection for Software: The Proper Role for Copyright," *StandardView* (3:2) 1995, pp 68-78.

Watts, D.J. "A simple model of global cascades on random networks," *Proceedings of the National Academy of Sciences USA* (99:9) 2002, pp 5766-5771.

Webster, J. "Networks of collaboration or conflict? Electronic data interchange and power in the supply chain," *Journal of Strategic Information Systems* (4:1) 1995, pp 31-42.

Weiber, R. *Diffusion von Telekommunikation: Problem der kritischen Masse* Deutscher Universitätsverlag, Wiesbaden, 1992.

Weitzel, T. "A Network ROI," Proceedings of the MISQ Academic Workshop on ICT standardization, Seattle WA, USA, 2003, pp. 62-79.

Weitzel, T. *Economics of Standards in Information Networks* Physica-Verlag, Heidelberg New York, 2004.

Weitzel, T., Beimborn, D., and König, W. "Coordination in Networks: An Economic Equilibrium Analysis," *Information Systems and e-Business Management* (1:2) 2003a, pp 189-211.

Weitzel, T., Son, S., and König, W. "Infrastrukturentscheidungen in vernetzten Unternehmen: Eine Wirtschaftlichkeitsanalyse am Beispiel von X.500 Directory Services," *WIRTSCHAFTSINFORMATIK* (4) 2001, pp 371-381.

Weitzel, T., Wendt, O., and Westarp, F.v. "Reconsidering Network Effect Theory," 8th European Conference on Information Systems (ECIS 2000), Vienna, Austria, 2000a, pp. 484-491.

Weitzel, T., Wendt, O., and Westarp, F.v. "Reconsidering Network Effect Theory," Proceedings of the 8th European Conference on Information Systems (ECIS 2000), Vienna, Austria, 2000b, pp. 484-491.

Weitzel, T., Wendt, O., Westarp, F.v., and König, W. "Network Effects and Diffusion Theory: Extending Economic Network Analysis," *Journal of IT Standards & Standardization Research* (1:2) 2003b, pp 1-21.

Wendt, O., and Westarp, F.v. "Determinants of Diffusion in Network Effect Markets," IRMA International Conference, Anchorage, USA, 2000.

Westarp, F.v. *Modeling Software Markets* Physica-Verlag, Heidelberg, New York, 2003.

Westarp, F.v., Weitzel, T., Buxmann, P., and König, W. "The Standardization Problem in Networks: A General Framework," in: *Standards and Standardization: A Global Perspective,* K. Jakobs (ed.), Idea Group Publishing, Hershey USA London UK, 1999, pp. 168-185.

Wiese, H. *Netzeffekte und Kompatibilität* Schäffer-Poeschel, Stuttgart, 1990.

Wigand, R.T. "Communication Network Analysis: A History and Overview," in: *Handbook of Organizational Communication,* G.M. Goldhaber and G.A. Barnett (eds.), Ablex Publishing, Norwood, New York, 1988, pp. 319-358.

Wigand, R.T. "Electronic Data Interchange in the United States of America: Selected Issues and Trends," in: *Electronic Data Interchange aus ökonomischer und juristischer Sicht: Forschungsbericht zu dem von der Volkswagenstiftung geförderten Forschungsprojekt ELTRADO (Elektronische Transaktionen von Dokumenten zwischen Organisationen)*, W. Kilian, A. Picot, R. Neuburger, J. Niggl, K.L. Scholtes and W. Seiler (eds.), Nomos Verlagsgesellschaft, Baden-Baden, Germany, 1994, pp. 369-391.

Wigand, R.T. "Emerging Electronic Markets at eBusiness Crossroads: Competitive and Regulatory Issues in the Electricity Industry," *Prometheus: The Journal of Issues in Technological Change, Innovation, Information Economics, Communications and Science Policy* (21:4) 2003, pp 415-428.

Wigand, R.T., and Frankwick, G.L. "Inter-organizational Communication and Technology Transfer: Industry-Government-University Linkages," *International Journal of Technology Management* (4:1) 1989, pp 63-79.

Williams, L.R., and Magee, G.D. "A Multidimensional View of EDI: Testing the Value of EDI Participation to Firms," *Journal of Business Logistics* (19:2) 1998, pp 73-87.

Williamson, O.E. *Markets and Hierarchies: Analysis and Antitrust Implications. A Study in the Economics of Internal Organization* The Free Press, New York, 1975.

Williamson, O.E. *The Economic Institutions of Capitalism: Firms, Markets, Relational Contracting* The Free Press, New York, 1985.

Williamson, O.E. "Comparative Economic Organization: The Analysis of Discrete Structural Alternatives," *Administrative Science Quarterly* (36:2) 1991, pp 269-296.

Witt, U. *Individualistische Grundlagen der evolutorischen Ökonomik* Mohr Siebeck Verlag, Tübingen, Germany, 1987.

Wong, P.-K. "ICT production and diffusion in Asia: Digital dividends or digital divide?," *Information Economics and Policy* (14) 2002, pp 167-187.

Y

Yang, Y.-N. "Essays on network effects," Utah State University, Logan, Utah, 1997.

Young, A.A. "Pigou´s Wealth and Welfare," *The Quarterly Journal of Economics* (27:4) 1913, pp 672-686.

Z

Zhu, K., Kraemer, K.L., Xu, S., and Dedrick, J. "Information Technology Payoff in E-Business Environments: An International Perspective on Value Creation of E-Business in the Financial Services Industry," *Journal of Management Information Systems* (21:1) 2004, pp 17-54.

Appendix: Global E-Commerce Survey

[READ:] Hello. My name is _____ and I'm calling on behalf of XXX and IDC, sister company to [local IDG magazine]. We would appreciate a few minutes of your time to help us understand your business's use of the Internet for a research study targeting all regions of the world. All responses will be used for research purposes only and are kept strictly confidential. We are not selling anything. In return for your time and help, we will send you an executive summary of our research findings. May I speak with the person at your site who is most qualified to answer questions about your site's use of the Internet and other technologies? [Wait for referral. Repeat intro and move to QA]

This will take 20 minutes or less. I'd like to begin by getting some background information.

QA   **ALL.** What is your current title?
     [Read as needed. Single response]
     1   President, Owner, Managing Director
     2   Chief Information Officer (CIO)/Chief Technology Officer/VP of Information Systems (IS)
     3   IS Manager, Director, Planner
     4   Other Manager in IS department
     5   Business Operations Manager
     6   Administration/Finance Manager, Controller
    97 Other [Specify in QAO, length=30]

RESPONDENT SELECTION/FILTER

Q1   **ALL.** Which industry best represents your site's primary business? [**Read. Single response.**]
     1   Manufacturing
     2   Retail or Wholesale Distribution
     3   Banking, Insurance or Other Finance
    97 Other [specify in Q1O, length=30]

Q2   **ALL.** An establishment is defined as a physical location. Does your organization have one or more than one establishment?
     1   One establishment
     2   More than one establishment

Q3   **ALL.** How many employees work at this establishment? **[Note to translators: employee means those with a work contract] [Note: Collect actual response. Ranges are not acceptable for this question. DK not acceptable response. All respondents must respond. Establishment is defined as that physical location where the respondent is based.]**

Q4   **IF Q2= (2).** Approximately, how many employees does your organization have in this country? **[PROGRAMMER: Q4 can't be less than Q3. Code "Don't know/refused" as –9.]**

Q5   **ALL.** Does your establishment use the Internet to buy, sell or support products or services?
     1   Yes
     2   No

GLOBALIZATION OF FIRM

Q6A   **IF Q2=2**. Does your organization have any establishments outside your country?
1   Yes
2   No
99   Don't know/Not answered

Q6B   **IF Q6A=1**. Approximately, how many employees does your organization have in total including all branches, divisions and subsidiaries? **[Interviewer: If exact value is not known, ask for rough estimate.]** [Programmer: Q6B can't be less than Q4. Code "Don't know/refused" as –9. If cannot say go to Q6C. Organization may be defined as the company or enterprise, the highest level of the entire worldwide entity.]

Q6C   **If cannot say**. Is it:
1   Less than 250
2   250-999
3   1,000 to 9,999
4   10,000+
99   Don't know

Q7   **IF Q6A=1**. Does your organization have its headquarters outside your country?
1   Yes
2   No
99   Don't know/Not answered

IF Q2=2. READ: For the rest of this survey, we would like you to consider only this establishment when answering questions about your organization.

GLOBALIZATION OF MARKETS/SOURCING

Q8   **ALL**. Does your establishment generate revenue from sales of products and/or services?
1   Yes
2   No
99   Don't know/refused

Q9   **IF Q8=1**. With the total equal to 100%, what percent of your establishment's sales are to business customers including commercial, government and education establishments versus consumers? **[Interviewer: If exact value is not known, ask for rough estimate. Less than 1% should be recorded as 1%. Enter 0 where appropriate.]** [Programmer: total must sum to 100%; label variables as Q9A, Q9B]
A. Percent to business, government, education
B. Percent to consumers
        Total = 100%

Q10   **IF Q8=1**. What percent of your establishment's total sales are from outside your country? **[Interviewer: If exact value is not known, ask for rough estimate. Less than 1% should be recorded as 1%.]** [Programmer: Record actual value. Code Don't know as -9.]

Q11   **ALL**. What percent of your establishment's total procurement spending is from outside your country? **[Interviewer: If exact value is not known, ask for rough estimate. Less than 1% should be recorded as 1%. Enter 0 if they do not procure from outside the country.]** [Programmer: Record actual value.]

Q12   **ALL**. Using a 5-point scale where 5 is significantly affected and 1 is not at all affected, please tell me how much your establishment is affected by ...? **[Scale: 1=Not at all affected, 5=Significantly affected. Code "Don't know/Refuse" as 99. Label variables as Q12A, Q12B, etc.]**
A. Competitors from outside your country

B. Competitors inside your country
C. Competitors in your local area

USE OF ECOMMERCE TECHNOLOGIES

End User Devices

Q13   **ALL.** Approximately how many personal computers are currently in use at your establishment? Again, establishment refers to this physical location. Please include both desktop and portable personal computers. **[Record actual value. Code "Don't know/Refuse" as –9]**

Access to E-Mail

Q15   **ALL.** Does your establishment use e-mail?
   1   Yes
   2   No
  99   Don't know/Not answered

Access to Web Site

Q16   **ALL.** Does your organization have a Web-site that is accessible by the public?
   1   Yes
   2   No
  99   Don't know/Not answered

Access to Intranet/Extranet

Q17   **ALL.** Does your establishment use an **Intranet**, that is, a private, internally-accessible Web site that provides information about the firm to employees?
   1   Yes
   2   No
  99   Don't know/Not answered

Q18   **ALL.** Does your establishment use an **Extranet**, that is, a private Web-site accessible by external organizations such as clients, business partners, and suppliers but not by the general public?
   1   Yes
   2   No
  99   Don't know/Not answered

Q19   **IF Q18=1**. Is this Extranet accessible by ...? **[1=Yes, 2=No, 99=DK]**
   A   Suppliers or Business Partners
   B   Customers Access to EDI

Q20   **ALL.** Does your establishment use EDI, that is, electronic data interchange? (Interview: If in doubt, quote definition: EDI involves information transfers between computers of different enterprises using a standardized format.)
   1   Yes
   2   No
  99   Don't know/Not answered

Q21   **IF Q20=1**. Is this standard EDI over private networks or Internet-based EDI or both?
   1   Standard EDI
   2   Internet-based EDI
   3   Both
  99   Don't know/Not answered

Access to EFT

Q22   **ALL.** Does your establishment use EFT, that is, electronic funds transfer?

1   Yes
2   No
99   Don't know/Not answered

Access to Call Center

Q23   **ALL**. Does your establishment use a call center, that is, a unit whose primary purpose is sales, technical support or services to customers?
1   Yes
2   No
99   Don't know/Not answered

USES OF THE INTERNET

Q24   **ALL**. Does your establishment use the Internet for ....
[Select all that apply. Scale: 1=Yes, 2=No, 99=Don't know/Refused. Label variables as Q24A, Q24B, etc.]
A. Advertising and marketing purposes?
B. Making sales online?
C. After sales customer service and support
D. Making purchases online?
E. Data exchange with suppliers?
F. Data exchange with customers?
G. Joint business processes with suppliers or cooperation partners?

Q25A   **ALL**. Have you ever heard of the concept of an Internet marketplace, exchange or trading community, through which multiple businesses buy and sell goods and services?
1   Yes
2   No
99   Don't know/Not answered

Q25B   **IF Q25A=1**. Does your establishment participate as a **buyer, as a seller, or both** in such an Internet-based trading community?
1   Buyer
2   Seller
3   Both
99   Don't know/Not answered

Q26   **IF Q24B=1 or Q25B=2**. Which of the following statements best characterizes how you are using the Internet to sell products and services?
1   Addresses new markets only.
2   Addresses our traditional distribution channels only
3   Competes directly with our traditional distribution channels
4   Replaces our traditional distribution channels
99   Don't know

Q27   **ALL**. Today it is possible to access content or services from various mobile devices such as mobile phones and handhelds such as Palms or Pocket PC devices. Does your organization provide or plan to provide content or services that mobile customers can access?
1   Already available
2   Plan to add mobile access within the next year
3   No, we have no current plans
99   Don't know

DRIVERS FOR INTERNET USE

Q28   **ALL**. Using a 5-point scale where 5 is "a very significant factor" and 1 is "not a factor at all," please rate how significant each of the following was to your organization's decision to begin using the Internet for business.

[Scale: 1=Not a factor at all, 5=A very significant factor, 99=Don't know/Refused. Label variables as Q28A, Q28B, etc.] How significant was ....
A. Customers demanded it
B. Major competitors were online
C. Suppliers required it
D. To reduce costs
E. To expand market for existing product/services
F. To enter new businesses or markets
G. To improve coordination with customers and suppliers
H. Required for government procurement
I. Government provided incentives

BARRIERS/DIFFICULTIES TO DOING BUSINESS ON THE INTERNET

Q29 ALL. Using a 5-point scale where 5 is "a very significant factor" and 1 is "not a factor at all," please rate how significant the following obstacles are to your establishment's ability to do business online. [Scale: 1=Not a factor at all, 5=A very significant factor, 99=Don't know/Refused. Label variables as Q29A, Q29B, Q29C etc.]
A. Need for face-to-face customer interaction to sell our products.
B. Concern about privacy of data or security issues.
C. Customers do not use this technology
D. Finding staff with e-commerce expertise.
E. Prevalence of credit card use in the country.
F. Costs of implementing an ecommerce site.
G. Making needed organizational changes.
H. Our level of ability to use the Internet as part of our business strategy.

Q30 ALL. Using the same 5-point scale, how much do the following affect your establishment's decision to do business online?
[Scale: 1=Not a factor at all, 5=Very significant factor, 99=Don't know/Refused. Label variables as Q30A, Q30B, Q30C.]
A. Cost of Internet access
B. Business laws do not support e-commerce.
C. Taxation of internet sales.
D. Inadequate legal protection for Internet purchases.

IMPACTS OF DOING BUSINESS ONLINE

Q31 ALL. Using a 5-point scale where 5 is "a great deal" and 1 is "not at all", please rate the degree to which your establishment has experienced the following impacts since it began doing business on the Internet?.
[Scale: 1=Not at all, 5=A great deal, 99=Don't know/Refused. Label variables as Q31A, Q31B, Q31C, etc.]
A. Internal processes more efficient
B. Staff productivity increased
C. Sales increased
D. Sales area widened
E. Customer service improved
F. International sales increased
G. Procurement costs decreased
H. Inventory costs decreased
I. Coordination with suppliers improved
J. Our competitive position improved.

Q32 ALL. Please indicate whether the following have increased, decreased or stayed the same in your establishment since it began doing business on the Internet.
[Scale: 1=Decreased, 2=Stayed the same, 3=Increased, 99=Don't know/Refused. Label variables as Q32A, Q32B, etc.]
A. Number of distribution channels

B. Number of suppliers
C. Number of competitors
D. Intensity of competition

ONLINE SALES

Online Sales section asked if Q24B=1 or Q25B=2,3, ELSE skip to Online Services section (Q37A)

[READ]: Now, turning to a few more questions regarding your establishment's online sales.

Q33   Are these online sales to other businesses or to consumers or to both?
     1   Businesses
     2   Consumers
     3   Both
   99   Don't know/Refused

Q34   **IF Q33=2, 3.** What percent of your establishment's total consumer sales are conducted online? **[If exact value is not known, ask for rough estimate. Less than 1% should be recorded as 1%. Code DK as -9]**

Q35   **IF Q33=1, 3.** What percent of your establishment's total business to business sales are conducted online? **[If exact value is not known, ask for rough estimate. Less than 1% should be recorded as 1%. Code DK as -9]**

Q36   Does the Web site support online payment?
     1   Yes
     2   No
   99   Don't know/Not answered

ONLINE SERVICES

Q37A   **IF Q1=1 and Q16=1(Manufacturing).** Does your organization's Web site support any of the following services?
    [Scale: 1=Yes, 2=No, 99=Don't know/Refused. Label variables as Q37AA, Q37AB, etc.]
    A. Product configuration
    B. Order tracking
    C. Service and technical support
    D. Product specification
    E. Account information

Q37B   **IF Q1=2 and Q16=1 (Retail or Distribution).** Does your organization's Web site support any of the following services?
    [Scale: 1=Yes, 2=No, 99=Don't know/Refused. Label variables as Q37BA, Q37BB, etc.]
    A. Gift certificates and/or registry
    B. Product catalogue
    C. Product reviews
    D. Individual customization
    E. Account information

Q37C   **IF Q1=3 and Q16=1 (Finance, Insurance).** Does your organization's Web site support any of the following services?
    [Scale: 1=Yes, 2=No, 99=Don't know/Refused. Label variables as Q37CA, Q37CB, etc.]
    A. Online services such as filing applications, filing claims, paying bills, transferring funds
    B. Access to account information
    C. Online tools such as research tools, planning tools, etc.

Q38   **IF ANY Q37AA-AE=1 or ANY Q37BA-BE=1 or ANY Q37CA-CC=1.** Are these online services to other businesses or to consumers or to both?
    1   Businesses
    2   Consumers
    3   Both
  99   Don't know/Refused

Q39   **IF Q38=2, 3.** What percent of your establishment's total consumer service volume is conducted online? **[If exact value is not known, ask for rough estimate. Less than 1% should be recorded as 1%.] [Programmer: Record actual value. Code DK as -9]**

Q40   **IF Q38=1, 3.** What percent of your establishment's total business to business service volume is conducted online? **[If exact value is not known, ask for rough estimate. Less than 1% should be recorded as 1%.] [Programmer: Record actual value. Code DK as -9]**

ONLINE PROCUREMENT

Online Procurement Section asked if Q24D=1 or Q25B=1,3. ELSE skip to Enterprise Application Strategy Section.

Q41   What percent of the dollar volume your establishment spends on supplies and equipment for doing business is ordered online?
    [Interviewer: If exact value is not known, ask for rough estimate. Less than 1% should be recorded as 1%. Enter 0 if they do not buy supplies and equipment for doing business online. Enter –9 if they do not don't know.] [Programmer: Record actual value.]

Q42   **IF Q1=1.** What percent of the dollar volume your establishment spends on direct goods for production, such as parts and components, is ordered online?
    [Interviewer: If exact value is not known, ask for rough estimate. Less than 1% should be recorded as 1%. Enter 0 if they do not buy direct goods for production, such as parts and components online. Enter –9 if they don't know.] [Programmer: Record actual value.]

Q43   **IF Q1=2.** What percent of the dollar volume your establishment spends on goods for resale is ordered online?
    [Interviewer: If exact value is not known, ask for rough estimate. Less than 1% should be recorded as 1%. Enter 0 if they do not buy goods for resale online. Enter –9 if they do not know.] [Programmer: Record actual value.]

ENTERPRISE APPLICATION STRATEGY

Q44   **IF Q16=1 or Q18=1.** Using a 5-point scale where 5 is "a great deal" and 1 is "not at all", please rate the extent to which your internet applications are electronically integrated with your internal databases and information systems. **[Scale: 1=Not at all, 5=A great deal, 99=Don't know/Refused.]**

Q45   **ALL.** Using a 5-point scale where 5 is "a great deal" and 1 is "not at all", please rate the extent to which your company's databases and information systems are electronically integrated with those of your suppliers and business customers. **[Scale: 1=Not at all, 5=A great deal, 99=Don't know/Refused.]**

SPENDING

Q46   **ALL.** What was your establishment's total revenue in 2001?

Q47   **ALL**. What would you estimate was your establishment's total IS operating budget as a percent of your establishment's revenue in 2001? **[Code "Don't know/Refuse" as –9. Cannot be >100%. Note: includes internal and external spending.].**

Q48   **ALL**. What percent of your establishment's IS operating budget in 2001 was devoted to Web-based, that is, Internet, extranet and intranet initiatives, including systems, software, IT services, consulting and internal staff? **[Code "Don't know/Refuse" as –9. Cannot be >100%. Enter 0 if no Web spending. Note: includes internal and external spending.].**

Q49   **ALL**. How many IT professionals are located in this establishment? **[Code "Don't know/Refuse" as –9. Can't be greater than Q3.]**

Q50   Would you be willing to allow us to provide the name of your establishment to the researchers so that they may link additional secondary data obtained from annual reports on your company to your responses? [If necessary, explain that their response would be linked to their organization's name for use in only in aggregated analysis and at no time would their response be reported by itself with the company identified.]
       1   Yes
       2   No

END OF SURVEY

GPSR Compliance
The European Union's (EU) General Product Safety Regulation (GPSR) is a set
of rules that requires consumer products to be safe and our obligations to
ensure this.

If you have any concerns about our products, you can contact us on

ProductSafety@springernature.com

In case Publisher is established outside the EU, the EU authorized
representative is:

Springer Nature Customer Service Center GmbH
Europaplatz 3
69115 Heidelberg, Germany